AF541362

External Affairs

External Affairs: Cross-Border Relations

OTHER LOTUS TITLES

Harinder Baweja (ed.)	*Most Wanted: Profiles of Terror*
Jawid Laiq	*The Maverick Republic*
M.J. Akbar	*Kashmir: Behind the Vale*
M.J. Akbar	*Nehru: The Making of India*
M.J. Akbar	*India: The Siege Within*
M.J. Akbar	*The Shade of Swords*
Rohan Gunaratna	*Inside Al Qaeda*
Rifaat Hussain, J.N. Dixit Julie Sirrs, Ajai Shukla Anand Giridharadas Rahimullah Yusufzai John Jennings	*Afghanistan and 9/11*
Satish Jacob	*Hotel Palestine Baghdad*
Anil K. Jaggia and Saurabh Shukla	*IC 814: Hijacked! The Inside Story*
Eric S. Margolis	*War at the Top of the World*
Maj. Gen. Ian Cardozo	*Param Vir: Our Heroes in Battle*
Mushirul Hasan	*India Partitioned. 2 Vols*
Mushirul Hasan	*John Company to the Republic*
Mushirul Hasan	*Knowledge Power and Politics*
Rachel Dwyer	*Yash Chopra: Fifty Years of Indian Cinema*
Sujata S. Sabnis	*A Twist in Destiny*
V.N. Rai	*Curfew in the City*

FORTHCOMING TITLES

Dr Humayun Khan Gopalaswami Parthasarathy	*Diplomatic Divide: Cross-Border Talks*
Maj. R.P. Singh	*Sawai Man Singh II*

External Affairs

Cross-Border Relations

General Editor: J.N. Dixit

S.K. Singh

J.N. Dixit

K.V. Rajan

C.V. Ranganathan

M.H. Ansari

Deb Mukharji

Salman Haidar

LOTUS COLLECTION

ROLI BOOKS

Lotus Collection

This edition first published in 2003
Second impression 2004
The Lotus Collection
An imprint of
Roli Books Pvt. Ltd.
M-75, G.K. II Market
New Delhi 110 048
Phones: ++91 (011) 29210886, 29212782
2921 2271, Fax: ++91 (011) 2921 7185
E-mail: roli@vsnl.com; Website: rolibooks.com
Also at
Varanasi, Agra, Jaipur and the Netherlands

ISBN: 81-7436-264-9
Rs 395

Typeset in Minion by Roli Books Pvt. Ltd. and
printed at Tan Prints (India) Pvt. Ltd., Jhajjar, Haryana

Contents

About the Authors

S.K. Singh, was Foreign Secretary from 1989 to 1990. He was also India's Ambassador to various countries including Afghanistan and Pakistan.

J.N. Dixit, former Foreign Secretary, also represented India in Sri Lanka during the crucial IPKF years. He has authored a book on his days in Sri Lanka called *Assignment Colombo.*

K.V. Rajan was India's Ambassador to Nepal from 1995 to 2000 and is now Director, Institute of Asian Studies.

C.V. Ranganathan was India's Ambassador to China from 1987 to 1991. Along with V.C. Khanna, he is the co-author of a book *India and China—The Way Ahead* published in January 2000.

M.H. Ansari served as India's Ambassador to Afghanistan, Iran and Saudi Arabia and also as Permanent Representative to the United Nations.

Deb Mukharji served in Islamabad from 1968 to 1971 where he saw the last days of the Ayub regime and the military crackdown in East Pakistan. He served as India's High Commissioner to Bangladesh from 1995 to 2000.

Salman Haidar served as India's Ambassador to Bhutan from 1980 to 1983 and was Foreign Secretary from 1995 to 1997.

Introduction

J.N. Dixit

I felt privileged when I was asked to be the General Editor of this collection of analytical essays on India's relations with its neighbours written by my distinguished colleagues in the Indian Foreign Service. The idea was to bring out a publication that focuses on contemporaneous developments in India's relations with each of its important neighbours in a historical context. This book focuses not only on the conventionally defined neighbourhood of India but also on the broader and relevant strategic neighbourhood and includes separate chapters on India's relations with Afghanistan and China.

The authors of these essays are not only known for their scholarly abilities but also for their knowledge about the historical, socio-cultural and economic impulses which have influenced India's relations with these countries. Their credentials have additional authenticity because most of them have hands-on experience as senior Indian Foreign Service officers who have been posted in these countries and who have played a direct and personal role in assessing political developments and advising the government on policy options.

An analysis of the relations between India and her neighbours, both in the bilateral framework and in terms of collective regional interaction, is pertinent and timely. At the beginning of the second millennium, the

South Asian region, stretching from Afghanistan in the northwest to Myanmar in the southeast, is at a watershed in terms of political developments and economic predicaments. India is—and will remain—a catalyst affecting the dynamics of inter-state relations in this region. It will also be a central factor affecting developmental and economic trends in this region.

There are several reasons why the countries of South Asia individually, and the region collectively, are at a watershed:

Despite the passage of half a century as independent countries, practically all the countries in South Asia are still in the process of individual national consolidation.

All the civil societies of these countries are subject to ethno-linguistic and religious centrifugal pressures. The people of this region have higher levels of political consciousness and expanding socio-economic aspirations that have resulted in an incremental desire amongst common people to participate in the power structures of their respective countries. This participatory ambition is more intense among the weaker sections of civil societies in all these countries.

Despite differing characteristics of the governments of these countries, the general trend is towards an institutional democracy, based on universal adult franchise—a trend which is backed up by increasing support from the international community, particularly the western democracies.

There has been a change in the ideological terms of reference on the basis of which the majority of South Asian states sought to fulfill their economic aspiration and developmental imperatives. The socialistic state-controlled orientations of economic policies have been replaced by a shift towards organising market economies based on competition, productivity, quality of products and liberalisation of processes of production and commerce.

Finally, the break-up of the Soviet Union and the end of the Cold War have brought about profound changes in international and regional power equations leading to the transformation of the geo-strategic environment of South Asia.

The characteristics of this change could be summed up as follows:

a) While the United States has emerged as the most important power in the world, this unipolarity will be tempered with multi-polar impulses and assertions of Japan, the European Union, China, Russia and, hopefully, India.

b) Economic considerations and developmental imperatives have become a matter of higher priority in public consciousness.
c) Globalisation has made territorial countries and nation-states fluid. The flow of ideas, people and goods is freer.
d) Rapid strides in technology, particularly information technology, are eroding the traditional concept of the nation-state. And, at the same time, these technologies are becoming the most substantive ingredients of national power.
e) Compared to other regions of the world, South Asia is an area of tension and conflict in terms of the current situation in Afghanistan, the hostility between India and Pakistan, the tensions between Bhutan and Nepal and the ethnic conflict in Sri Lanka, which has ramifications for India. Moreover, India and Pakistan becoming *de facto* nuclear weapons states has heightened tensions as well as focused on the importance of strategic environment in the South Asian region.

Added to all this is the evolving international consensus in dealing with certain issues which have an impact on countries transcending national borders and national concerns. Foremost among these is the issue of tackling global terrorism as a threat to civil cohesion of state structures. Concerns regarding respect for human rights, creating and nurturing democracies and managing the entire scenario in all its multi-dimensional implications now animate the policies of the international community—this is particularly so in countries of the South Asian region where these issues are of particular concern in the context of the political and socio-economic predicament of the people in these countries.

It should also be noted that the patterns of multilateral cooperation are in the process of being replaced by new patterns of regional and sub-regional cooperation. The South Asian region is lagging behind the other regional groupings in terms of levels of cooperation when compared to the progress made by the ASEAN, APEC and so on. Regional security and regional development are the two macro-level objectives that govern regional interaction and inter-state relations in South Asia.

The essays in this book, written by eminent civil servants, diplomats and analysts, who have not only theoretical knowledge but direct functional experience of dealing with South Asian relations, is a relevant and timely exercise in introspection and prognosis about the political and economic prospects of South Asia at this critical juncture.

When we talk about prospects of South Asian security, stability and economic development, we discuss the well-being of nearly 1.3 to 1.5 billion people, constituting roughly one-sixth of mankind in the broadest and the deepest sense of the word. Security does not simply mean mutual or collective self-protection in military terms of the people living in the different countries of South Asia. It involves, in the first place, the preservation of their respective national identities in political and territorial terms. It also involves ensuring their economic well-being, covering a long-term environment for durable peace, political stability and cooperation.

India, while advocating regional cooperation, did not make any proposal for institutional cooperation because it anticipated resistance from its neighbours, particularly Pakistan. The disparity in size, demography, resources and levels of development between India and all its immediate neighbours led to this approach. The additional factor of a number of political issues on which there were (and are) controversies between India and its neighbours underpinned India's reticence in this matter.

Hence, it was with caution that India viewed the proposal for South Asian regional cooperation put forward by the late Bangladesh President, Zia-ur-Rahman, in January 1980. There was the perception that, in view of the perennial tensions between India and Pakistan, and the distance that characterised India's relations with Bangladesh and Sri Lanka, Zia-ur Rahman's proposal would be a purely cosmetic exercise. There was also the apprehension that the forum, if created, would be a regional platform for 'India bashing'—for putting collective pressure on India on matters of individual concern to each of the participant countries.

Non-participation would have laid India open to the accusation of scuttling an innovative proposal for regional cooperation, despite being the most socio-economically endowed country in the region. Taking all factors into consideration, India ultimately joined the negotiations for the creation of the South Asian Association for Regional Cooperation (SAARC). It came into being in December 1985 after four years of sustained negotiations.

Physical proximity invariably results in interaction. This, however, need not necessarily be positive in content. Interaction can be negative and adversarial, as our experience has shown. In the course of time, the futility and wastage of an adversarial relationship will be realised as revealed by experience and developments in different parts of the world—especially since the early 1970s when there was a thaw in the Cold War culminating in a total transformation of the global scenario after 1989.

The point to be noted is that the geographical parameters of regional or sub-regional cooperation are not determined by the logic or public perception of national or regional boundaries, but by political inclinations and economic requirements. In this context, there is ambiguity in defining the South Asian region. The enthusiasm or willingness of various countries to be part of a South Asian arrangement, therefore, depends more on economic and political considerations.

In addition, there is a dichotomy between the size of the national economies of the region and their resource and technological bases. In this respect, India is a category by itself. Pakistan and Bangladesh have large economies in terms of geography, resources and population. In contrast, Bhutan and Nepal have unidimensional smaller economies. Sri Lanka has developed a more diversified economy.

Ethno-cultural affinity or similarity provides an intellectual, emotional and social impetus to regional cooperation. There are both positive and negative elements affecting this factor in South Asia. Linguistic, ethnic, religious and cultural traits of the people of South Asia transcend the national frontiers of the seven member countries. The people of these countries also follow the same religions. All this should be a potent impulse for cooperation.

Paradoxically, it is the very commonality of the ethno-cultural and religious heritage that has created problems of national political identity among India's neighbours especially Pakistan and, more recently, Bangladesh. Despite shared socio-cultural and religious inheritance, the assertion of a separate political identity necessitates and results in countries of the region pulling back from processes of economic and socio-cultural cooperation. The apprehension of being merged with or marginalised by India remains an obstacle in the process of consolidating regional cooperation.

Cohesiveness in terms of the institutional framework of the power of the region, shared ideas about the organisation of government and shared values about shaping the political system of countries in the region add to the prospects of cooperation. We in South Asia, have to strive towards realising this cohesion. There still remains some distance to be covered before this objective can be realised.

Finally, but also the most important consideration, impinging on regional or sub-regional cooperation in any part of the world is a commonality of perceptions concerning the manner in which regional stability can be ensured, and a shared approach to strategic and security issues affecting the region. Objectivity requires that India clinically analyse the attitude of its neighbours towards it while deciding on the manner and extent to which it should participate in the regional cooperation effort. While Bhutan and Nepal have no palpable reservations about India in matters relating to strategic and security concerns, Pakistan, Bangladesh and Sri Lanka do. Whether or not these reservations and concerns on their part are valid or justified is beside the point.

It follows, therefore, that until a number of complex bilateral political issues between India and its neighbours are resolved, these countries will (a) continue to look for balancing equations with other countries outside the region and (b) to that extent, their willingness to participate in regional cooperation effort will be both limited and inhibited. In the foreseeable future, therefore, the process of cooperation will be gradual.

Prospects of security have to be assessed in a comprehensive manner, both in terms of the security concerns of the individual South Asian states and in the South Asian regional context. While security concerns for the individual states may be rooted in the nature of inter-state relations within the region and in the political and territorial issues which stand unresolved, countries of South Asia face a number of challenges in terms of broader issues.

Traditionally, states have been inclined to deal with security issues that they face by political or diplomatic tactics that are competitive or confrontational, or through the application of incrementally coercive force culminating in military force. But if people in South Asian countries, through a process of political education and enlightenment, are persuaded to move away from norms of confrontation and application of coercive force, a more creative system of managing both national and regional security could be forged. A beginning can be made in areas of security that are not subject to direct competitive political or territorial threat perceptions.

Threats from the political ideological factors, security against supra-nation integration, threats to international society and law and order from fundamentalist forces form part of political security. They need to be examined in their local, regional and global security dimensions. Is there a possibility in South Asia of such threats getting out of hand and becoming a security risk of high order? Can regional mobilisation take place against the threats of a state's destabilisation through political subversion?

Political compulsions affect the prospects of South Asian security negatively.

First and foremost is the asymmetry between India and its South Asian neighbours, in terms of demography, natural resources, levels of economic development, technological capacities and military strength. India has to undertake some very special efforts to remedy the threat perceptions amongst its neighbours -- which are a logical consequence of this asymmetry.

Second, the nuclear weaponisation of India and Pakistan has profoundly affected the security environment in the region, not only in terms of regional security perceptions but also in terms of the strategic response of important nuclear powers like the US, the Russian Federation and China.

It is imperative that India and Pakistan undertake early negotiations within the framework of the Lahore Memorandum of February 1999 to formulate proposals for mutual restraint and to implement them. It is also essential that India structure a relationship with China, Russia and the US to stabilise the strategic environment in the context of the nuclear weaponisation of the region. The influence that these important countries can exert on Pakistan to come to an understanding with India on this specific issue is, and will remain, a matter of high priority.

The threats from cross-border terrorism, narco-crimes, violent religious extremism etc., pose a common challenge to all South Asian countries including even Pakistan. A systematic and continuous effort should be made to forge inter-state South Asian regional cooperation to counter and eliminate these threats.

The demographic pressure on land in all the countries of the region will generate spontaneous migration which individual governments may not be able to contain in the coming decades. This can create social tensions and economic instability if not managed through mutual cooperation. It would be pertinent for the governments in South Asia to initiate early discussions to make arrangements for an economic community and an integrated economic region that would enable freedom of travel, free movement of goods and services and the movement of peoples on the basis of consent and cooperation within the region for specific periods for specific socio-economic purpose.

The South Asian Association for Regional Cooperation itself should revise its agenda and charter to facilitate discussions on all political, economic and territorial issues that create tension between the countries of the region. The terms of reference for discussing these issues should be calibrated in a manner where unity and territorial integrity of individual states of the region do not get challenged in the process. The objective should be limited to examining possible compromises without affecting the vital interests of the SAARC members, and to acknowledging the fact that there would be difference of perceptions between different countries in these vital interests.

Broadening the agenda of SAARC to cover collective security issues and institutionally strengthening the organisation to galvanise cooperation between South Asian states are objectives that should be seriously adopted by member states to ensure durable security in the region.

The South Asia experiment in the creation and consolidation of nation-states has different origins, different impulses and different limitations. The South Asian Nation-states originated from the processes of imperial consolidation of the colonial period. Each such state had a plural ethnic, religious and linguistic demography that is in the process of being cemented through comparatively new concepts of national identity. The limitations are many, more so because what South Asia is trying to do in a span of 50 or 10 years was done in Europe over a period of nearly three-and-a-half to four centuries.

In fact, South Asian nation-states are subject to a profound contradiction. Their collective historical memory is that of their fragmented ethno-linguistic and religious societies, with smaller territorial identities being overcome by imperial integration and colonial rule. So, there is an impulse towards creating themselves into strong nation-states. On the other hand, the ethnic, cultural linguistic and religious identities have the strength of tradition and history that transcends the emergence of nation-states on the international scene. These identities have been reinvigorated in a new atmosphere of freedom and self-rule that has characterised South Asia since the end of the World War II. There are situations where the impulses toward building a strong nation-state are challenged by narrower aspirations of ethnic and sub-national identities.

This is the difference that the South Asian states and the South Asian people have to now resolve.

Pakistan

S.K. Singh

While assessing the resilience and durability of new sovereign states, historians and political scientists often make a review of the way their peoples have accorded respect or otherwise to the heroes and founders of such new states and nations: those who had wielded the supreme or sovereign state power during the early days of their existence.

An analytical review of the story of the early decades of a new state indicates a great deal about the character, idealism and ideology of its people. Studies of post-1776 USA, or post-1917 Soviet Union, or of the leaderships of post-colonial Indonesia, India, Nigeria and Ghana have provided an assessment of the future of these nations, especially the principles and philosophy that motivated the founding fathers, the intrinsic national character and grit of those who followed these early leaders and the ethical values and human attitudes of the societies that emerged as nation states.

Let us apply this yardstick to Pakistan and see how its leaders and peoples managed their state sovereignty, their heroes and themselves.

Mohammad Ali Jinnah, the founder and first head of state of Pakistan died in September 1948, less than 13 months after he had anointed himself governor general of Pakistan. He was advised by his doctors to spend several quiet weeks in Ziarat, the only hill station of Baluchistan province, resting and recuperating far from the madding crowd. His health continued to deteriorate despite this rest; his doctors got alarmed, and subjected him to a thorough medical check-up in Ziarat. They were appalled to find him suffering from both, tuberculosis and cancer of the lungs. They panicked and ordered his early return to Karachi where he could receive more systematic medical attention and be kept under observation by the best medical experts.

His return flight to Karachi was shrouded in secrecy. By then he had become thoroughly suspicious and distrustful of his old comrade and prime minister, Liaquat Ali Khan. Jinnah is on record as having told his doctor once Liaquat Ali Khan had departed after visiting him in Ziarat, during the Quaid's last illness: 'He came because he wants to know how serious my illness is; how long I will last.'

While Jinnah was being driven in an unmarked ambulance from Karachi's Mauripur Airport to the governor general's official residence in Karachi, the vehicle broke down. As a consequence, the governor general lay for a couple of hours, unbeknown to people, under the hot Karachi sun of the month of September, until alternative arrangements could secretly and quietly be made for taking him home. In the course of that night, Jinnah died.

Three years later, on 16 October 1951, while addressing a public meeting in Rawalpindi, Liaquat Ali Khan himself was assassinated by a hired gunman. The gunman, in turn, was instantly shot dead and, therefore, none of the powerful individuals suspected to have been involved in the conspiracy to assassinate the prime minister were arrested or charged with a murder which had taken place in full public view.

The documents concerning the investigation and the official enquiry about this assassination got destroyed, as the aircraft in which the forensic team and their records were being taken from Rawalpindi to the capital, Karachi, blew up in mid-air. Thereafter, there was a deliberate effort to obliterate the incident from public memory. Begum Liaquat's bitterness on this score was never hidden.

After Liaquat's murder and before General Ayub Khan's *coup d'état* in 1958 that helped him declare himself chief martial law administrator, and the president of Pakistan, a veritable cavalcade of governors general and prime ministers made their brief appearances on the stage that was Pakistan. These were Ghulam Mohammad, Khawaja Nazimuddin, General Iskandar Mirza, Mohammad Ali Bogra, Chowdhury Mohammad Ali, I.I. Chundrigar, Sir Feroze Khan Noon and Hussain Shahid Suhrawardi. All these were players who strutted and fretted their brief hour on the stage and then were heard no more. They enjoyed state power for short periods but were subjected to opprobrium and humiliation for much longer. Most of them died as they had lived—without attempting or achieving anything worthwhile, or contributing to any improvement of the lot of their people.

The first foreign minister of Pakistan, Sir Mohammad Zafarullah Khan, was considered a man of considerable legal acumen and some political substance. Once out of office he was ignored, and had to spend his last dozen years or more derided and humiliated as a Qadiani, an apostate and a non-Muslim. He died in the 1980s, neglected and rendered nearly anonymous, a deeply frustrated and sad man, almost a un-person. My last two conversations with him in Lahore, just before he passed away, were painful for him and instructive for me.

Incidentally, the only scientist of any significance produced in Pakistan, Dr. Abdus Salam, who won the Nobel Prize for Physics, was also a Qadiani and he too died in Trieste, where I had the privilege of knowing him. He, too, was derided as a non-Muslim, without the nation ever celebrating his contributions to either science or to his fatherland, Pakistan.

Field Marshal Ayub Khan had been president of Pakistan for 11 years, when he was forced to hand over power to his erstwhile deputy, General Yahya Khan, in March 1969. While leaving the presidential residence, under the pressure of some justifiable and many unfair allegations, Ayub said with some bitterness to his assembled ministers and generals: 'The rest of the world was beginning to look up to us, but our politicians said, "Don't be in a hurry. We will show you what we really are." Pakistan was able to bluff the world, but the Pakistani people themselves called our bluff. We do not know the value of freedom. In freedom our people feel exposed and unhappy. When I found that they wanted to go back to slavery, I quietly stepped aside.'

His successor, General Yahya Khan, by his actions in 1971, invited his own nemesis, and condemned his country to lose its eastern half. He was then forced by public opinion to move aside and transfer power in December that year to Zulfiqar Ali Bhutto, the only civilian ever to be called the chief martial law administrator. Yahya was denounced by his successor, Bhutto, as 'a liar, a drunkard, a fraud and a traitor' and was put under house arrest.

Bhutto was diligent in exercising authority as the president. And, precisely 25 years after Pakistan attained independence, he was able finally to get the National Assembly to provide the country its Constitution. This development resulted in his appointing himself as prime minister.

He, however, never stopped playing political and power games, deriding and distrusting his own party colleagues and ministers, arresting several of them; rigging elections purposelessly (for he would have won even in a fair and free election); and publicly insulting his hand-picked, specially chosen chief of army staff General Zia-ul-Haq, often calling him a 'performing monkey'.

It is no wonder that on the first possible opportunity Zia

showed Bhutto the door gleefully and promptly. He, thereafter, kept him under house arrest in Murree and elsewhere, until he was able to ensure that Bhutto was accused and formally charged with abetting and ordering the murder of Ahmad Raza Kasuri. After that, Zia sat quietly and allowed the legal machinery to grind on until the Pakistan Supreme Court condemned Bhutto to death for murder. On 4 July 1979 the former President and former Prime Minister Z.A. Bhutto, Quaid-I-Awam (the Great Leader of the People) was hanged as a common criminal in Rawalpindi Jail.

Bhutto's successor, President Zia, himself died in an air crash, which has never been fully investigated, nor ever fully explained. Interestingly, the presidential aircraft, a Pakistan Air Force C-130 crashed within 150 seconds of having taken off from Bawahalpur Airport.

After having watched the crash from another plane in the vicinity, General Mirza Aslam Beg, who soon became Zia's successor as the next chief of army staff, coolly flew on to Islamabad. He had a major role in arranging the succession of the president of Pakistan Senate, Ghulam Ishaq Khan, as the next president of Pakistan.

General Zia's burial place near the Faisal Mosque in Islamabad has all along been referred to rather vulgarly as Jabara Sharief or Jabara Chowk—as many believe that very little of his body had survived the plane crash and the resulting fire, and the one visible and prominent part of President Zia that got buried in that grave was his *jabara* (jaw in Urdu).

A former Pakistani civil servant, with some claim to intellectual attainments and good literary style, has in his book referred to Pakistan as a Dream Gone Sour. He quotes the following lines from William Wordsworth:

'. . . Oft said I then, and not then
only, what a mockery this
Of history; the past and that to come!
Now do I feel how I have been deceived.

> *Reading of Nations and their works, in faith,*
> *Faith given to vanity and emptiness*
> *Oh! Laughter for the Page that would reflect*
> *To future times the face of what now is!'*

State power in Pakistan has all along been attended by Machiavellian intrigue and violence, resembling curiously all that had followed in Arabia after the death of the Prophet, when violence attended all but one of the Caliphs who succeeded the Prophet.

The first Caliph Abu Bakr presided over Islamic society in its infancy, for just two-and-a-half years, from Medina and died peacefully. After that, his successor, Omar, led Islam for 10 years. Under his stewardship, Islamic society spread from being the city-state of Medina to becoming a virtual empire covering Palestine, Egypt, and parts of Iran and Azerbaijan. He was killed with a knife by his Persian valet.

The next Caliph Uthman was an Ummayyad, and succeeded Omar when he was already 70 years old. His caliphate lasted a dozen years. These were turbulent years of controversy and expansion during which, unfortunately for the young faith, allegations of corruption multiplied. In AD 656 he was brutally assassinated by a group that included the Prophet's youngest wife, Aisha, as also several of his older companions. Aisha's own brother, also named Mohammad, too was an accomplice.

Ali, who was the Prophet's nephew as well as son-in-law, had long felt that, by right, he should have been the Caliph after the Prophet's passing away. By now, he was already middle-aged, embittered and much disenchanted, not too keen to inherit the Caliphate. However, he was persuaded to assume the Caliphate. Ali left Medina and made Kufa in Iraq his capital. There he had to face an army of Muslims led by his step-mother-in-law Aisha. Soon the authoritarian ruler of Iraq, Muawiya, joined her. Ali was in the process of making a political compromise with Muawiya, when one of his own followers, a Khwarij, killed him for betraying the faith by accepting a compromise. Ali's son Hasan, who then took his father's mantle, was persuaded by Muawiya to step aside and pass on the Caliphate to him. Muawiya poisoned Hasan soon after. And thus began the second chapter of the long and complex tale of the Caliphate, which lasted until the early decades of the twentieth century.

Pakistan and India emerged into their partitioned but sovereign status in August 1947. Their national objectives, ethos, societal philosophies and pursuits thereafter have differed vastly, one from the other. They have persisted in disapproving each other's pursuits and ambitions strongly, and have found it impossible to cultivate any mutual sympathy. Their near-visceral distrust and disapproval of each other has been tinged with some nostalgia about a united and composite existence and growth that might have been. Even though many Pakistanis have privately given voice to this feeling, a nostalgia about living in a composite multi-cultural society (and this gets reflected occasionally in poetry, theatre and music), Pakistan has all along refused to acknowledge any such feeling.

This mutual antipathy derives from the divergent views, pursuits and assessments which our two leaderships, then struggling in two different styles, with two separate sets of objectives, cultivated over several decades against colonial rule. This happened even while the two communities were living together as part of a composite Indian society sharing the common history and culture of the sub-continent.

At the time of parting in 1947, while the progenitors of Partition were demanding separation, both leaderships were aware of how easy it could have been to erase mutual misunderstandings and antipathy. And, retain a common united existence, which would have inevitably left the post-colonial, united India a greater and vastly stronger political, economic and technological presence in the post-Second World War, post-Charter United Nations impacted, Cold War era.

The Hindus and Muslims of India had, in the last seven centuries, achieved much together; quarrelled and bickered viciously hundreds of times, and yet had managed to build deep mutual appreciation, sensitivity, even affection. The angry and passionate proponents of separation, determined to fracture the country and divide it into communal portions—one for the Hindus and the other principally, almost exclusively, for the Muslims, however, ignored this. These two Indian leaderships, with many notable exceptions, rejected in the 1930s and 1940s a united future even as they were preoccupied with evicting the foreigner from their land. Naturally, the wily foreigner recognised his potential for mischief making and deliberately carved out his own vested interests, which in the future were to damage the possibility of a united existence.

These contradictory emotional and rational assessments were real for the generation that inherited Pakistan and tried, during the '50s and '60s, to flesh out its strength. They tried to do so even while memories of pre-Partition composite India were still fresh and the pride in their new Pakistan as a separate, independent Islamic nation was unadulterated.

A number of Pakistanis were puzzled as to why such a large proportion of their co-religionists belonging to the very provinces that continued to remain part of India had elected to continue living with the distrusted, despised and yet admired Hindu majority, and refused to migrate to the areas that now constituted their new Pakistan.

There was, however, a segment of the new political and intellectual establishment in India that persisted in hoping, and even expecting, a broader South Asian Confederal state to emerge once the passion and anger that had motivated the original makers and builders of Pakistan had simmered down. This feeling persisted until the emergence of Bangladesh in the early '70s. But it evaporated after India saw how, even in Bangladesh, there was no great enthusiasm for joining India, only an inchoate appreciation that India had stood with them in the dark days of Pakistani cruelty and repression.

The sagacious Frontier Gandhi, Khan Abdul Ghaffar Khan, comrade of the Mahatma, the Father of the Indian Nation, had passionately opposed the concept of partitioning India. In later years, as declining health provided intimations of mortality to him, Baba, as he was called, used to explain: 'What political folly was committed by Jinnah Saheb. He was unable to look into the future or understand what a powerful and significant state free and undivided India should have been. Just imagine, today there are 145 million Muslims living in Bangladesh, and 135 million in India, and 130 million in Pakistan. These, in a united India, would have totalled up to 410 million people, and who could have dared treat the Mussalmans of a united India as a minority. Jinnah Saheb was a shrewd, difficult politician, always calculating, always arguing, and debating. Why could he not calculate with wisdom and understand this simple fact, something that was clear to us all even in the 1943-1947 period.'

During the '50s and '60s, the Pakistani establishment had some curiosity and much anxiety about their identity as a nation. The basic question demanding a clear answer was: Was this new country, Pakistan, a modern country inhabited by Muslims; or was it an Islamic society, shunning liberal secularism, unable to relate with the Shariah?

Numerous international and national conferences, dialogues and seminars were organised in Karachi, Lahore, Pindi and even Multan, for some soul searching and to receive other people's assessments about their brand-new state of Pakistan, and the identity and potential of the Pakistani nation.

What were they? Where precisely in the world did they stand? What was their place in the sun? What direction was their society and nation likely to take? Were they South Asians first or Islamic first? And last, what was their place in the emerging Afro-Asian context? Had they boxed themselves in by joining the CENTO and SEATO, or did these two alliances provide them with the power and potential to expand? Were their people going to be comfortable in these two pro-Western and anti-communist treaty organisations? What direction would be best for their state to take about their future economy, societal balance and constitutional practices, viewed against the background of their geography, history, culture, and their strategic imperatives?

This exercise failed to yield any clear or unambiguous answers for that generation of Pakistanis. No clear vision emerged from these well-orchestrated exercises meant to define their national identity and prognosticating the direction the new state could or should take. Should they be Maulana Maudoodi's Islamic State on the one hand, or seek Quaid-I-Azam Jinnah's liberal, modern and democratic model? This reflected the original schizophrenia, resulting from their wanting both simultaneously—an Islamic, Shariah-oriented state, and a modern Muslim one. And, this dilemma persists until today.

They were aware too that Mr. Jinnah, immediately after Partition, had declared himself in favour of structuring a democratic, not theocratic, liberal, modern and industrialised Pakistan. This dilemma or schizophrenia prevented the country from getting its Constitution speedily. With great difficulty they gave themselves a Constitution in 1956, almost a decade after attaining independence and a separate sovereignty. It was never promulgated and put into operation. Their second Constitution of 1962 was replaced in 1973 by a third version, which went through an extensive process of recasting and rewriting in 1981. After that date it has been kept in suspended animation off and on.

Ever since its separation from India, Pakistan has been spelling out the difference between its identity and that of India. It has tried to structure a culture of its own; a culture different from India's, and has been anxious to ensure that it is seen as something so distinctive that the entire world would acknowledge its separate and distinct identity. In 1947, it finally succeeded in inventing a nation for itself. This nation, and the state that was created, were unable to discover a positive identity. Their negative identity, however, lay in asserting that they stood for everything that India was not. And, in due course, their strong anti-Indian nationalism became the only one they could claim and cherish.

It realised that, even with its separate territory, it was impossible to devise a different and distinctive ethnicity, or language, or music, or culture, or literature that it could claim as exclusively Pakistani. The country discovered in the first two decades that they could not claim a separate identity—divorced from that of India—even in the context of Islam or of South Asia.

How to carve out a distinct social construct for themselves without reference to India, became the principal preoccupation for Pakistan. Their rejection of everything and anything Indian soon translated itself into full-blooded hostility to India and Indians. This rejection and hatred of India has by now congealed into something concrete, palpable, visible and tangible. The unstated demand of their country is that India should be avoided or destroyed.

Pakistan has never been able to overcome the desire or temptation, in every area and facet of their national life, pursuits and attainments, of comparing themselves favourably with India. This comparison often comes dressed as their quest for parity, or sometimes a vigorous competition in certain areas. The conscious and subconscious desire in Pakistan has always been to seek parity with India in every way, in every field and in every segment of life. This forces them to strive all the time to negate and obliterate the disparity of the two sizes in whatever way they can.

They have never been too shy to beg, borrow or steal from third parties, to seek and receive assistance from any external actor who, for whatever reason and for however short a duration, was prepared to humour or help them along.

In the earliest period of Pakistan's existence it was the two Anglo-Saxon powers, UK and USA. Somewhat later, during the post-Nasser era, they pursued the OIC countries. And, ever since the early '60s, they have cherished and nurtured what they call their 'all-weather and seamless friendship' with the People's Republic of China and, just by chance, exploited their common objective of enfeebling India. The pursuit of parity with India, especially in terms of military capability, has been an unalterable quest for all the leaderships of Pakistan, all through its existence.

Right from their inauguration as a state they have never relented in their pursuit of the territory of the Indian state of Jammu and Kashmir. It was, to them, fair game as a Muslim majority constituent state of India. Within weeks of its emergence as a separate state, Pakistan signed a 'standstill' agreement with the maharaja of Jammu and Kashmir, pending a final determination about which of the two countries—India or Pakistan—he wished to accede to. Pakistan, however, sent its armed personnel into the state with a view to capturing some territory, pretending that the infiltrators were not Pakistani armed forces but certain over-zealous tribals, Afridis etc., from the tribal areas of the NWFP, who insisted on waging jehad against the notion of a predominantly Muslim state joining non-Muslim India.

Kashmir has become Pakistan's constant, even eternal and passionate quest, complaint, and *casus belli* against India. It has never denied or hidden that it has stoked the fires of the pro-Pakistan passion of the Kashmiris and also provided them their permanent enemy without whose fearsome and menacing proximity the nation could have fallen into a relaxed slothful slumber.

It has gone to war with India four times for Kashmir, and to the UN Security Council half a dozen times. It was this cause that gave the Pakistanis the courage and the passion for the pursuit of nuclear weapons and missiles as their means of delivery. In the last dozen years and more, they have imposed a proxy war on India by exporting cross-border terrorism into Jammu and Kashmir from the Pak-occupied portion of Kashmir that, they hope, will bleed India to death.

They have, since the birth of their state, also tried recklessly to sow disaffection amongst the 145 million Muslim minorities in India. They have done so without caring for the consequences for their own future prosperity as a state or the security and future of their own cousins, the Muslim community in India.

Pakistan and India have had scores of disputes, hundreds of negotiations, and have signed a very large number of agreements in the last half-century. Most of these have lapsed or remained ignored. In the post-independence era, the two heads of government and state, foreign ministers, finance and commerce ministers, foreign and other secretaries etc., have met bilaterally or multilaterally on several hundred occasions.

However, no mutual trust exists and no measures for establishing any confidence-building measures or nuclear-risk-reduction-measures have been undertaken till now. They have failed to coordinate their thinking and concepts on peace and security in general. And, this despite the fact that, through the Tashkent Agreement of 1966 and the Simla Agreement of 1972, both countries are committed never to use war again as an instrument for determining issues or settling differences. Both have continued taking war-like measures whether in Siachin or in Kargil. Artillery, mortar and machine-gun fire across the line of control have been endemic.

All this is punctuated from time to time by friendly visits, conferences, bilateral talks and summits. Good examples of these were General Zia-ul-Haq's visit to Jaipur to watch a cricket match in 1987, Prime Minister Vajpayee's bus journey to Nawaz Sharif in Lahore in 1999 and the Vajpayee-Musharraf summit in Agra 2001.

Indo-Pak relations have been complex, disturbed and distressing from the time of Pakistan's birth. Pakistan is a country closest to India geographically, ethnically, linguistically, and culturally but it remains a difficult neighbour. There is intense distrust and, on occasion, each calls the other its most implacable adversary or foe. When, however, Indian and Pakistani citizens meet on neutral ground, in a non-political atmosphere, they find it easy to be warm, even affectionate, and generous at a personal level and extremely hospitable to one another. It is true that the internal tensions and problems of Pakistan have grown over the years. It is also true that India has not been able to render them any help. Pakistan derives great satisfaction from creating problems for India.

Little has changed, it would appear, in this bilateral relationship since Jawaharlal Nehru's time from Independence until the mid-'60s. Nehru was convinced that Pakistan's birth was due to a negative attitude to Indian nationalism and that Pakistan remained rootless and lacking in positive content.

Nehru arrived at some wrong conclusions. For example, he and several leaders of the Indian National Congress were convinced that Pakistan's separation from India was a temporary phenomenon and that ultimately both wings of Pakistan could not avoid gravitating towards some sort of confederal arrangement with India. After Field Marshal Ayub assumed power in Pakistan, Nehru thought that military rule could not but be a short-lived experiment. Both these judgements were flawed.

On Kashmir, Nehru could foresee no easy progress towards any settlement. He hoped (once again mistakenly) that Pakistan authorities would cease incidents of sabotage in Kashmir. At the same time, however, he publicly acknowledged that no government in India could agree to hand over to Pakistan any territories in Jammu and Kashmir, or even agree to a process that might lead to such an outcome. He once candidly told Ayub that the only practicable and feasible course was to permit matters where they were, that the basic *status quo* would need to be allowed to continue for some more time with minor adjustments to the ceasefire line. He added that any major territorial adjustment would 'affect injuriously' the Muslims in India and would have a destabilising effect not merely in Kashmir, but all over India.

Pakistan maintained its ill-will towards India and deliberately dragged Kashmir into Cold War politics. Nehru felt that this development denied both countries an opportunity for settlement. In the last two years of his life, Nehru appeared disinclined to leave the Kashmir problem for his successors to cope with. Pakistan took a rigid posture then and managed to convince itself that, as China's Himalayan war had brought India to its knees, it could peg up its demands on the Kashmir issue and let India squirm.

Pakistan needs to be persuaded that its effort to keep this issue at a boiling point would defeat its purpose of negotiating a settlement. Some years need to be given to this issue, to let emotions and passions calm down, and ensure that the two countries do not feel the need to move towards irrationality and friction. Without a better ambience in Indo-Pak relations, more day-to-day cooperation in diverse fields, and a scenario where the two countries acquire a vested interest in each other's prosperity and happiness, this dispute cannot move towards any resolution.

Any dispute with a long and complex history, in which religion, ethnicity and geo-political differences are involved, where territory is being sought, cannot be solved unless an amicable atmosphere is created as a precondition for meaningful negotiations.

An excellent example is that of two friendly governments, Ireland and England, who both agree that the Northern Ireland issue should be resolved. Admittedly, they have not been able to move towards a solution during the last dozen or so years of joint endeavour, but they do realise that a few more years of persistence will get them there. The history of the dispute, emotions, the traditional use of violence, ethnicity and religious emotions have been busy defeating the two friendly sovereign states and their governments until now, by the history of past violence, and the noisy and inimical present, that is kept alive by non-state actors.

In his writings just before his execution, Bhutto hinted that his most abiding and significant legacy for Pakistan was the commitment he extracted for China's help in the nuclear and missile fields. India's peaceful nuclear explosion of 1974 had perturbed Bhutto and his collaborators. In his usual flamboyant style he had vowed to 'eat grass' and to face all hardships to build his Islamic bomb.

Clearly, by the mid-'80s Pakistan had acquired nuclear weapons capability. Its national and indigenous research base for this was narrow and, in general, the world suspected that much of its capability was imported. For years they had been importing nuclear items, heavy water, other ancillaries and equipment secretly through their special, clandestine purchase organisations functioning in Europe and in North America. Technology and components were provided by China. Certain Arab countries were suspected of having helped them with financial resources.

After the five Indian nuclear tests of May 11 and 13 1998, Pakistan promptly responded on May 28 and 30 1998, with six tests of its own. Pakistan derived considerable satisfaction from these tests as they enabled it to come out of the nuclear closet and to openly assert its nuclear weapons capability. Pakistan could also now claim symmetrical deterrence capability vis-à-vis India. Pakistan was pleased with itself as the first Muslim country to have acquired this capability.

In the earlier days, it used to claim that its bomb was the bomb for the Islamic world. It now underplays this aspect. Pakistan feels that while other Islamic countries have more oil, or a higher GDP, Pakistan's leadership in the Islamic world cannot be challenged or underestimated due to their being the sole Islamic possessors of nuclear weapons.

China, too, makes little secret of being Pakistan's provider of ready-made missiles and of having gifted the missile-making capability to Pakistan. Islamabad, in these fields, does not aspire to match India but merely wishes to sustain its deterrence capability, and be of some utility to its benefactor, China.

In bilateral politico-strategic terms, Pakistan now possesses a wider variety of options both in terms of its relations with the great powers as also with the countries of Central Asia and the Persian Gulf. It has chosen, until now, to ignore and avoid getting into a dialogue with India on nuclear doctrine, or about bilateral confidence building measures.

The process India had commenced in Lahore with General Musharraf's predecessor, Nawaz Sharif, has been totally ignored by him. His Kargil effort erased the hope Lahore had kindled. And Kargil, which was believed to have been General Musharraf's brainchild—followed by sustained activity of jehadi groups in Kashmir, organised and managed by the ISI—has worsened the bilateral relationship and stalled bilateral dialogue. Pakistan is even now entirely unwilling to move towards anything like a no-first-use declaration.

Political turbulence has been a constant in the story of Pakistan. It is difficult to comprehend unless we observe the manner in which various social groups and classes have tried to capture and control state power, right from the country's establishment as a sovereign entity.

At the time of Partition in 1947-48, eight million Muslim refugees migrated to Pakistan, replacing the six million Hindus and Sikhs who, on being squeezed out of Pakistan, left for India. The Muslim refugees represented a social force because it was acknowledged that they had spearheaded the struggle for and had played a major role in the creation of Pakistan.

The new political leadership and the senior-most echelons of bureaucracy in this new country were from amongst these new arrivals and were accepted as authentic original leaders of the new state. They were not indigenous inhabitants of the provinces in which Pakistan was now born and established. During the bulk of Jinnah's agitation and clamour for separation, the political and bureaucratic leaders of the original and indigenous areas of Pakistan, (Punjab, Sindh, Baluchistan and Frontier Province) had remained indifferent or lukewarm to the idea of Pakistan. It was the refugees from India who managed, even dominated, Pakistan immediately after its birth—socially, economically and politically—providing the country's political and bureaucratic establishment.

Thus, during the first decade of its existence, the indigenous elite and common people of the new state of Pakistan found the refugees from India (who were referred to as 'Mohajirs' and were only one-quarter of the population) playing the dominant rôle in the new state.

However, three-fourths of the indigenous population soon developed a certain antipathy to the Mohajirs, and became conscious of their distinct interests that, with time, became their vested interests. These outsiders were born in Uttar Pradesh, Bihar, Madhya Pradesh, Rajasthan, Hyderabad (Deccan), Karnataka, Kerala, Gujarat, etc. Thus, right from its commencement, the Pakistani political system was afflicted by tensions and disequilibrium.

Meanwhile, authentic Pakistanis, especially their traditional elites from those parts that comprised this new country, demanded their own share in the power, glory and wealth of the newly invented nation and state. These were the big feudals of the Punjab, the Waderos of Sindh, the tribal Maliks and chiefs of Baluchistan and the Sardars and Khans of the NWFP. During the colonial period, they had gotten used to feudal privileges, wealth and perks that were never questioned or disturbed by the British. All of them were opposed to any idea of land reform.

General Ayub Khan's military takeover in 1958 and the beginning of Pakistan's industrialisation coincidentally came about at about the same time. Both these processes of military dictatorship and industrialisation helped to make real the other trend of indigenising Pakistani politics.

Industrialisation led to the earliest urbanisation. This also helped in the process of the Pakistani military dominating civil society, and assuming political authority, indeed the entire structure of governance. All these changes led to unavoidable shifts of socio-economic authority and influence from the landlords and tribal chiefs towards the industrialising urban classes and the captains of industry.

Since landlords and the feudal class, industrialists, bankers, leaders of commerce and the attenuated politico-bureaucratic gentry all saw that they could derive their profits, perks and respectability in society from their military overlords, the emergence of a new kind of social balance became easy. It, however, depended on a real and permanent disequilibrium in the Pakistani state and society. Through the processes of easement, practice and tradition, this has tended to be more or less automatically understood and acceptable in Pakistan.

As we discuss the impact of the first military ruler of Pakistan, Ayub, on the political evolution of Pakistan, we must note that he managed to enjoy public confidence even approval somewhat longer than each one of his military successors—General Yayha Khan (1969-71), General Zia-ul-Haq (1977-88) and General Pervez Musharraf (1999-continuing). Each of them enjoyed just a few months of applause and a happy honeymoon with the people and the media and thereafter, each came under two pressures: one, the demand that democracy better be restored at the earliest and sending the military marching back to its barracks to achieve this; and two, the current military ruler should better announce the date schedule for the next elections to ensure restoration of the Central Parliament or National Assembly, and the provincial legislatures.

The present chief-of-army-cum-president has been calling himself just the chief executive of the country and has refused to assume the grandiose but accurate title of the chief martial law administrator. He has also made the shrewd but unpopular move of getting himself confirmed through a referendum for a further five-year term.

General Musharraf insists that his two immediate predecessors as prime ministers chief executives continue to remain in exile. Benazir Bhutto keeps shuttling between Washington, London and Dubai to avoid being arrested on charges of corruption, etc., in case and whenever she returns home.

Nawaz Sharif and his family, much like the former Ugandan military dictator, General Idi Amin Dada, has been consigned to the care (and confinement) of the Saudi royal family, unlikely to be sent home in a hurry. He, too, in the event of somehow landing in Pakistan, could face serious charges like attempting to murder Musharraf and, of course, many allegations and charges of corruption.

This effectively means that the two principal political parties of the country, the People's Party of Pakistan (PPP) and the Pakistan Muslim League (PML), which are also the largest and oldest ones in the land, are kept in a kind of suspended political animation.

For good measure Mohajir Musharraf (he was born in Delhi and his family was originally from Lucknow, before they migrated to Pakistan in 1947) has also ensured that the Mohajir Quami Mahaz (MQM) leader, Altaf Hussain also continues to cool his heels in comfortable exile in London.

This leaves Musharraf to deal with various splinter groups and offshoots of these three parties, as well as with parties like Wali Khan's Awami National Party, which had aligned itself to Nawaz Sharif's PML and was originally an expression of the Pakhtun nationalist movement. Likewise, the Baluch nationalist movement also consists of groups that are all Baluchi nationalists but attach themselves to various tribal chiefs. Baluchi populations are somewhat scattered, divided between Pakistan, Iran, Afghanistan and Turkmenistan.

The whole scene in recent years has been confused and muddied by the politics of the mosque and of Islamists, most of them claiming to be jehadis. Some of them have sought strength by aligning themselves with the Afghan Talibans, who come and go out of Pakistan at will.

When Bhutto arrived on the scene with his slogan of '*Roti, Kapda aur Makaan*', both the middle class and the working class in urban areas became conscious of the imminence of their exclusion from the fruits of Pakistan's developmental and national wealth.

Unfortunately, Bhutto went in for a somewhat arbitrary process of nationalising the larger industries, banks and insurance companies, without having prepared the nation or the system. And, also without having acquired an in-depth understanding of the new and real constituencies, which had by then emerged within the nation and were busy defining their respective areas of influence and authority.

While attempting nationalisation he failed to notice that, in India, this process had been arrived at after considerable preparation and debate at more serious intellectual, social and political levels, and over a number of years. As a result, society in Pakistan was caught unawares by the kind of reforms that Bhutto was now working to put into the statute book, including the new labour laws for ensuring additional benefits for the working class.

He soon discovered that the feudals' constituency, which had helped him acquire authority, would not permit him to head into the new pro-labour and pro-urban directions. Bhutto's dilemma stemmed from the fact that he had more or less consciously permitted the old elite to continue holding political power. This elite class comprised feudals and large landholders like himself, including the tribal chiefs in the NWFP and Baluchistan. This effectively prevented him from doing anything that could help him gain popularity amongst the labour and other industrial urban constituencies.

He was too intelligent not to recognise that the path taken by the Indian leadership had been entirely different from that in Pakistan. One of the Congress Party's earliest economic reforms in India had been their comprehensive and nation-wide land reforms implemented with considerable flexibility. It had commenced in 1937, when the Congress assumed governance in seven provinces under the Government of India Act. Landlordism was abolished and much of the arable land was distributed amongst the landless peasantry.

Bhutto went on to curtail the decision-making powers of the civil service, and further compromised the already-compromised concept of the independence of the judiciary.

While taking over state power in the country, General Zia defined the objective of his stewardship as Islamisation of the nation, including specifically the areas of jurisprudence and economic work of governance. This won him the loyalty of devout Mussalmans around the country, including a fair percentage belonging to the middle class. Bhutto had alienated a large proportion of the urban middle class by accepting and promoting the authority and privileges of the landed feudal class and the tribal chieftains, who too were conservative and strongly Islamic. This middle class could now afford to forget Bhutto and effortlessly begin following Zia in Islamising the system. Many middle-class Pakistanis admired and appreciated Zia's style of punctilious humility and saw in him a leader who was a simple and devout Muslim. Many were fooled into imagining that Zia's tenets of Islam were bound to promote more ethical conduct in governance.

In the long run, societal management on a day-to-day basis required, first of all, resolving the contradictions of Pakistan wishing to be seen both as a modern, industrial nation and as a devout Islamic society.

During our partitioned existence, Pakistanis have tended to see in our country a continuity of the Hindu majority which their old Muslim League leadership had found it difficult to cope, and impossible to live with, in our pre-Independence era. Many are nevertheless conscious of India's political and economic achievements during the post-Independence era. They still feel, however, that India's military defeat(s) at the hands of China and Pakistan (they regarded the brief Kutch skirmish as a clear military triumph!) showed how feeble this country remains militarily. Except in the Bangladesh War of 1971, Pakistan has all along claimed that it has overcome India, or at least contained it militarily in each armed contest, despite the enormous variation in our respective sizes. Even during the recent mobilisation of the two armed forces on the Line of Control, they have never tired of asserting that the Pakistan army will successfully and with ease, deal with and defeat our armed forces. For their military humiliation of 1971 they blame the 'treacherous Bangladeshis' who helped India to dismember Pakistan, by de-linking the Eastern part of the country. They rejoice also that the USA and India, together were unable to prevent Pakistan from emerging as a significant nuclear-weapon-and-missile-wielding power. From all this, they have convinced themselves that these bilateral wars and battles and competition, are a continuation of their success and prowess in the Hindu-Muslim rioting which persisted during the British era. They feel that India is weighed down by too much historical rancour and too much resentment against them. Also that we feel some kind of inferiority vis-à-vis themselves having been under Islamic rule for almost 800 years.

It was a trick played by the British against them that at the end of colonial rule, they left the Hindus, as a so-called majority, the largest and best part of India; and to them a 'truncated' Pakistan. The British had grabbed India from the Mughals (who were Muslims) and should have returned the entire country to them.

They believe that Hindus are never truthful in political matters. It is patently false that the Hindu is tolerant, secular or democratic. The caste system and the Hindu traditions about untouchables prove this point conclusively for them. They see a major conspiracy behind the contradictory actions of India's leadership who, on the one hand, accepted Partition, and on the other hand proceeded to lure a large number of Muslims to stay on in India as their hostages. They see in the philosophy of the Sangh Parivar a proof of their correct assessments about India and the duplicity of the Hindus. Now that the Hindu is unabashedly establishing his majority status the Sangh Parivar theories are beginning to show the extent to which the Hindus now accept Jinnah's old

Two Nation Theory, as they recognise themselves as different from the Muslims. They see Gujarat as a continuing phenomenon. They hope that with their capacity to anticipate things, they will be able to defend themselves through fracturing India, by building a Khalistan in the Punjab, a Tamil Eelam in Southern India and several separate republics in the North-East of the country.

They are also pleased that they have greater influence, and greater credibility as friendly neighbours with the other SAARC and other nations especially China, Nepal, Sri Lanka and Bangladesh, than India. They are always 'delighted' to be able constantly to expose India's hegemonic designs to all India's closest nieghbours, as also to all major powers of the world including the USA. They feel reassured about their safety and security, as it is being guarded by the mighty Pakistan army, which has the will power, and prowess to triumph over the much larger Hindu Armed Forces. They believe that the Indian Armed Forces are inherently feeble, because they have no self-confidence, no self-assurance and respect, and therefore, they view the rest of the world with the psychology of fear, many apprehensions, and resentments. This is bound once again, and one day soon, to bring India under their control, after certain parts of India de-link themselves from their present country. This theme of their insuperable bravery and India's weakness at arms has been constant. Indeed, from time to time they get the feeling that the Indian Republic is about to self-destruct or selfishly break itself up through disunity. This happened when Nehru died and a little later when the political pressures on Indian law and order had become severe. On such occasions their military personnel is sent to India, to break it up.

With the exception of some members of the intelligentsia, Pakistanis are not impressed with India's economic, commercial, scientific or technological achievements. The mullah-military combine which is the principal factor in formulating the public opinion within Pakistan, is convinced that this is a miasma and made up as a tissue of lies.

This could also explain why the Pakistanis living outside the tyranny of this mullah-military combine, anywhere abroad, find it easy to be rational in comparing the two societies in all their major dimensions and facets. This would also explain that once they are outside the subcontinent, they find it easy and natural to befriend the Indians in their common ambience and localities abroad.

The period, in which Bhutto was the supreme leader of Pakistan, coincided with the oil and construction booms in the Gulf region. The oil-rich Arab lands (and Iran) helped create a huge demand in those countries for blue-collar skilled labour and technically qualified personnel from South Asia. Once Pakistani workers secured new and lucrative employment in West Asia and North Africa and the migration of large numbers of Pakistani workers to these Eldorados of opportunity and wealth got established, a significant and prosperous remittance economy grew speedily in Pakistan. It changed, even transformed, the economic and social landscape of the country. Soon the Pakistani state discovered how significantly the size of their middle class had expanded—and with what speed.

The Pakistani military also saw in this trend a huge opportunity for themselves. They rejoiced in being Muslims and belonging to the same faith as the people of the oil-rich countries and regions. The Pakistani military enjoyed the reputation of a disciplined, modern, well-equipped force in all these countries and, therefore, the military leadership of Pakistan succeeded in creating lot of opportunities for themselves to function in these countries as trainers, promoters, and protectors of the nascent and often small Arab military forces. They took charge of the process of the maintenance and repair of the Arabs' modern technological arms, armament, gadgets and equipment in the area of defence. This created the military component of Pakistan's remittance economy and also built greater cooperation and camaraderie with Islamic militaries, thus expanding the area of intelligence functioning for the Pakistani Inter-Services Intelligence and Military Intelligence branches.

Simultaneously, within Pakistan, they rapidly expanded their direct involvement in a variety of civilian industrial ventures that became part of the nation's new industrialisation. All this fuelled the creation and expansion of the Fauji Foundation of Pakistan and the emergence of the Shaheen (i.e., Air Force) and Bahri (Navy related) Foundations.

In the meanwhile, however, large amounts of foreign capital flowed into Pakistan, as a result of it becoming a frontline state for the Americans and Western powers that were fuelling the struggle of the Afghan Mujahideen against the Soviets—a factor in the ultimate demise of the Soviet system and State.

The guerrilla warfare in Afghanistan, so diligently assisted by Pakistan, resulted in the US providing approximately $7.8 billion worth of military equipment and other assistance to Pakistan between 1980 and 1989. Many more billions were distributed in and around Afghanistan through the conduit provided by Pakistan and the instrumentality of its intelligence groups, which collaborated, with zeal and loyalty, with the CIA for dismantling the Soviet Union. A fair percentage of this cash did stick to Pakistani fingers while they were distributing and apportioning this assistance.

A lot of unaccounted humanitarian assistance, clandestine funds for various intelligence operations and other covert purposes also came Pakistan's way through the munificence in caution and carelessness of the West. And, then there was the foreign developmental aid, humanitarian assistance, food and medicines, etc., which needed to be distributed amongst the approximately 3 million Afghan refugees who had taken shelter in Pakistan from Afghanistan.

The secret service subventions for clandestine work in

Afghanistan did not come merely from the CIA, but also from other secret services including those of Saudi Arabia, Libya, Abu Dhabi and several Western countries. All the arms and ammunition, the so-called humanitarian assistance, the secret service funds for playing the Great Game that rapidly became the Greater Game of dismantling the number two superpower, required necessarily to be channelled through Pakistan. This was due as much to its geography as to the USA's confidence in the Pakistani military.

According to some estimates, approximately $15 billion over a period of seven years was handled by Pakistan. One major consequence of this was the creation of approximately one million jobs for Pakistanis.

General Zia's survival, indeed his ability to win the loyalty of a majority of his people, owed principally to the extraordinarily high rates of economic growth that resulted from the huge influx of foreign capital into the country. President Zia once confided that, within the OIC, Pakistan's authority and primacy as a member of that fraternity was based on two factors: one, on the country's military prowess and size which, in some ways, he considered either superior to, or in certain aspects as rivalling the military apparatuses of Egypt and Turkey; and two, on the superiority of Pakistan's technological credentials within the Islamic community of nations.

He was proud, he once told me, of having insisted on maintaining Pakistan's chairmanship of the OIC's Committee on Science and Technology. Apparently, Saudi Arabia had wished to annex this chairmanship, as a prize for its major financial contribution and assistance. Pakistan resisted this successfully.

Pakistan gradually frittered away part of these resources. In recent years, its economy has had a low growth rate and an increasing debt burden. And, its economy has also suffered through poor crops, political turmoil, social unrest and corruption. The sanctions imposed by the Western powers, especially the US, after Pakistan's May 1998 nuclear tests in Chagai, were further expanded due to additional American sanctions imposed after General Musharraf's military takeover after the *coup d'état* of October 1999—when he brusquely abolished Pakistan's democracy such as it might have been.

The terrorist attack of 9/11 on the US created a new global situation. Also, a new regional situation was created by Pakistan joining the global coalition in support of the American fight against terrorism. As a result, most of the sanctions against Pakistan were withdrawn and the economic and financial support of the international community to the country was restored. Pakistan has once again started receiving aid, loans and financial concessions from the US, Britain, Canada, Japan and other nations.

These nations have also ensured similar opening up of economic support for Pakistan by the ADB, IMF and the World Bank. In the fiscal year 2000-01 Pakistan's aggregate growth rate had been just 2.6 per cent. The World Bank had put Pakistan in the same category as Congo and Ethiopia as amongst the world's most severely indebted and low-income countries.

According to the World Bank, in that year Pakistan was a country, (one of only three countries in the world) whose debt burden had deteriorated in a perilous manner. The other two were Benin and the Kyrgyz Republic. It must be mentioned that, as a result of the two sets of sanctions that had crippled Pakistan, the overall level of foreign assistance (which had peaked to $3.3 billion in 1988-90 period) had been reduced to $1.5 billion in 1999-2000.

The country's economy suffocated due to the fact that in 1999-2000 it spent almost 12 per cent of its total GDP on debt servicing alone. During this period of economic hardship, the bulk of the foreigners working on different projects in Pakistan started leaving the country. A large proportion of orders that had been placed with Pakistani industries were also cancelled, without their receiving any fresh orders. Pakistan's ready-made garment industry estimated that its total textile exports, which used to be 65 per cent of their total exports of $9 billion, sustained a loss of $3 billion in export earnings alone during the year 1999-2000.

Insurance companies added war risk charges on all trade to and from Pakistan's shipping ports. A number of foreign airlines withdrew from the country entirely or partially. The travel and hotel industries were badly affected. And, the national airline PIA (Pak International Airways) suffered a loss of Rs. 30 million in one year.

To crown it all, the Pakistani military between 1996-97 and 2000-01 insisted on increasing its defence expenditure from Rs. 127 billion to Rs. 157 billion (approximately $2.5 billion to $3.3 billion), an expansion of nearly 25 per cent. This, however, is nothing new or novel for Pakistan. Almost all through its existence the country has been controlled and ruled by military dictators, who have wielded great influence and a variety of vetoes, even during those brief periods when civilians were at the helm. And, their officer corps has all along insisted on the country giving priority to expenditure on arms and armed men over the expenditure on development and nation building. They have already indicated to their own country, and to the Western powers, which have treated them as a frontline nation that has joined their fight against terrorism, that they will need an additional $2.5 billion during the fiscal year 2001–2002.

Once Pakistan joined the US and other countries of the West in the global war against terror, the IMF, the World Bank and the Asian Development Bank all started coming up with financial support packages for Pakistan. The World Bank has sent a strong message to Pakistan that it wants to see Pakistan promoting positive reforms in the management of its economy. Several dialogues are on for additional funds for the country. The package of the ADB is expected to be around $1.25 billion.

In December 2001, the Paris Club creditors agreed to

restructure their public external debt. This agreement provides for a comprehensive restructuring of a stock of debt amounting to $12.5 billion as of 1 December 2001. Out of their total debt, commercial credits are to be repaid over 23 years, with five years of grace, and progressive payment at the appropriate market rate. ODA credits are to be repaid over 38 years with 15 years of grace at rates that are concessional and generous.

These promises of financial support, along with various free grant funds released by the US and other Western countries, the rescheduling of several of Pakistan's debts, the $1 billion support assistance (terms for this are not yet known) and actions such as Canada converting a $300 million loan into development funding, have eased the pressures on Pakistan's economy. Pakistan and its economists have already started hiking up their demands. They now plead that they need at least $5 billion that is free of conditionalities to provide themselves some fiscal space.

The European Union, in the meanwhile, has offered to help Pakistan by providing it wider access to its markets. Pakistan is hopeful that the US will also offer similar access to its market.

Japan has declined write-offs due to its legal constraints, but has offered rescheduling of debt and aid package along lines that are similar to those offered by the US. The US has been discussing with other creditors debt relief, which will be a mix of write-offs, reschedulings, renegotiations of terms of repayment and servicing.

In realistic terms, this is indicative of the possibility that Pakistan's anti-India adventurism could rise as a result of these inputs from abroad, just in case their economic situation improves. Unless a superhuman effort is made to curb Pakistan's enthusiasm for keeping India under pressure through backing and promoting terrorist activities in Jammu and Kashmir, otherwise called Pakistan's proxy-war against India, their military budget is bound to see further expansion.

Even after one has taken all these concessions into account, Pakistani economists like Dr. Akbar Zaidi feel that the kind of economic revival that is being anticipated or hoped for by the government may not take place. This is principally because the government is likely to continue facing revenue shortfall due to the recessionary trend in the economy and falling inputs.

It is by now clear that the real law and order authority and political influence in Pakistan are likely to remain in the hands of the military establishment—whether Pakistan has a military general who calls himself chief martial law administrator or one who is addressed as chief executive or an elected prime minister. Over the years, the military have ensured that the Pakistani people have become used to this.

What is less well known is that the Pakistan army has also made itself the largest employer of manpower in the country. By and large, the man in the street remains unaware of how important their military's corporate interests in the Pakistani society have become. This provides the Pakistani military a major interest in retaining political influence and power in the governance of the country, whatever the form of government may be called.

The starting point for what has by now emerged as the behemoth Fauji Foundation in Pakistan was the establishment of the Army Welfare Trust in 1954 under the Societies Registration Act. The mandate of the trust was to generate funds for the welfare and rehabilitation of the orphans and widows of the '*shaheeds*' and the disabled personnel of the Pakistan army and their dependents. The trust was also charged with creating job opportunities for retired personnel of the army. The idea obviously was to continue generating funds for welfare and rehabilitation, without the trust itself undertaking welfare activities directly. This was left to the General Headquarters. The funds or the profits generated from the various industrial ventures become available to the Welfare and Rehabilitation Directorate of Pakistan's GHQ for utilisation on welfare activities as determined by the military leadership of the land.

A corollary of this is that commercial ventures have been organised (in the name of welfare) by the Pakistani military, which now considers itself also as a major engine for socio-economic and political growth. All these industries are managed by serving army officers, along with recently retired and some not so recently retired senior officers, in a proportion of one-third serving and two-third retired officers. From time to time, during the tenure of political (as opposed to military) governments, the former have acquiesced in the expansion of the military-controlled industrial and commercial ventures, a kind of political bribe to win the military's support.

Over the years the original Fauji Foundation and its Army Welfare Trust have been joined by two other foundations—the Shaheen Foundation for air force officers and the Bahria Foundation controlled by the Pakistan navy. Both are on the same pattern as the Fauji Foundation.

Together, the industries controlled by these foundations represent the largest business and industrial conglomerate in Pakistan. The entire enterprise is organised and arranged in a manner that there is little, if any, trace of public accountability in respect of their overall operating and controlling mechanisms. The ruling principle is that if the chief of army staff can be trusted to run the entire army (and often even the country) properly, surely he can be trusted to do likewise in respect of the profits and produce of the Fauji Foundation!

A constitutional question had arisen some years ago about the juridical propriety of the military's major and close involvement in the country's commercial and industrial spheres. This question arose because the 1973 Constitution of Pakistan limits the role of the defence forces exclusively to maintaining and managing the international security of Pakistan. Due to its power and influence, the military, however, ignored such theoretical, esoteric questions of jurisprudence and managed to continue expanding unchecked its role in the context of the Fauji Foundation's commercial and industrial ventures. Such minor matters as a constitutional disability were best forgotten.

Long-term political governance in the hands of the military often results in the military expanding its direct role in commercial, industrial and manpower management spheres. At last count, the total assets and investments controlled by the Fauji Foundations of the three forces were over Rs. 200 billion.

Public sector operations such as the National Logistics Cell (NLC) and the Frontier Works Organisation (FWO), which fall under the Fauji Foundation, have gradually become major monopolies. The NLC, for example, has a fleet of 2,000 vehicles and employs almost 2,500 serving army officers and 4,100 retired officers. This organisation controls all food grain movement in the country and several similar bulk commodities, heavy in weight and bulk. It also meets the transport requirements of all military supplies. The FWO has been given the responsibility of road construction and civil works on a profit-making basis. Even so, both these organisations continue to receive financial infusions from the public sector. For example, in 1993-94, NLC was provided with Rs. 245 million to invest in stocks and bonds.

Most of these business ventures, however, have been making losses; and some of them have been a burden on the public sector by drawing funds from the annual defence budget. Over the years, government auditors raised certain objections about a number of financial discrepancies. Most of these objections were dropped after intervention at the highest official levels.

Jobs are provided to senior officers in these foundations, to specially favoured retired personnel or to those on the verge of retirement, as rewards. They are taken away if and when some of them need to be punished. President Zia made generous use of top positions in the foundations to reward officers for earlier services and obedience rendered and loyalty displayed, and sidelined those in service who posed a potential threat to him or to his system.

Most of these retired military officers are untainted by any specialised knowledge or training for their jobs. This leads to a considerable wastage of resources. The profitability of most of these organisations is questionable. There is major loss of tax revenue through the operation of these industrial and commercial ventures as they are tax-free, since the welfare foundations fall under the Charitable Endowment Act 1989. Under public pressure, this rule was changed in 1991, but the taxes levied were not calculated on an equitable basis. The profits claimed by the Shaheen and the Bahria Foundations are being taxed at the rate of 33 per cent, while the Fauji Foundation and the Corporations under the Army Welfare Trust are taxed at a lower rate i.e., only 20 per cent. This makes it obvious that it is the army that has the real clout, even in the matter of calculating the tax rates, and not the other two services.

Recently, the UNDP has been tempted to assist these favoured and fortunate foundations. In 1995-96, the UNDP created a Pilot Business Incubation Centre for retired officers of the Pakistan army, with a view to training them to run and manage businesses, and encouraging them to make their own enterprises profitable. Their justification for involvement was that since 400 officers in their early forties with good education retire each year from the Pakistan army and, since the Army Welfare Trust runs numerous business activities—especially ones connected with sugar, rice, oil mills, cotton farms, travel agencies, in addition to managing Askari Commercial Bank (Soldiers Commercial Bank), and certain leasing and insurance companies—a developing country like Pakistan would benefit by the UN setting up such a centre.

The welfare projects and programmes of the Fauji, Shaheen and Bahria Foundations are managed and funded through fully owned commercial and industrial projects. The fully owned industrial projects of the Fauji Foundation are: Three sugar mills, Fauji Cereals, Foundation Gas, several Foundation Commercial Projects, Fauji Polypropylene Bags Manufacturing Plant, etc.

The Fauji Foundation's fully-owned commercial projects are: Fauji Sugarcane Farm, Fauji Security Services, Overseas Employment Services, National Identity Card Project, Fauji Institute of Management and Computer Science, Foundation College of Education and Foundation Medical College. All these have subsidiary projects which include: Fauji Fertiliser Company, Fauji Oil Terminal and Distribution Co., Fauji Kabirwallah Project Co., Fauji Cement Co., Fauji-Jordan Fertilizer Co., Mari Gas Co. and Fauji Software Co.

The foundation has also established two intermediate colleges, 81 Model Schools for children of ex-servicemen, one textbook bank, 13 hospitals, 23 day-health centres, 41 mobile dispensaries, 23 static dispensaries, two mobile health units and one artificial limb centre.

The justification for running the Fauji, Shaheen, and Bahria Foundations is that these help encourage individual responsibilities and independence for 8.5 million ex-servicemen and their dependents, all of whom total up to 7.5 per cent of the country's population.

Some Pakistani military men concede that this entire set-up has injected a 'flaw in the system' because it does not operate on any principles of equal trade and equal access. As long as the playing field is tilted in favour of the military, and protection and cover is available to them from womb to tomb, it will remain difficult to contemplate any truly non-military governance in the country.

Sheikh Salim Chishti is known as the *pir* (savant-saint) venerated by Emperor Akbar. But he was not the only one. There is one other mentioned in the *Akbar-Namah*. He gave the young emperor solace and help when he was a teenager. The emperor had been recently orphaned by Humayun's sudden death, was inexperienced and surrounded by the armies of Sher Shah Suri from Bihar, Hemu, the Hindu warrior-commander from Haryana and the leftover Lodhi princes. Akbar was militarily squeezed out of Allahabad, Agra, Delhi and Ambala, pushed into northern Punjab—young, vulnerable, hopeless, helpless, lonely and without friends and allies. He met a Muslim Sufi *pir* who gave him solace and counsel.

Neither today's anxieties and pain, nor today's joys and happiness, said the *pir* to Akbar, should be seen as permanent. Ignore them, for this world is but a bridge. Build upon it not, cross over it in peace and humility.

'Today's pleasures and problems shall pass, everything passes, everything changes. When in trouble, remember that help is round the corner and misfortune shall disappear. Whenever you rejoice in your success, remember that too shall pass.'

These lessons given to Akbar by his *pir* apply also to our current disappointments and distress with Pakistan. How long will it take for this tiresome, difficult neighbour to change its nature? What gift from us will make it alter its hostility, anger and loathing against India?

I am reminded of President Zia-ul-Haq whom I got to know at close quarters, during my four years in Islamabad. Zia was no Akbar. However, on two occasions he came close to affirming to me that he wanted to change the mutual attitudes of the two peoples. That, as a soldier, he knew the perils and pains of war and he was conscious that nothing can change on the ground unless the two peoples find it in themselves to appreciate, trust and admire one another. It was difficult for me at that stage to trust General Zia because those were the very days when he was actively and personally fomenting Khalistani agitation in India.

In retrospect, today I feel that maybe he was candid with me. There was no need for him to make certain confessions about the methods he had employed in wooing some of the Indian Sikh leaders, even sharing certain names with me.

He tried to persuade me to understand his peace plan, despite my insistence that like many I also wondered if his advisors would allow him to move 'peace wards' with India.

He often asserted that whenever peace came to the subcontinent, it would be because of the initiative of a Pakistani military leader who could see the futility of quarrelling and bickering, and recognise that Pakistan's long-term national interests could be served only in peace with India, and not by seeking revenge. He agreed to the idea of the Indo-Pakistan Joint Commission so that it could be made the pretext for annual consultations between himself and Indira Gandhi.

During one four-week period, President Zia asked me to five informal and intimate lunches and dinners at his residence. At these meals, the other invitees were his military cronies not merely generals, admirals and air marshals but also a number of more modest retired brigadiers, colonels, air force wing commanders, and captains of the navy, from amongst his own personal friends of long standing.

On all these occasions, I was the sole outsider and the only foreigner. I asked him in puzzlement why me, and what was the purpose of having me intrude on these intimate occasions. His reply was dignified and disarming, and apparently sincere. He said he wanted me to understand who his 'rufaqah' (friends) were; the people whose welfare and whose children meant much to a friend like Zia. He added that he wanted me to witness how ordinary and mediocre all these friends were and how important their loyalty was to him. Some of them were successful while the others not. They remained worthwhile to him as his friends. He wanted me to see for myself, he added, how they behave and talk amongst themselves, what their real feelings and attitudes are. 'It is for their children and mine, neither for myself nor for a Nobel Peace Prize that I crave India's friendship. I often ask myself whether I am less of a Stephanian, now that I am the president of Pakistan.'

He took the same line when he insisted that I must travel with him to Jaipur when, by watching a cricket match, he indicated to the world that the crisis of the Operation Brasstacks was buried for good. On that occasion, Prime Minister Rajiv Gandhi did not invite him to Jaipur. That invitation was from N.K.P. Salve, President of India's Cricket Control Board. Zia insisted on visiting Jaipur nevertheless. He told me that he wanted to set a precedent that, in South Asia as in Europe, a head of state can travel to a neighbouring country to witness a match, watch a play, or listen to a qawwali session in a normal healthy manner.

Maybe he was fooling India and me. Maybe not. Maybe our two countries will learn to look at one another without anger or suspicion or distrust. Maybe. Maybe not.

Sri Lanka

J.N. Dixit

India has a unique relationship with this island nation. Take ethnic identities, for instance—the people of Orissa, Andhra Pradesh and West Bengal have links with the Sinhalese. And, the people of Tamil Nadu have long-standing links with Sri Lankan Tamils of all categories going back to Antiquity. Moreover, the people of India share the three major religions of the Sri Lankan people—Hinduism, Buddhism and Islam. This is a symbiosis characterised by competitive claims to loyalty and contradictions in attitudes of the people of the two countries towards each other.

It is in this context that one analyses Indo-Sri Lankan relations. However, it would be pertinent to go into a little bit of the historical background first.

The original sources of Sri Lankan history—the Mahavansa and the *Chulavansa*—say that a legendary prince either from southern Bengal or Orissa conquered the island's original tribal population. Prince Vijaya reportedly came with 700-odd followers to Sri Lanka around the third century BC after having displeased his father. He first married a local tribal princess, and then a princess from either Andhra Pradesh or Tamil Nadu. His flock followed suit by marrying South Indian girls and thus began the Sinhala race.

Several years later, towards the end of third and the beginning of the second century BC, the people of Sri Lanka were converted to Buddhism by Prince Mahindra—son of Emperor Ashoka—who went as a Buddhist missionary to the island. Over the last two millennia, the majority of Sri Lanka's population have become staunch followers of Hinayana Buddhism.

The Tamil presence in Sri Lanka, particularly in the northern region, dates back to roughly 2,000 years. The northern areas of Sri Lanka were reportedly part of various South Indian empires, or a part of an independent Tamil kingdom, particularly the kingdom of Jaffna.

Sri Lanka's history, till the arrival of the Portuguese and Dutch in the sixteenth and seventeenth century, was a chequered one with a number of Sinhalese kingdoms co-existing with the Tamil kingdom of the north. The antagonism between the Tamils, who were Hindus, and the Sinhalese, who were Buddhists, can be taken to have existed from the olden times—if you consider the legend of the fight between Sinhalese King Dutagamanu and Tamil King Ellara.

Legend has it that Dutagamanu came to dominate most of the island after killing Ellara in a single combat. The armies of Dutagamanu and Ellara reportedly confronted each other. As the battle was about to begin, Ellara, who wanted to avoid large-scale violence and bloodshed, challenged Dutagamanu to a single combat. He suggested that the victor claim full jurisdiction over the kingdom. Dutagamanu killed Ellara. It is an interesting footnote in history that at the time of this combat, King Dutagamanu was in his mid-twenties and King Ellara was in his early eighties.

The island remained under fragmented political rule during the colonial period till the British defeated the Sinhalese king of Kandy in the late eighteenth century and unified the island. By this time, the original Sri Lankan Tamil population was spreading out to the east coast of Sri Lanka.

The origins of the prejudices and antagonism between the two communities lie in the role of the Tamils during the British colonial period. Having subjugated the Sinhalese majority, the British naturally did not trust them very much in the initial stages of the consolidation of their empire in what was then called Ceylon. They also played on the apprehensions of the Tamil minority and used them as an instrument of their colonial regime. Another factor contributing to the good British-Tamil equation was the British familiarity with the Tamils because of their century-old connection with the Coromandel Coast of India.

The result was that the Tamils, despite being a minority, became disproportionately influential in the management of the Sri Lankan political and economic affairs right till the time of the country's independence. The Tamils also became economically successful in the non-agricultural sectors of Sri Lankan society because of their association with colonial rulers and their comparatively aggressive entrepreneurship. So, the historic, ethnic and religious antagonisms were compounded by the Sinhalese feeling of being discriminated against and unfairly treated by the British with the support of the Tamils.

These undercurrents of mutual suspicion and distrust were a characteristic of Sri Lankan politics in the first half of last century despite the semblance of general harmony and co-existence between the two ethnic communities that constituted society in the island nation.

Once Sri Lanka became independent, the Sinhalese majority took control of the power structure. And, the

Tamils came under increasing pressure to pay the price for the role they had played in the past in the colonial power structure. Despite the legal and constitutional attempts made in the Donnoghmore and Jennings constitutional structures to balance ethnic interests in the newly emerging polity, Sri Lankan politics continued to be mired in ethnic hostilities and suspicions.

Matters came to a head in the mid-fifties when S.W.R.D. Bandaranaike failed to succeed D.S. Senanayake whose son Dudley, and then Sir John Kotelawala, cornered the prime ministership. Bandaranaike decided to use the potent ethnicity card to come to power. The Sri Lankan Freedom Party led by him won the elections in the late fifties on the 'Sinhala only' platform.

Bandaranaike converted the Sri Lankan polity to a Sinhalese Buddhist state. Sinhalese was declared the only official language. Knowledge of it was made compulsory in higher education and for entry into government services. And, Sri Lanka, which was basically a multilingual, multiethnic society became subject to the pernicious forces of ethnic discrimination and communal antagonism. It is ironical that Bandaranaike was assassinated by a Buddhist monk soon after becoming prime minister on the count that he had not moved far enough towards making Sri Lanka a sufficiently assertive Buddhist state and society.

True, this is only a capsuled and simplistic description of Sri Lankan history up to the late fifties of the last century. But there can be no quarrel on the general details. Sinhala-Tamil antagonism increased during the decades of the sixties and seventies because of various attempts made by Tamil leaders like Chelvanayakam and the senior Thiruchelvam, to evolve constitutional and administrative formulae to ensure fair play for the Tamils. The agreements signed by these two leaders with successive Sri Lankan prime ministers were not implemented. Tamils legitimately felt betrayed and there was a sense of alienation. There was growing frustration borne of political discrimination and lack of opportunities for education and economic well-being amongst the Tamils, especially the youth.

The Sri Lankan government's declaration, labelling the large number of Tamils living in plantations in the central highlands of the country as 'stateless persons without any citizenship rights', heightened the Tamil sense of deprivation. The declaration came despite their having been residents of Sri Lanka for more than a hundred years. This segment of Tamils was brought in as indentured labour by the British from Tamil Nadu from the second decade of the nineteenth century onwards. This particular development also became an issue between Sri Lanka and India in the post-Independence period. Despite the agreements signed after difficult negotiations to resolve the issue of granting Sri Lankan citizenship to a portion of these Tamils, it still remains problematic in terms of ground realities.

The general elections of 1977, in which Prime Minister Srimavo Bandaranaike was defeated, also coincided with higher levels of political agitation amongst the Tamils of Sri Lanka. The election campaign in the north and east of the country was tense and characterised by violence. A high point of the tragedy was the burning down of the Jaffna Library by Sri Lankan security personnel. The library had one of the most exclusive and valuable collection of Tamil books, Tamil literature and manuscripts, particularly about Sri Lankan Tamils. The incident was perceived as an unforgivable act of cultural vandalism against the Tamils.

Thereafter from 1977-78 onwards, Tamil agitation took a violent turn. The first notable incident was the present leader of the LTTE Vellupillai Prabhakaran reportedly killing the pro-government mayor of Jaffna, Durriappa in 1978.

The UNP, led by Jayewardene, came to power. He amended the Sri Lankan Constitution converting the government to a presidential form with the president enjoying extensive executive powers. The Constitution also affirmed Sinhalese as the official language and Buddhism as the state religion.

And when there was a rise in violence by Tamil youth in Jaffna, the government reacted with coercive measures instead of attempting a political dialogue with the moderate segments of the population represented by the Tamil United Liberation Front (TULF)—which still showed a willingness to participate in the political processes to negotiate some practical arrangements for the autonomy and devolution of power to the Tamil areas. This was of no avail. The TULF had participated in the 1977 elections and had emerged as a strong force in the new Sri Lankan Parliament, on the platform of provincial autonomy and the removal of discriminatory measures against Tamils.

Jayewardene followed the tactic of suppressing Tamil violence by force and, at the same time, delaying negotiations with the Tamil leaders to find a political solution that was responsive to their aspirations.

These trends continued between 1977 and 1983 when, in late June and early July, intensive security operations were undertaken against Tamil militants. The latter reacted with equal ferocity. Thirteen soldiers were killed in an ambush in the last week of July 1983. This was the first time that the Sinhalese security forces had faced such a level of fatal casualties. The bodies of the soldiers were brought back to Colombo for cremation—sparking off the horrendous anti-Tamil riots of July 1983.

Colombo was the worst affected. Even the houses of some officers and staff of the Indian High Commission were attacked. The riots also spread to other Sinhalese majority areas where Tamils were residing. The Sri Lankan government was either helpless or conniving with the Sinhalese in letting off steam over the killings of the soldiers. Worse, in retaliation, the government simultaneously undertook an extensive crackdown on Tamils in Jaffna. The consequence was the large-scale migration of Tamils from Sri Lanka to Tamil Nadu. Between 200,000 and 250,000 Tamils came to India as refugees. Those who could afford it migrated further afield to the US, West Europe and Australia. The most significant development in this Tamil exodus to India was the establishment of bases by Tamil militant youth groups moving into Tamil Nadu.

President Jayewardene seemed inexplicably paralysed. Instead of using the media to calm down the situation, he did not appear on Rupavahini (the government television channel) for nearly six days after the riots. And, when he did appear, his message to the nation was nondescript and somewhat defensive.

It must be mentioned that there was a deeper subconscious apprehension in the Sinhalese psyche about Sri Lanka Tamils. I would call it 'the minority complex of a majority'. Though the Sinhalese Buddhists constitute over 85 per cent of the population of Sri Lanka, they viewed the Tamil minority not as a minority but as part of the looming Tamil political and demographic presence to the north of the island. Tamil Nadu, with a population of 55-60 million Tamils, was seen as the natural support base for Sri Lankan Tamils.

A combination of historical memories of Chola incursions into the island and the linguistic political and cultural links that the Sri Lankan Tamils had with Tamil Nadu, made the Sinhalese feel that they were threatened with dismemberment of their country—which would be initiated by India under pressure from its own Tamil citizens. Hence, the deeply felt aversion to respond to any Tamil demand for devolution of power or to their desire of being acknowledged as a separate ethnic group within Sri Lankan polity. These subconscious apprehensions came to the fore after Mrs. Gandhi returned to power in January 1980.

Jayewardene came to power in 1977, around the same time when Mrs. Gandhi lost the elections and Morarji Desai replaced her. There were a number of reasons that made her concerned about Sri Lanka's attitudes and policies. She was deeply conscious of the strong sense of Tamil political and cultural identity felt by the people of Tamil Nadu. It was the first state of India to threaten secession during the period when attempts were made to impose Hindi as a compulsory national and official language of India. She was aware that all the political parties in the state and the people were sympathetic to the aspirations of Sri Lankan Tamils. She could not ignore these factors while reacting to developments in Sri Lanka.

Jayewardene, being equally conscious of the factors that would affect India's motivations and attitudes, took a number of pre-emptive steps in his foreign policy that did not help matters. He sought and received help from Pakistan and Israel to suppress Tamil agitation between 1977 and 1983. He also signed agreements with the US offering broadcasting facilities to the Voice of America on the west central coast of Sri Lanka around Chilaw. Though apparently declared a broadcasting facility, the government of India had definite information that it would also be a base for electronic intelligence operations.

Jayewerdene also gave the contract for the repair and restoration of what is known as the Trincomalee Oil Tank Farms to the Americans. These are large oil storage facilities constructed by the Allies during World War II near the port of Trincomalee to support operations of the South and South East Asian Command of the Allied Forces. They had fallen into disuse and then into disrepair. India had also bid for this project. Ours was the most reasonable price offered but the Jayewardene government gave the contract to a consortium of companies led by Americans after taking various political and other factors into consideration. This provided a potential base for the American strategic presence around the important port of Trincomalee.

Sri Lanka's emerging security, economic and intelligence connections with Pakistan, Israel and the US were perceived by Mrs. Gandhi as a strategic challenge and threat. The combination of the Tamil Nadu political factor and these patterns of Sri Lanka's international connections led her to generate pressure on Jayewardene.

Another factor, at a human level, which created a distance between President Jayawardene and Mrs. Gandhi was the nature of the interaction between him and President Sanjeeva Reddy, and between him and Prime Minister Morarji Desai. Both Reddy and Desai visited Sri Lanka in the late seventies. The fact that Reddy and Desai were no admirers of Mrs. Gandhi needs no belabouring.

Senior Sri Lankan political figures told me that when Jayewardene interacted with Reddy and Desai, they cracked jokes and made caustic comments about Mrs. Gandhi and her capability to rule India. These conversations were mentioned to Mrs. Gandhi by various sources. It was natural for Mrs. Gandhi to perceive Jayewardene in an antagonistic light. This antagonism also had its basis in the long-standing friendship between Mrs. Gandhi and Mrs. Bandaranaike.

The first step that Mrs. Gandhi took was to give support to Sri Lankan Tamil parties and Tamil militant groups from 1980 onwards, details of which have been mentioned in a number of articles and books over the last nine years. There is no need for me to repeat them. The 1983 riots gave Mrs. Gandhi not only the necessary handle but also a justification for cautioning President Jayewardene about his non-responsive attitude towards Tamil aspirations.

Jayewardene's main advisers in his strong-arm tactics towards the Tamils were his National Security Minister Lalith Athulathmudali and his Prime Minister Premadasa. Oxford-educated Athulathmudali was a suave politician. Before coming to power, he was teaching law in Singapore and Israel. Personally ambitious, his assessment was that a strong anti-Tamil stance would further his popularity and success in Sri Lankan politics. Premadasa, despite his claims of believing in the ideals of Mahatma Gandhi and peaceful co-existence of different ethnic communities in Sri Lanka, had a strong anti-Tamil and anti-Indian orientation in his political thinking. He was also deeply suspicious of Tamil demands because he was convinced that accepting them would be the first step towards Sri Lankan Tamils successfully engineering the break-up of the country.

Mrs. Gandhi was perturbed enough about the intensity and level of violence in Sri Lanka to issue an official statement that India could not remain unconcerned about developments in a neighbouring country as close as Sri Lanka. On July 26, within three days of the riots breaking out, she sent the then Foreign Minister Narasimha Rao as her special envoy to Jayewardene. Mrs. Gandhi's expression of concern after the riots was not a manifestation of her sudden awareness of the crisis in Sri Lanka.

As the situation in Jaffna became more tense with Sri Lankan forces clashing with Tamil militants, secretary (east) in the Ministry of External Affairs K.S. Bajpai had expressed concern over the violence in the north of the island. Mrs. Gandhi's decision to send Narasimha Rao was preceded by a telephone conversation with Jayewardene in which she told him that his consultations with the Indian representative would bring down temperatures and perhaps reduce Tamil apprehensions. Jayewardene received Rao and gave him a factual description of the events and an assessment of their political implications. As a matter of courtesy, Rao also sought a meeting with Prime Minister

Premadasa that was granted. But Premadasa who had serious objections to Rao's visit to Colombo, threw political tact to the winds and acted churlishly. He kept the Indian minister waiting in his ante-room for about 20 minutes before receiving him. This had its own ramifications as far as India's attitudes were concerned.

Rao's visit laid the foundation for India's assistance to Sri Lanka in resolving the ethnic problem. Many Sinhalese political leaders and members of the decision-making elite, however, felt that India was assuming the role of a self-appointed mediator and interventionist in Sri Lankan affairs. The points which they missed were Sri Lanka's geographical proximity to India, and the deep socio-cultural link between Sri Lankan Tamils and Indian Tamils—which compelled India to perceive critical developments in the island as an issue that could affect India's own unity and territorial integrity if it did not respect the sentiments of its Tamil citizens, and not just as leave a neighbouring country deal with its internal problems. Moreover, Jayewardene's structuring international equations that could potentially be a strategic challenge to Indian security made India perceive Sri Lankan developments as a critical embryonic regional crisis that called for some decisive action.

The objective of the Rao visit was to persuade Jayewardene to reconsider his options on the basis of ground realities and the logic of regional geopolitics. The message was that India did not desire a break-up of Sri Lanka but it would not countenance policies that posed a strategic threat. And, that India was quite willing to mediate between the Sri Lankan government and its Tamil citizens to evolve a realistic compromise.

Seven years after the withdrawal of the IPKF and the change in governments in both countries leading to changes in Indian policies towards Sri Lanka, it is time to put matters in perspective and examine how valid the criticisms are. The first category of questions requiring answers is whether Indian support to Tamil aspirations and its assumption of the role of a mediator between the Tamils and the Sinhalese were avoidable? Was there any necessity at all for India to get involved in Sri Lanka's ethnic crisis? Was Indira Gandhi's move to generate pressure on the Jayewardene government to meet Tamil objectives legitimate, particularly between 1983 and 1984?

India's involvement in Sri Lanka, in my assessment, was unavoidable not only due to the ramifications of Colombo's oppressive and discriminatory policies against its Tamil citizens but also in terms of India's national security concerns due to the Sri Lankan government's security connections with the US, Pakistan and Israel.

It would be relevant to analyse India's motivations and actions in the larger perspective of the international and national strategic environment between 1980 and 1984.

President Reagan was in power and the Soviet Union was going through the post-Brezhnev uncertainties preceding Gorbachev's arrival on the scene. Reagan was talking 'Evil Empire' and 'Strategic Defence Initiatives' to contain this empire's pernicious intentions. The Soviet Union under Chernenko and Andropov was equally confrontational. The conflict in Afghanistan following Soviet military intervention was at the height of its intensity. Pakistan was an ally of the US and the latter's main instrument in containing Soviet advance into Afghanistan. Zia-ul-Haq in Pakistan was taking full advantage of American interests in utilising Pakistan as a frontline state to further US strategic objectives in the Central Asian region. The *quid pro quo* that Pakistan demanded was political, material and military support to enhance Pakistan's strategic capacities against India. Israel continued to be the northern point of the arc of containment that the US government was creating on the southwestern flank of the Soviet Union, stretching from Turkey and Israel via the Gulf up to Pakistan.

Sino-Indian relations remained uneasy despite the restoration of full diplomatic relations between the two countries in 1976. Americans and Chinese interests had a parallel interest in containing Russian attempts at extending its area of influence in Afghanistan. India, being perceived as a supporter of Russian movement into Afghanistan, was being subjected to political and economic pressures to reduce Soviet-Indian strategic equations as well as political and technological cooperation. China and Pakistan were encouraging suspicions about India in Nepal and Bangladesh as part of this exercise.

The rise of Tamil militancy in Sri Lanka and the Jayewardene government's serious apprehensions about this were used by the US and Pakistan to create a pressure point against India in the island on the strategically sensitive coast of peninsular India. Jayewardene was apprehensive about support from Tamil Nadu to Sri Lankan Tamils. He was personally averse to Mrs. Gandhi and was of the view that she should not condone Indian Tamil support to Sri Lankan Tamils. He, therefore, established substantive defensive and intelligence contacts with the US, Pakistan and Israel.

The government of India was also subject to internal centrifugal pressures in Punjab and Kashmir and parts of the northeast. There was widespread sympathy in Tamil Nadu for the plight of Sri Lankan Tamils. An ethnic Tamil political party, the AIADMK, led by M.G. Ramachandran or MGR as he was popularly known, was governing Tamil Nadu at the time. Having positive political equations with MGR was important for Mrs. Gandhi. The fact that Tamil Nadu was the first state in India that threatened to secede was part of Mrs. Gandhi's political memory—the DMK had threatened secession when Hindi was sought to be imposed as the national as well as official language of the states of India in the mid-sixties.

There was a perception that if India did not support the Tamil cause in Sri Lanka and if the Indian government tried to question the political and emotional feelings of Tamil Nadu, there would be a resurgence of Tamil separatism in the country. India, therefore, could not remain unconcerned about Sri Lankan developments during Mrs. Gandhi's second tenure. She chose the option of supporting the Sri Lankan Tamils.

As far as I can judge, it was not her intention to support the demand for Eelam, a separate Tamil state in Sri Lanka that would have resulted in the break-up of that country. If India were to endorse the demand for the establishment of a separate state on the basis of ethnicity and religion—that would disintegrate a neighbouring multi-ethnic, multi-religious and multi-lingual state—then it would find it difficult to maintain its own unity and integrity facing as it did the challenges of separatism in Punjab and Kashmir.

Its intention was only to provide support to the Sri Lankan Tamils to generate pressure on the Jayewardene government to make it responsive to Tamil aspirations so that Sri Lanka did not disintegrate. The political exchanges between India and Sri Lanka between 1980 and 1983 confirm this assessment. The anti-Tamil riots of 1983 and the Sri Lankan government's draconian response to the violence, resulting in large numbers of refugees coming to India, changed the content of Indian policies in Sri Lanka. Tamil militancy received support both from Tamil Nadu and the Central government, not only as a response to the Sri Lankan government's military assertiveness against its Tamils, but also as a response to Jayewardene orchestrating the military intelligence presence of Israel, Pakistan and the US in Sri Lanka. The assessment was that this presence would pose a strategic threat to India, as they might encourage fissiparous movements in the southern states of India. Had the anti-Tamil riots not occurred, the Jayewardene government's plan was to steadily increase military pressure on Sri Lankan Tamils by providing the three countries a continuing presence in Sri Lanka.

One ripple effect of this would have been Tamil Nadu's disenchantment with India if New Delhi had remained detached and taken the formally correct attitude about Sri Lankan developments. This, in turn, could lead to some sort of Tamil secessionist movement in India, a process that could have found encouragement from Pakistan and the US given India's experience with their policies over Kashmir and Punjab.

In normative terms and in terms of international law and principles of morality, was Mrs. Gandhi correct in giving political and material support to the Sri Lankan Tamils? The answer, obviously, has to be in the negative. Sri Lanka should have been allowed to sort out its own problems. India should not have interfered in any way even if developments in Sri Lanka and its government's policies endangered Indian interests.

Had Sri Lanka been several hundred miles away from the coast of India, this approach could have been adopted. But Sri Lanka was only 18 miles away from Tamil Nadu. Inter-state relations are not governed by logic or morality. They were and remain an amoral phenomenon. Unilateral adherence to morality, even when it affects your very existence as a nation, may be admitted as an adorable principle. But it is neither desirable nor practical if another country deliberately indulges in policies that are immoral and, at the same time, pose a threat to you. Practical and corrective action in such a situation has to be taken. The Sri Lankan government's discrimination against its Tamils could not be considered correct or moral on any grounds.

Tamils were under continuous discriminatory pressure for nearly three decades after Sri Lanka achieved independence. The Sri Lankan government compounded the situation by establishing external political and security equations to further Sinhalese policies that posed a threat to Indian security. The Indian response was not just inevitable, it was imperative from New Delhi's point of view.

The Indian mediatory effort almost succeeded. The all-party conference convened by Jayewardene had agreed on a devolution package which Mrs. Gandhi's chairman of policy planning, G. Parthasarathy, had fashioned in consultation with the Sri Lankan president and with the Tamil leaders. It was Jayewardene who scuttled the proposals using the instrumentality of the Buddhist clergy and opposition parties. He claimed that he could not implement the proposals because there was no national consensus on them. It was at this stage that Mrs. Gandhi was tragically assassinated.

The next, and more intense phase, of Indian involvement in Sri Lanka was borne of the failure of the all-party conference when Rajiv Gandhi assumed power in December 1984. He maintained continuity in Indian policies but with certain significant shifts in emphasis and nuances. His assessment was that while Indian mediatory efforts are necessary and useful, India must assume a more impartial stand in the conflict between the Sinhalese and the Tamils. And, that it must reduce the pro-Tamil slant in its approach in order for the efforts to succeed. The then Foreign Secretary Romesh Chandra described the shift as: 'India intends to have an Indian rather than a Tamil Nadu policy towards Sri Lanka.'

Meetings, discussions and negotiations on the Sri Lankan ethnic issue, which took place between March 1985 and December 1988, were part of the persistent and painstaking efforts made by India to persuade Sri Lankan Tamils to move back from their extremist demand of a separate Tamil state and to give up violence and terrorism to secure their demands. India's advice to them was to accept a compromise that would substantially meet their aspirations and give them devolved authority to manage their own affairs within the framework of a united Sri Lanka. At the same time, our effort with the Sri Lanka government was to persuade them to give up their xenophobic, ethnic approach towards their own Tamil citizens and to restructure their political system in a manner which would meet the aspirations of the minority in their own country. Our suggestion was that compromises should be reached that would make Sri Lanka safe for its socio-ethnic diversities and that would preserve its unity and territorial integrity.

While the Sri Lankan government continued the pretence of negotiations, it prepared itself for a long and aggressive military stance against its own citizens. The ambiguities indulged in by the Sri Lankan government in negotiations at Thimpu, Colombo, Delhi and Bangalore amply prove this point.

Tamil political and militant groups—with their historical memory of the repeated betrayal of Sinhalese-Tamil agreements by the Sri Lankan government, their knowledge of its real intentions and their deeply felt and sub-conscious apprehension that Colombo would not implement the compromises even if they were reached—refused to agree to definite compromises unless India took the direct responsibility of guaranteeing their implementation.

By December 1988, the Indian mediatory role was stuck in the doldrums of the Sri Lankan government's obfuscation and the recalcitrant attitude of Sri Lankan Tamil political and militant groups. The massive military campaign, launched by the Sri Lankan government against Jaffna as well as the blockade of the Jaffna Peninsula, confirmed Sri Lankan Tamil apprehensions and the validity of their suspicions about Jayewardene's intentions. It would be pertinent to recall that the military operations launched in January 1987 by Lalith Athulathmudali commenced within 25 days of Chidambaram and Natwar Singh's visit to Colombo and the finalisation of what was called 'The 19th December proposals'.

These military operations convinced Rajiv Gandhi that

Indian policies on Sri Lankan issues required changes. These were: (a) India should firmly oppose the Sri Lankan government's military operations against Tamils. (b) More direct political pressure had to be generated against Jayewardene to implement the devolution package that had been finalised in negotiations between 1985 and 1986. (c) If India succeeded in the above two objectives, it should persuade Tamils to come back to the negotiating table. (d) If these negotiations succeeded and a set of solutions resulted from the discussions, India should directly guarantee the implementation of the solution in one form or the other through appropriate agreements. (e) India, apart from being a mediator, should become the guarantor of compromises to give a tangible sense of security to Sri Lankan Tamils and to ensure that Colombo implements the solutions agreed upon.

These elements in the evolving policies of India were the result of a series of internal discussions that Rajiv Gandhi held with his political and civil service advisers. Making these operative depended on somehow persuading Sri Lanka to discontinue its military campaign against Tamil militants that was causing enormous hardship to the Tamil civil population in Jaffna. Rajiv Gandhi was, therefore, concentrating on meeting this primary objective between January and June 1987.

One wishes that these objectives were met by political means. But that was not to be. It took a direct semi-military effort by India to break the blockade against Jaffna—namely the air dropping of supplies on 4 June 1987. Many countries were critical of this operation. It has to be remembered that India first tried to send these supplies by sea on the basis of bilateral consultations. It was only when Sri Lanka refused to resolve the problem by bilateral political discussions that India had to take unilateral action. There are precedents of states and governments taking such action for humanitarian as well as political purpose. Technically, it might have been a violation of international law in terms of humanitarian necessities but the action, in my view, was both politically necessary and morally justified. I would add that India's decisive action generated enough confidence among Sri Lankan Tamils that led to the LTTE sending the message (via Singapore) laying down conditions for a compromise with the Sri Lankan government. It was also perhaps a signal of decisiveness by India that persuaded Jayewardene to initiate negotiations with the Tamils that found expression in the Indo-Sri Lanka Agreement of 27 July 1987.

Speaking about precedents, the Berlin airlift in 1961 is the closest parallel that I can recall to the airdrop of civil supplies by India. One can compare this Indian operation with the Russian intervention in Hungary and Czechoslovakia; the British-French intervention in Egypt leading to the Suez crisis; Turkey's intervention in Cyprus; the US's uninhibited interventions in Cuba, Grenada, Panama, Libya and Haiti; China's intrusion into Vietnam in 1979 and in South China Sea to lay claims to the Spratly Islands. Keeping in mind these intrusions, it is incontrovertible that our intrusion was neither lethal, nor intended to dissipate the legitimate government of Sri Lanka or to erode the unity or territorial integrity of that country.

The criticism against India for providing supplies required for the very survival of the beleaguered Tamil population of Jaffna was and is a patent exercise in political and moral hypocrisy. The only party that was justified in being critical in objective terms was the Sri Lanka government. I accept the validity of the Sri Lankan government's critical reaction because it was their authority and jurisdiction that was questioned by the Indian airdrop. Nevertheless, it was also the same government's own obstinacy and prejudices which compelled India to take unilateral action. Providing rice, kerosene, oil, and life-saving medicines to a population of nearly a quarter of a million people deprived of these for nearly five months was certainly not a crime compared to the invasion of countries, bombing them and imposing governments on them—which was the motive of the other instances which I have mentioned above.

There has been widespread and repeated criticism of the Indo-Sri Lanka Agreement of 1987. The points of criticism are: (1) Since India's mediatory efforts had failed, it need not have taken on the direct responsibility of resolving the domestic, ethnic crisis of another country. (2) Rajiv Gandhi desired the diplomatic success of pushing through such an agreement to divert attention from mounting domestic criticism against him about Bofors and several other issues. (3) He insisted on the agreement despite advice from intelligence agencies and the armed forces not to take on the responsibilities envisaged in the agreement. (4) He should not have sent in the peacekeeping forces to Sri Lanka. It was an unjustified military intervention in a neighbouring country. The alleged failure of the IPKF in neutralising the LTTE and its withdrawal signified a major foreign policy failure for India that Rajiv Gandhi could have avoided.

To deal with these criticisms point wise: The consequence of the failure of India's mediatory effort by December 1986 was the Sri Lankan government's military operations against Tamils. It was clear that there could be a massive inflow of refugees from Sri Lanka into Tamil Nadu again and the state government took a unilateral decision supporting the Tamil cause in Sri Lanka. Any coercive attempt by the Central Government to stop the Tamil Nadu authorities from supporting the cause in the face of the Sri Lankan government's militaristic intentions would have resulted in the revival of Tamil secessionism in India.

In fact, the government of India had come across ideological long-term policy documents prepared by the

LTTE towards the end of 1986, which talked about the creation of a 'Greater Eelam' consisting of Tamil Nadu, northeastern provinces of Sri Lanka and even certain areas in Malaysia and Singapore where there were sizable Tamil populations. If India had not take further initiatives after the end of the mediatory efforts in December 1988, Sri Lanka would have continued the consolidation of its intelligence and security relationships with the US, Israel and Pakistan.

So, when the opportunity for a renewed effort to resolve the ethnic crisis arose following messages exchanged between the LTTE and N. Ram of *The Hindu* and between N. Ram and Gamini Dissanayake, it was logical for Rajiv Gandhi to respond to the opportunity. The message from the Tamils clearly stated that they would agree to a compromise only if India became a direct party to the agreement with the Sri Lankan government guaranteeing the implementation of the proposals. Consequently, India agreed to take on this extended responsibility for the larger cause of the unity and integrity of Sri Lanka, the creation of harmony between Tamils and Sinhalese, and to bring about normalcy and stability in India's neighborhood. Sri Lanka was geographically proximate and the Tamil ethnic issue sufficiently sensitive in terms of India's domestic politics compelling Rajiv Gandhi to undertake the serious attempt manifested in the Indo-Sri Lanka Agreement. India's national security concerns contributing to the process have already been mentioned.

The second criticism that Rajiv Gandhi rushed into the agreement coercing Jayewardene as well as the Tamils to participate in the agreement is neither politically accurate nor factually correct. It was a rushed agreement only in terms of the chronological time frame in which it was negotiated and signed. The development package and the constitutional amendments proposed in the Indo-Sri Lanka Agreement to meet Tamil aspirations had been under discussions for nearly four years before negotiations on the agreement commenced. The agreement was discussed with all the Tamil groups and with President Jayewardene clause by clause.

Though both the Sri Lankans and the Tamils articulated their reluctance and doubts, their official representatives agreed to the provisions of the agreement and endorsed its signing. The agreement was preceded by Rajiv Gandhi holding discussions with all concerned in the Central Government, the Tamil Nadu government and the Sri Lankan government. The process of consultations, negotiations on the agreement and its finalisation was completed in a period of little over a month. But the background of contacts and detailed discussions between India, the Sri Lankan government and various Tamil groups since July 1983, should not and cannot be ignored. Rajiv Gandhi decided to sign the agreement only after all concerned, especially Jayewardene and Prabhakaran, consented to the agreement. That they sabotaged the agreement and pulled back later is a different point.

The allegation that Rajiv Gandhi wanted a diplomatic success to divert attention from the domestic criticism that he was facing over Bofors and other issues is not valid from what I recall of the events and discussions of that period. I participated in consultations and discussions on the Sri Lankan situation at the highest levels of the government of India. I had more meetings with Rajiv Gandhi, compared to my interaction with his predecessors when I was in Dhaka, Washington, Delhi and Kabul. I never discerned any subconscious motivation or undercurrent of thought processes on the part of Rajiv Gandhi linking his involvement in the Sri Lankan situation with his domestic political predicament.

In my assessment, his motivations were clear. He wanted to ensure that no alienation takes place in Tamil Nadu. He desired India's national security concerns to be safeguarded from any negative ramifications of the Jayewardene government's ethno-phobia. He was also committed to the unity and territorial integrity of Sri Lanka.

Even if I take note of the argument that Rajiv Gandhi was unlikely to be frank with me about his domestic predicament and the desirability of redressing it by a foreign policy achievement, the fact remains that his closest political and civil service advisers would have give some expression to this concern of his in informal discussions and consultations. I do not recall a single instance when any of the ministers or any of my service colleagues mentioned this motivation on the part of Rajiv Gandhi

The theory that Rajiv Gandhi insisted on the agreement despite advice against it, is wrong. Intelligence agencies, armed forces and the Ministry of External Affairs, as well as I had told him that the initiatives being taken for signing the agreement were valid and practical. My advice to him was that it was time to bypass the LTTE if they remained obstinate, garner support from other Tamil groups and sign the agreement directly with the Jayewardene government.

Representatives of the Research and Analysis Wing told him that the agreement could be signed since it had been explained to all Tamil groups, including the LTTE, and since they had given their overall consent. In response to specific doubts raised by my colleagues in the Information Bureau and myself, on the likelihood of LTTE pulling back from the agreement, the representatives of RAW told Rajiv Gandhi that they had sufficient influence with the LTTE to prevent them from resiling from the agreement once Prabhakaran gave his commitment. The phrase used was: 'These are the youth whom we have dealt with. We can manage this eventuality.'

In the same vein, when a query was raised about the likelihood of the Indian armed forces having to militarily confront the LTTE and the possibility of these forces getting involved in guerilla or anti-insurgency operations in Sri Lanka, the then chief of Army staff General K. Sunderji told Rajiv: 'This should not be a matter of concern. The Indian armed forces can neutralise the LTTE in a fortnight or three to four weeks.'

It was on these confident assertions that Rajiv Gandhi went ahead with the agreement. He did not overrule the professional advice given to him. That the advice was wrong and the political judgement on which this advice was based was erroneous has to be acknowledged with the benefit of hindsight.

The criticism that Rajiv Gandhi should not have militarily intervened in Sri Lanka following the signing of the agreement, begs the definitional question—was it a military intervention or military assistance given in response to a specific and formal request from the Sri Lankan government to meet the situation emerging in the country after the agreement was signed? The basis on which the IPKF went to Sri Lanka cannot be called a coercive act or unilateral intervention by any criteria.

The criticism that the agreement did not fulfill its objectives and that the IPKF's withdrawal without completion of its tasks was a foreign policy failure is valid. The reasons for this failure need an analysis in different terms. Let me attempt this: Firstly, Indian interests and resulting motivations leading to involvement in the Sri Lanka ethnic crisis were logical and therefore valid. That they did not succeed in executing our policies and in managing our involvement in a coordinated manner was the first cause of our failure. More importantly, the moment the agreement faced hurdles, Indian public opinion did not show sufficient political awareness about the implications for Sri Lanka and India were the agreement to fail. It became critical of Rajiv Gandhi, which resulted in the erosion of our collective political will to sustain our policy objectives.

The V.P. Singh government, which succeeded Rajiv Gandhi, transmuted this lack of political will into operational decisions that reversed Indian policies towards Sri Lanka and resulted in the failure of the agreement. This process might have gained us appreciation from the Sinhalese and spurious good conduct certificates from other countries, but it did not serve Sri Lanka and India's long-term interests.

The agreement failed because Rajiv Gandhi took the decision to sign the agreement on the basis of predications and advice conveyed to him by his advisers, which in retrospect were inaccurate and over-optimistic. He can be blamed for the decision to sign the agreement but not for the collective judgement of the Indian establishment.

The agreement also failed because there was no cohesion in the operational aspects of Indian policies and no harmonious coordination between different agencies of the government of India dealing with the Sri Lankan crisis. In fact, there were periods when the Indian defence establishment, the intelligence agencies and the Ministry of External Affairs were working at cross-purposes. The Sri Lankan operation is in glaringly negative contrast to the harmony, cohesiveness and coordination that characterised Indian policies related to the Bangladesh crisis in 1970-71.

Rajiv Gandhi could be partially blamed for the contradictions that characterised Indian policies. He had to instruct the armed forces to confront the LTTE. But once they reverted to terrorism, there was perhaps an emotional and psychological inhibition on his part to take drastic action against the LTTE. He had an innate sympathy for the legitimate rights and aspirations of the Tamils. It is perhaps because of this mindset that he permitted representatives of our intelligence agencies to continue negotiations with the LTTE even as the Indian forces were engaged in military operations against them. The consequence was that the LTTE and the Sri Lankan government took advantage of this two-track policy and its contradictions, and, thereby reduced the efficacy of the IPKF operations.

The intriguing motivations and misperceptions of the Sri Lankan government and the LTTE respectively, negatively affected the prospects of success for the India-Sri Lanka Agreement. Jayewardene's motivation was to pretend to implement a solution so that Indian antagonism was neutralised. He did not wish to alienate Sinhalese public opinion from his party. He indulged in delaying tactics and did not take decisive and firm enough action against Premadasa and Lalith Athulathmudali, who systematically sabotaged the agreement soon after it was signed. The engineered suicide by LTTE cadres led by Pulendran, followed by covert discussions with the material support given to the LTTE reflected this phenomenon.

India and the LTTE itself had different perceptions about New Delhi's intentions behind the signing of the agreement. Prabhakaran, from the initial period of his emergence into leadership, emotively perceived that India's real intention was to support his ambition of creating 'Eelam'—a separate Tamil state in Sri Lanka. His understanding was that by signing the agreement and becoming its direct guarantor, India would acquire a legitimate direct politico-military presence in Sri Lanka. Once this presence was consolidated, India would give his struggle against the Sri Lankan government full support, leading to the creation of Eelam. Prabhakaran discovered that Rajiv Gandhi's motivations, as manifested in the Indo-Sri Lanka Agreement, were genuine and sincere and that India had no plans of clandestinely helping him create a separate Tamil state. He was not just disappointed but bitter. He waited for the first opportunity available to go back from the agreement and revert to violence.

He was helped in the process by the activities of Premadasa and Lalith Athulathmudali and the continuing support that he received from the leaders of Tamil Nadu across the spectrum both politically and materially. In fact, Rajiv Gandhi's expectations that, once M.G. Ramachandran supported the agreement (which he did), he would have full cooperation from Tamil Nadu in implementing his policies in Sri Lanka, proved to be wrong.

Prabhakaran refused to take on direct responsibility for running the Tamil provincial government that continuously delayed the formation of the interim provincial government. This was possible because of his confidence about support from Tamil Nadu and his knowledge that the IPKF, even if it undertook military operations, would act with inhibition and would be subject to restraints because of India's deep sympathy for the Sri Lankan Tamils.

The discipline of the LTTE cadres and their inclination to exercise extreme coercive violence generated such a level of fear among the Sri Lankan Tamil population that they came out fully in support against the group's violent tactics. There was also widespread conviction amongst Sri Lankan Tamils that though they had India's sympathy and support, the LTTE was the only Tamil group that could effectively resist the depredations of the Sinhalese security forces. They, therefore, were disinclined to criticise the LTTE or to pressurise it to join the mainstream of democratic politics till they were absolutely sure about their security and till the entire devolution package was fully operational.

The Sri Lankan government deliberately and consistently acted against this objective of the Sri Lankan Tamils. According to the impression I gathered from IPKF officers at the highest levels of command, the IPKF was itself handicapped in terms of the brief given to them about the objectives of their mission. They carried out operations in a disciplined manner according to instructions received, but I was constantly queried as to why they found themselves in a situation where they were fighting Tamils whom they were supposed to protect and whose cause they were supposed to uphold by helping implement the Indo-Sri Lanka Agreement.

Somehow there was a failure in giving them a detailed and multi-dimensional briefing about the complexity of the task they had undertaken. Their actions were therefore not backed up by a shared and informed conviction about the purpose of their operations. I must qualify this value judgement by underlining that there was no such contradiction affecting cooperation and coordination between the Ministry of External Affairs and the Ministry of Defence or the High Commission of India and the IPKF. There was trust and constant cooperation between these agencies in Delhi and between Lt. Gen. Kalkat, Commander of the IPKF.

I don't have detailed knowledge of the many problems that the IPKF faced as articulated by some of the divisional commanders who functioned under Lt. Gen. Kalkat. Some of these commanders themselves were not convinced about the logic of the IPKF presence and operations in Sri Lanka.

Their second complaint was that sufficient operational authority had not been delegated to them to carry on their operations. There was unnecessary interference in field operations from the IPKF high command according to some of our divisional and brigade commanders. According to these officers, command and control was highly centralised between the Army Headquarters and IPKF headquarters. I do not have sufficient factual information to confirm this assessment of the divisional commanders. Generals Sunderji Sharma and Rodrigues, who were at the Army Headquarters at that point of time, and Lt. Gen. Depender Singh, Ashok Chatterjee and Kalkat, who were in the Southern Command and involved in the Sri Lankan operations should be able to provide a more accurate evaluation of this critical value judgement by their junior colleagues. I hope they do so as both the Indian armed forces and the Indian public have a right to know the details about what happened and how we managed the situation.

Regardless of these handicaps and limitations, the IPKF performed its tasks with discipline, dedication and a sense of purpose as long as they were allowed to continue in Sri Lanka. They brought order and stability in the northern and eastern parts of the island. The IPKF was the main enabling factor behind elections in the Tamil-dominated regions of Sri Lanka and the creation and establishment of a Tamil provincial government. They were an equally important factor in assisting the Sri Lankan government to hold the presidential elections in 1988 and 1989.

By the end of 1988 and beginning of 1989, they were in the final phase of containing and neutralising the LTTE. It is my assessment that had the IPKF been allowed to stay on in Sri Lanka for another six months or so, the LTTE would have been under sufficient pressure to give up violence and join mainstream politics. It is also my assessment that the V.P. Singh government's decision to succumb to Premadasa's pressure and withdraw the IPKF was detrimental both to Indian and Sri Lankan interests. The *de facto* withdrawal of the IPKF scuttled the Indo-Sri Lanka Agreement. It revived the ethnic conflict and prolonged violence and instability in Sri Lanka.

One overarching miscalculation of India was our underestimating Prabhakaran's passionate, even obsessive, commitment to the cause of Tamil Eelam, his authoritarian and single-minded nature, his tactical cleverness and his resilience in adversity. The second miscalculation about him and his cadres was that India and Sri Lanka together could persuade other Tamil groups and the Tamil population in general to join the mainstream of democratic politics bypassing the LTTE. The governments of India and Sri Lanka partially succeeded in the second exercise. But the contradictions of their own policies prevented tangible success in this respect.

I myself overestimated the sincerity and political will of Jayewardene to come to a genuine compromise with the Tamils with the help of the Indian government. I knew the pressures that led to his endorsement of the Indo-Sri Lanka Agreement and the limitations he faced by signing it. But I thought that, having gone through a highly critical experience in relation to the ethnic crisis, he would sincerely fulfill his commitments as envisaged in the agreement. I gave this assessment to Rajiv Gandhi.

I was convinced that the LTTE would not participate in any negotiated settlement. I, therefore, felt that India should deal with other Tamil groups, bypassing the LTTE and isolating it. My assessment at the time was that if other Tamil groups joined the Indian initiative, the LTTE could be successfully isolated which would compel it to join the peace process. I was wrong in this assessment. The LTTE played out the tactic of joining in the initiative and then sabotaging it—whatever their reasons.

My expectation that the LTTE could be successfully isolated from Sri Lankan Tamils also proved to be wrong. I did not anticipate the various undercurrents and motivations in Sri Lankan and Indian politics that would contribute to the LTTE's survival and its continuing capacity for struggle. It was also my assessment that Indian public opinion and political parties would rise above their apprehensions and interim difficulties and would be fully supportive of a comprehensive practical compromise—safeguarding Sri Lankan interests, Tamil aspirations and India's regional security concerns. I was wrong in this anticipation.

While the agreement was euphorically welcomed for the first two-and-a-half months, when everything was apparently moving as planned, our media and political circles started criticising one of the most important diplomatic initiatives taken by Rajiv Gandhi—the objectives of which were necessary and logical on all counts. My anticipation, that once Jayewardene signs the agreement he would be decisive in neutralising Premadasa and Lalith Athulathmudali and their policies against Tamils and the agreement, also proved to be wrong. Jayewardene either did not have the political will or his approach was that of tactical intrigue because of which he refrained from reining in Lalith and Premadasa.

There is also the criticism that Rajiv relied more on bureaucrats, intelligence officers and the armed forces in the formulation of his Sri Lankan policies rather than on his political colleagues. I do not know how valid this criticism is. It is true that Rajiv Gandhi consulted his civil service, intelligence and armed forces officers on Sri Lankan affairs more than Mrs. Gandhi or her predecessors had on major foreign policy initiatives. However, it is not true that he did not consult his political colleagues. I have personal knowledge of the fact that he consulted Narasimha Rao, Shiv Shankar and N.D. Tiwari, the three serving or former Foreign Ministers, who dealt with the Sri Lankan crisis between 1985 and 1989. To the best of my knowledge, he also consulted K.C. Pant who was the Defence Minister, as well as a member of the cabinet committee on political affairs, on all major steps that he took on Sri Lanka. How influential were the inputs of his political colleagues in the decisions which he took is a matter on which I cannot pronounce a value judgement. All I can say is that I did not notice any voice of dissent on any of the important aspects of Rajiv Gandhi's Sri Lankan policies from his political colleagues.

Despite the murky atmospherics of the Sri Lankan crisis and the contradictions in Indian and Sri Lankan policies, the Indo-Sri Lanka Agreement would have succeeded had Jayewardene been sincere in implementing it, had Premadasa been endowed with the wisdom to acknowledge that the agreement provided a practical compromise on a very complex issue, and had he not insisted on the withdrawal of the IPKF and the replacement of the agreement with the so called Treaty of Friendship which he suggested.

Above all, the agreement would have succeeded had India shown political will and grit to complete the task that it had assumed. And, had it fulfilled the commitments it had given to the government and the Tamils of Sri Lanka to normalise the situation in the island country as envisaged in the agreement. The manner in which our Sri Lankan policy between 1983 and 1990 failed, once again confirmed the international perception of India being a soft state. Not a very happy thought. History will judge Rajiv Gandhi's Sri Lanka involvement with greater precision and objectivity with the passage of time. In my perception, in dealing with Sri Lanka his motive was fair and as just as he could be in his policies. He was courageous in taking on responsibilities to safeguard Indian interests and the well-being of a small neighbouring country despite the complexity of the issues involved and the onerous nature of the responsibilities. He took upon himself a thankless job for the well-being of the people of India and Sri Lanka and paid for it with his life. He may be judged as a failure as far as his Sri Lanka policies are concerned but the logic of his purpose and his deep commitment to India's national interests and regional peace at that point of time cannot be questioned.

The Sinhalese, despite being the majority community in the country, have a deeply felt minority complex in relation to the links between Sri Lankan Tamils and the Tamils of Tamil Nadu in India. A conscious effort to remove this complex is a prerequisite for any solution of the Sri Lankan ethnic problem.

The governments of both India and Sri Lanka have to undertake specific measures to create mutual trust, to educate public opinion and to evolve policies that will guarantee the existence of Sri Lanka as a plural society.

The Indian endeavour should be to continuously and tangibly assure Sri Lanka about its commitment to the island nation's independence, unity and territorial integrity.

The Sri Lankan government must move out of its suspicious and xenophobic mindset and be genuinely responsive to Tamil political aspirations. Any expectation that Tamil concerns can be neutralised by a process of political and military confrontation, is not realistic.

The Indo-Sri Lanka Agreement failed because the Sri Lankan government and the LTTE agreed to it only for tactical purposes and with contradictory motives, while India pushed through the accord due to lack of patience after nearly four years of mediatory efforts

The Sri Lankan government entered the agreement in the hope that India's direct involvement would help it in militarily suppressing the LTTE. And, the LTTE initially accepted the agreement under the misconception that the agreement would be the umbrella under which India would directly intervene in Sri Lanka and help in the creation of Eelam. India entered the agreement in the hope that by directly participating in the agreement, it would overcome the competing obstinacies of the Sinhalese and the Tamils and thereby help stabilise the situation in Sri Lanka. The predications on which the agreement was signed and the expectations on which it was based proved to be inaccurate

Neither the Sinhalese nor the Indian public gave sustained support to the Indo-Sri Lanka Agreement despite the valid motives and correct objectives. Sri Lankan Tamils, while generally supportive of the agreement and the Indian involvement, did not have sufficient resources or the will to resist the fear and violence generated by the LTTE, thereby weakening the agreement. Their deeply felt suspicions about the Sinhalese majority also contributed to their stilted cooperation in implementing the agreement.

Rajiv Gandhi was given inaccurate advice about the political, military and intelligence factors affecting the implementability of the agreement. He decided to go ahead with the agreement on wrong predications by his military, intelligence and foreign service advisers, which led to the hurdles the agreement ultimately faced.

The Jayawardene and Premadasa governments did not completely fulfill the government's obligations under the agreement. Nor did the LTTE.

The large-scale induction of the IPKF into Sri Lanka was, in some respects, an unexpected contingency. The result was the IPKF undertaking a task without clear briefings and clear definition of objectives. The situation on the ground itself changed the objectives and tasks of the IPKF—compared to what was originally envisaged. The IPKF did not have the full backing of the Indian public opinion and faced hostile Sinhalese public opinion. The IPKF was also viewed with some amount of reservation and suspicion by the Sri Lankan Tamil population. In short, the IPKF performed its tasks in excruciatingly adverse circumstances.

Inter-departmental rivalries in the government of India resulted in a lack of cohesion and coordination between different agencies engaged in the implementation of the Indo-Sri Lanka Agreement.

The situation was further compounded by senior figures of the Sri Lankan government actively sabotaging the agreement for their own political purposes.

There were vested interests abroad that desired a continuation of the civil war-like situation in Sri Lanka—in terms of sales of arms, drugs, safeguarding refugee status and political asylum status as well as for maintaining intelligence and security links with foreign entities on the basis of the continuation of the ethnic crisis.

The religious and ethnic reluctance of the Sinhalese majority to meet Tamil aspirations remains a major hurdle. Only a change of heart and mind can eradicate this fundamental defect. India's interest in developments in Sri Lanka is unavoidable. But India should not get directly involved in the internal affairs of Sri Lanka except when developments in the country pose a direct and immediate threat to its security and territorial integrity. The Indian involvement in Sri Lanka between 1983 and 1987 was perhaps precipitate, now that we have the benefit of hindsight.

Having said all this, it is to be emphasised that the motivations behind New Delhi's involvement in Sri Lanka between 1983 and 1990 was based on concrete apprehensions about India's national security and its sincere desire to safeguard the unity and territorial integrity of Sri Lanka. The more important lesson which Sri Lanka should take note of is this—that if it has to survive as a unified country, the Sinhalese majority will have to make genuine efforts to respect the multi-ethnic, multi-religious and multi-linguistic plurality of Sri Lankan polity. This acknowledgement can be achieved only through political processes and not by military means.

In the final analysis, India's Sri Lanka experience in those six years proves the validity of an axiomatic principle in international relations, which I have learnt during my long years in the Indian Foreign Service—adhering to absolute principles of morality is the safest and the most non-controversial stance in foreign relations. This, however, is not possible because of the amoral nature of international relations. Safeguarding one's national interests may result in compulsions that necessitate departure from absolute principles of morality.

Once you depart from these principles to fashion and implement policies to meet your interests, you must have the grit, patience and stamina to follow these policies till they achieve their objectives. If a country, or a people, does not have this forbearance and political will, then the policies will remain inadequate and will fail.

Mrs. Gandhi, during her long years as Prime Minister

of India, had acquired this grit and stamina and could impart this political will to Indian public opinion. Rajiv Gandhi had the same capacity to a great measure, but he lived in more volatile times and in a more fractious ambience. Despite this, he was purposive in meeting India's national interests. It was the government that succeeded him which decided to choose good conduct certificates from abroad as a more desirable objective than completing a foreign policy task that was of utmost importance for India's interests in South Asia and for stabilising the situation in Sri Lanka. Sri Lanka's drift to continuing violence till now has been the consequence of this dubious choice.

Having indulged in this critical introspection, one still ruminates on why India failed, and where it went wrong. The flaws in our Sri Lankan policies in holistic and moral terms were:

1. While Mrs. Gandhi's support for Sri Lankan Tamil aspirations was correct and justified, her policy of materially supporting Tamil militant separatists was wrong. India's interests and the Tamil cause, which oriented her towards generating pressure on Jayewardene, could have been pursued by political and diplomatic means instead of extending material support to Tamil militants.
2. Rajiv Gandhi's approach was more impartial when it came to the Sinhalese and the Tamils. He pulled back from giving material support to Tamil militants. He, and all of us who advised him, were, however, not perceptive enough to fathom the deep psychological and emotional chasm between the Sinhalese and Sri Lankan Tamils—something, which went beyond socio-economic and political factors.
3. We were over optimistic about the change of mind in the Jayewardene government and about the capacity for reasonableness amongst Tamil militant groups and Sri Lankan Tamils generally, which led India to sign the Indo-Sri Lanka Agreement. Both Jayewardene and the Sri Lankan Tamils acquiesced to the agreement only for tactical purposes. Though being aware of this undercurrent,

we expected that our political will backed by military force would overcome this lack of sincerity and reasonableness on the part of the Sinhalese and the Sri Lankan Tamils. Our predications and expectations in these regards were wrong.

4. The Indian mediatory effort, leading to the signing of the Indo-Sri Lanka Agreement, and the dispatch of the IPKF to Sri Lanka were the inevitable consequences of the activist posture that we took on the internal affairs of Sri Lanka due to our strategic concerns and domestic ethno-political compulsions.

The power structure in India was initially unable to totally pull back from involvement in Sri Lankan affairs. Moreover, all of us in the government involved in Sri Lankan developments between 1983 and 1990, did not comprehend the collective mindset and political psyche of the Indian people that has generally been averse to assertive or intrusive postures in inter-states relations, even if it affected our national interests.

The Indian state, despite structuring a balance of power to the creation of a new world order that was no longer subject to the aberrations of and suspicions of ideological confrontations. Issues of major interest and concern were the creation of a new world economic order based on the principles of free market economy. Structuring an international security environment, that would be rooted in international regimes and disciplined aimed at non-proliferation of weapons of mass destruction. A general agreement emerged among the major powers that no single country should be allowed to be hegemonistic or excessively communal in any region of the world.

A consensus also emerged that political and military trends, contributing to destabilisation of established state structures, should be contained and eradicated. These trends were cross-border terrorism, narcotic crimes, adventurous manipulation of international stock exchanges and currency arrangements, management of ecology and environment within the framework of international regimes and the encouragement of human rights and democracy as the basic principles of governance.

One consequence was that the old suspicions and reservations about inter-state relationships got replaced by new considerations affecting the national interests of the countries in the South Asian region. For instance, India's reservations about countries like Israel and the white-dominated South African government disappeared. With the complete erosion of the special political-strategic relationship between India and the former Soviet Union, New Delhi opened up contacts with the US, although reservations about Washington's political and security environment in the South Asian region also came to an end.

The P.V. Narasimha Rao government and the government of H.D. Gowda, Inder Kumar Gujral and Atal Behari Vajpayee have been more detached about Sri Lanka developments and emotionally less involved with the aspirations of Sri Lankan Tamils for a separate and independent homeland. The anger and bitterness about the LTTE assassinating Prime Minister Rajiv Gandhi have diminished over the passage of time and with the accused having been tried and sentenced by Indian courts.

India became more enmeshed in the difficulties of its relationship with Pakistan, particularly after the nuclear weaponisation of the two countries in the summer of 1998 and the conflict in Kargil between April and July 1999.

While the general interest and involvement of the people of Tamil Nadu in the Sri Lankan Tamil cause diminished after the assassination of Rajiv Gandhi and the continuing adherence to violence by the LTTE, certain political parties of Tamil Nadu revived their contacts with the LTTE and became supportive of its struggle for self-determination and Eelam. The LTTE continues to have connections with Tamil Nadu. Its cadres are still finding support and territorial refugees in the southern states. A disturbing development has been the emerging links between the LTTE and Indian secessionist movements, particularly in the northern states of India.

This has led to a certain convergence of interests in security matters between India and Sri Lanka. While remaining supportive of the legitimate ethno-linguistic and political aspirations of Sri Lankan Tamils for greater delegation of power, autonomy and so on, India remains equally firmly committed to the unity and territorial integrity of Sri Lanka. The Indian view is that whatever solution is found has to be within the framework of the constitutional arrangements that preserve Sri Lanka's territorial unity and integrity, a logic which India applies to its own violent separatist movements in different parts of the country.

To move on to the broad patterns of internal developments in Sri Lanka, one takes note of the fact that barring Chandrika Kumaratunga and the LTTE leader Velupillai Prabahakran and his adviser Anton Balasingham, all the major political figures involved in the ethnic crisis from 1988 to 2001 have passed from the scene. Many of them have been killed. President J.R. Jayewardene and Mrs. Srimavo Bandaranaike were exceptions, both dying due to old age. But most of the major Sinhalese and Tamil political leaders, including military leaders, were killed. Even comparatively non-controversial political figures like Dr. Neelam Thiruchelam were assassinated. The killing of Sinhalese political and military leaders, particularly during the last half of President Premadasa's tenure, is subject to doubts and suspicions as to who engineered these assassinations. Internal rivalries in Sinhalese politics seem to have contributed to these violent tragedies.

Sri Lanka has had a comparatively stable government under President Chandrika Kumaratunga since 1994. She has managed to retain a tenuous majority in the parliamentary elections held in 2000. She herself will face elections in the near future—the results of which will have a crucial impact on Sri Lankan politics in the next decade. The point to be acknowledged is that both the major political parties in Sri Lanka, the United National Party (UNP) and the Kumaratunga-led People's Democratic Alliance are subject to internal conflicts and factional pressures. There is an absence of an overarching political leadership in these political parties that would enable them to move purposefully in cooperating with each other to negotiate a durable solution to the ethnic problem.

Developments in Sri Lankan Tamil politics are equally problematic. The LTTE has undoubtedly emerged as the dominant politico-military organisation in Tamil politics. All the other Tamil militant groups stand dispersed. The TULF and the EPDP are only playing a marginal role in parliamentary politics in that country. There are remnants of other Tamil groups in existence but they are marginalised and have a miniscule credibility with the Tamil population. The LTTE's negotiating stand remains ambiguous except for the firm commitment to the ultimate objective of an independent Tamil state in Sri Lanka.

A critical development in the politics of Tamil ethnicity are the Sri Lankan Muslims, most of whom are Tamil speaking, claiming a separate ethno-religious identity and asserting that any delegation of powers and new territorial arrangements within Sri Lanka should ensure a separate homeland for Tamil Muslims in the Eastern Provinces of Amparai, Batticaloa and portions of Trincomalee. Muslim politics has also become volatile and violent as evidenced by the death of the leader of the major Sri Lankan Muslim party Mohammed Ashra, who was killed in a helicopter crash about two years ago,

An interesting facet of Tamil politics in Sri Lanka is that both, the Muslim segment as well as the majority of other Tamils led by the LTTE, are not short of funds to carry on their political or military activities. The sources of financing vary from donations from the Tamil diaspora abroad to earnings from narcotics and overt and covert financial donations from foreign countries that Sri Lanka has not been able to monitor or control effectively.

The constitutional proposals for the delegation of powers to the Tamils to meet their territorial and administrative demands are in doldrums. First, because the package offered by President Kumaratunga between 1995 and 1999 has not been backed up by a general Sinhalese consensus despite efforts within the Parliament and outside. These proposals went into a tailspin with the UNP pulling out from discussions aimed at evolving a consensus by the end of 1999 due to electoral considerations (the parliamentary elections of 2000 and the forthcoming presidential elections).

The Buddhist clergy remains insensitive and obdurate about granting any substantive concessions to the Tamils. The armed forces of Sri Lanka, though exhausted by the continuing military conflict, have become an influential factor in fashioning a political solution. There is a school of thought in the military establishment that, having been engaged in fighting the LTTE for such a long period, compromises are not the solution: the solution should be based on the Sinhalese negotiating from the position of strength.

Another critical development has been the incremental linkages between the youth amongst the Tamils of Indian origin in the central highlands of Sri Lanka and the LTTE. A comparative moderation of the Tamils of Indian origin in political matters is giving way to incremental militancy after the death of their leader Thondaman. His Ceylon Workers Congress is a divided and faction-ridden political entity.

It is because of these factors that a structured discussion for constitutional and political compromises has not succeeded. One, therefore, does not see any durable compromise emerging in the foreseeable future. One speculates that even any substantive discussion on this subject can begin only after the presidential elections in Sri Lanka. It is against this background that one surveys the internal situation in Sri Lanka and the military conflict between the LTTE and the Sri Lankan government.

The period between 1999 and 2000 witnessed dramatic confrontations between the LTTE and Sri Lankan armed forces. After the LTTE's successful destruction of the major military base at Ponnerin and its capture of the Elephant Pass, there was a brief period when the Sri Lankan troops managed to push back the LTTE. But in 2000, LTTE cadres managed to annihilate major Sri Lankan military bases in the northern Wanni region and in various approaches to the Jaffna peninsula. The fall of Jaffna was considered imminent. The Sri Lankan government was deeply concerned. President Kumaratunga took personal interest and oversaw the offensive against the LTTE. Sri Lanka simultaneously sought large-scale military assistance from abroad.

While India offered to safeguard the sea-lanes in the Palk Strait, Indian military supplies were reported to be nominal. Sri Lanka, however, got extensive range of military supplies from Israel, Pakistan, both Koreas, the US and Britain. Such assistance came readily in the context of the LTTE being armed with more sophisticated weapons systems, including naval craft, anti-aircraft guns and high quality infantry weapons. The Sri Lankan government managed to check the LTTE offensive to capture Jaffna. The military campaign in 2000 also resulted in high levels of casualties for the LTTE.

As these lines are being written, the Sri Lankan government remains enmeshed in a tense military predicament. It is perhaps because of its failure to achieve military dominance in Jaffna that the LTTE agreed to mediation by Norway—the talks were conducted by senior

Norwegian diplomat Solheim since the second half of 2000. Solheim first met Prabhakaran's adviser Balasingham in London and through him established contact with the LTTE leader in Sri Lanka. The Norwegian government held parallel discussions with the Sri Lankan government.

Solheim's earlier initiative had brought about compromises between the PLO and Israel. Norway had the advantage of not having any emotional political or ethnic links with the Sinhalese or Tamils. Nor did it have any colonial connections with Sri Lanka. The Norwegians felt they had high credibility (a valid presumption). Over the last eight months, Solheim has been travelling between London, Colombo and the Wanni region in Sri Lanka, where Prabhakran reportedly resides. He has had meetings with President Kumaratunga and Sri Lankan Finance Minister Lakshman Kadirgamar. He has also been holding parallel discussions with Balasingham and Prabhakaran.

The Norwegians acknowledge the relevance of Indian influence in Sri Lankan developments. They have been keeping India fully informed of their discussions through the Indian High Commissioner in Colombo and the Ministry of External Affairs in New Delhi. Solheim himself has visited New Delhi twice.

A significant point to be kept in mind is that the Norwegians have declared that their initiative has only two limited objectives—first, to organise a long-term ceasefire, and second, to facilitate direct bilateral negotiations between the LTTE and the Sri Lankan government. They have assiduously disclaimed any intention of suggesting constitutional formulae or proposals for a political settlement. Their argument is that such proposals should come out of direct negotiations between the LTTE and the Sri Lankan government.

The outcome of this initiative remains uncertain because of the LTTE refusing to give up its military campaign, despite its off-again, on-again declarations of a unilateral ceasefire. Keeping in mind the trends in Sri Lankan public opinion, Mrs. Kumaratunga has also had to make her truce offers conditional on the LTTE giving up arms and the military campaign. The Sri Lankan government is also not willing to accept the LTTE as the sole representative of the Sri Lankan Tamils. (One can discern an interesting similarity between India's approach to the Kashmiri militants and the Sri Lankan government's attitude.)

Though India remains detached and unwilling to get actively involved, Sri Lankan government leaders remain concerned about the equations in Tamil Nadu politics—namely relations between political groups in the state supporting the LTTE and the major political parties, the DMK and the AIADMK. As a result, both Kumaratunga and UNP President Ranil Wickramasinghe have visited India more than once over the last two years to keep New Delhi informed of their assessment of political affairs in their country and to assess the details and nuances of India's policies.

It must be mentioned that the Sri Lankan government unofficially sounded out India about giving direct military assistance to resist the LTTE. Ironically, sections of the Buddhist clergy suggested that Indian armed forces be called back to Sri Lanka. However, there was no formal official request. India wisely declined to get involved, given the last experience of participating in the peacekeeping process in the country between 1987 and 1990.

Sri Lanka's ethnic crisis, while having a certain permanence in terms of its basic process, is subject to rapid changes and unpredictable developments. The dynamics of the Sri Lankan predicament is so volatile that even a short-term exercise at arriving at conclusions cannot be entirely successful. Developments since the beginning of 2001, particularly during March and April, have to be taken note of.

While the LTTE continued to have sufficient finances and

a flow of arms supplies, its trained cadre strength diminished during 2000 due to casualties and other military pressures generated by the Sri Lankan army. Its international acceptability as a legitimate armed struggle to attain ethnic self-determination has also been diminishing. The US had already declared it a terrorist organisation. The British government also banned it in 2000. It remains a banned organisation in India. The Sri Lankan ban on the group, imposed after the LTTE's bomb attack on the Buddhist temple at Kandy in 1998, has continued.

The general assessment is that the LTTE has been under pressure since the last quarter of 2000. This assessment is based on the following factors:

First, the LTTE's willingness to allow the Norwegians to mediate. Second, the LTTE declaring a unilateral ceasefire in December 2000 and extending it, month by month, till the summer of 2001 despite the Sri Lankan government's refusal to reciprocate. Third, repeated efforts to resume a dialogue provided two pre-conditions are met—that the Sri Lankan government lift the ban on the LTTE, acknowledging it as a political organisation, and, that the LTTE be treated as the sole representative of Sri Lankan Tamils.

The second precondition, though questioned by other Tamil political groups in Sri Lanka, is not a tough proposition because the LTTE is now acknowledged by Sri Lankan Tamils as their main representative political organisation. Whether this acceptance and acknowledgement of LTTE's role is based on a fair or general support is a relevant question because the LTTE has neutralised the political and organisational capabilities and influence of other Tamil groups.

The other fact to be acknowledged is that the LTTE's political credibility has increased as far as Sri Lankan Tamils go because its discipline is ideologically integrated in its singleness of purpose of achieving self-determination for the Tamils. And, also because of the resilience with which it has carried out its struggle over nearly two decades. Moreover, the fact that it survived the IPKF operations and has fought the Sri Lankan army to a virtual standstill has given the LTTE military credibility, not only among the Tamils but also, to some extent, internationally as well even though it is criticised for being a secessionist terrorist organisation.

The LTTE's political acumen is also acknowledged due to the manner in which Prabahakaran has managed negotiations with the Sri Lankan government and the adroitness with which the organisation handled the mediatory role adopted by India in the 1980s as well as the present round of discussions with the Norwegians.

There has also been a significant transformation in the leadership of the LTTE. Prabhakaran remains supreme leader of both the political and military aspects of the LTTE campaign but practically all its senior advisers are new in the sense that they have come on the scene from the mid-'90s. Except for Balasingham, all the other prominent but subordinate colleagues of the LTTE chief have died or have been eliminated by him. The more junior among them have been delegated to military and political backwardness. Individuals like Mahatya, Yogi and Kittu are no longer on the scene. They have been replaced by leaders like S.P. Tamil Chelvan, who is Prabhakaran's senior political adviser. There have also been changes at the regional and sub-regional levels and command of LTTE cadres.

The thread of continuity in these developments is that Prabhakaran has been successful in increasing and consolidating his authority as the supreme leader of the organisation. His public perception, among Sri Lankan Tamils, ranges from a folk hero to a highly competent military commander and a very adroit political leader, profoundly committed to the welfare of his people. His aversion to joining mainstream democratic processes, his deep mistrust and paranoia about the Sinhalese, his intolerance of dissent and his record of violence and terrorist acts are overlooked or submerged in the context of his commitment to the well-being of the Sri Lankan Tamils.

It is pertinent at this juncture to examine the orientations of India's Sri Lanka policies before speculating on future prospects of political developments in that country. There has been a certain continuity in India's Sri Lanka policies since the failure of the Indian mediatory effort, which culminated in the withdrawal of the IPKF from Sri Lanka in March 1990.

India's Sri Lanka policy can be summed up in the following lines:

India is fully supportive of the legitimate political, social, economic and cultural aspirations of the Tamils of Sri Lanka (of both categories, the native Tamils and the Tamils of Indian origin settled in Sri Lanka since the middle of the nineteenth century). However, India opposes the LTTE's violent and terrorist campaign to achieve these aspirations. India would be supportive of initiatives for resolving the ethnic crisis in Sri Lanka through a political dialogue.

India is of the view that any compromise achieved should be within the framework of the unity and territorial integrity of Sri Lanka.

In the context of past failed efforts in the 1980s and 1990s, India would not take any active and direct part in any mediatory exercise in Sri Lanka in the foreseeable future. But it will not oppose similar facilitating efforts undertaken by other countries or international organisations, provided such initiatives are accepted by the Sri Lankan government and the LTTE. India is of the view that any solution would ultimately have to be negotiated between Sri Lankans themselves, that is, the Sinhalese and the Tamils.

The LTTE's direct involvement in the assassination of Rajiv Gandhi means that India would be reluctant to deal with the organisation till those guilty, including its top leadership, are brought to book. Apart from this, specifics in Indian politics towards Sri Lanka would be to strengthen and extend bilateral relations and economic cooperation—to the extent that Colombo wishes such cooperation and subject to its sensitivities about any excessive Indian involvement in Sri Lanka.

One element in India's Sri Lanka policies of the 1990s seems to be getting diluted. This was the decision by the government of India and Tamil Nadu to ensure (to the extent possible) that the LTTE does not have bases or sanctuaries in the country, since India remains opposed to any secessionist or terrorist group operating from its territory. However, from the end of March this year, there have been reports that some Tamil political parties, like the MDMK and the Tamil Nationalist Movement, are initiating action to help the LTTE. Mr. Vaiko, the leader of MDMK, and Mr. P. Nedumaran, who heads the Tamil Nationalist Movement in Tamil Nadu, have sought the support of the convenor of the ruling National Democratic Alliance of India, former Defence Minister George Fernandes, in their initiative to rehabilitate the LTTE.

Fernandes has had a background of supporting the LTTE struggle even before he became a member of the Vajpayee government. According to newspaper reports in India, he had a long meeting with Vaiko and Nedumaran in Chennai on 6 April 2001 to work out a strategy for the political rehabilitation of the LTTE. The reason for this move was that the LTTE was on the defensive and not getting sufficient support even from Tamil Nadu, under the Karunanidhi government. Nedumaran has been arguing with the coalition government in New Delhi that India's has a substantive interest in supporting the LTTE because, at the ground level, the Indian Tamil's sympathy lies with the Sri Lankan Tamils and not with the Sinhalese. There is a slow groundswell of public opinion in Tamil Nadu to modify India's general policy line summarised above. If the Sri Lankan government musters a military solution or indulges in extensive violence against Sri Lankan Tamils, this pro-LTTE view will be revived with very negative consequences for Indo-Sri Lankan relations.

In the meantime, two Norwegian diplomats, special envoy Solheim and Norwegian Ambassador to Sri Lanka, Joan Westborg, have had discussions with Prabhakaran and S.P. Tamil Chelvan to commence negotiations with the Sri Lankan government without preconditions. As mentioned earlier, the LTTE has, however, stipulated preconditions.

President Kumaratunga's response to the preconditions had been to assert that she was willing to deal with the LTTE as one of the most important organisations representing Sri Lankan Tamils but not as the sole representative of the Tamils. As far as the lifting of the ban on the LTTE is concerned, she had not rejected the suggestion but stipulated that the LTTE should first come to the negotiating table.

She faces obvious difficulties in responding to the demand for lifting the ban, The LTTE has not indicated any willingness to lay down arms and abjure violence. It has also not given any signal about being flexible about its demand for a separate and independent homeland. It will be difficult for Kumaratunga to persuade the Sinhalese majority, particularly the Buddhist clergy and the Sri Lankan armed forces, to endorse a decision to lift the ban, given the LTTE's past record of violence and the context in which the ban was imposed (the attack on the holiest of Buddhist shrines in Kandy). There is also the perception that the LTTE is responding to the Norwegians only to regroup, re-equip and strengthen itself before launching its next military campaign.

Equally significant is the perception that leaders of the Tamil community across the board seem to be supportive of the LTTE's approach towards a solution. This was manifest in their reaction to the public statement by the US Ambassador to Sri Lanka, Ashley Wills, during a visit to Jaffna in the third week of March. He did not say anything in support of the Sri Lankan government's attitude towards the LTTE. All he said was that the US is committed to the unity and territorial integrity of Sri Lanka; that the US opposes the LTTE's violent campaign and that it is not willing to accept that the LTTE is the sole representative organisation of Sri Lankan Tamils. Leaders of the Tamil community in Jaffna, Trincomalee and Batticaloa criticised the US ambassador, accusing him of supporting the Sinhalese against the Tamils. (It was a factually incorrect criticism). These public statements were made not only by Tamil political figures, but the Christian and Hindu clergy in these provinces as well.

The Tamil diaspora in Westerm Europe, the Scandinavian countries, North America and South East Asia are actively interested in the success of the Norwegian effort. But they also feel that the responsibility for the delay in arriving at a solution lies with the Sri Lankan government rather than with the LTTE.

Given this situation, what are the prospects for peace?

First and foremost, it should be repeated that the Norwegian mission is aimed only at bringing the Sri Lankan government and the LTTE to the negotiating table. The actual problems/solutions will finally have to be negotiated by the Tamils and the Sinhalese directly. Negotiations therefore are bound to be prolonged and tortuous because the solution sought by the LTTE completely contradicts the solution the Sri Lankan government has in mind. It is difficult to foresee peace and normalcy in Sri Lanka in the near future unless there is a dramatic and miraculous change in the mindset of the LTTE and the Sri Lankan leadership.

Nepal

K.V. Rajan

The past five decades of India-Nepal relations have witnessed many lost opportunities, costly misjudgments and avoidable misunderstandings. It is remarkable that successive governments in both countries have so comprehensively failed to establish a stable, mature relationship based on mutual trust and a long-term vision of cooperation.

This is despite both the countries sharing unique assets like centuries-old shared cultural affinities, a 1,751 km open border and powerful economic complementarities in water resources, energy, trade, investment and tourism. As a result, a relationship, which could have served as a model of ties between neighbouring countries, attracts little respect or interest within India or outside; and, a sub-region which should by now have become the most prosperous in South Asia, remains one of the poorest in the world.

The series of crises, which have shaken the Himalayan kingdom in the past two years, and the shadows that have been cast on the bilateral relationship as a consequence, offer an opportunity for soul-searching on both sides of the border, and perhaps mark a new beginning.

Three events—the hijacking of the Indian Airlines flight from Kathmandu on 24 December 1999, the royal tragedy of June 1 2001, and the declaration of Emergency in November 2001 to end the Maoist insurgency—have underlined the depth and complexity of the crisis confronting Nepal.

They have exposed massive failures in governance; widespread disillusionment with a decade of multi-party democracy; the new vulnerability of the institution of monarchy; the real danger of an irreversible radicalisation of Nepal; the increasing use of Nepalese soil for terrorist-related activity; and the continuing fragility of the India-Nepal relationship, even when there are friendly democratic governments in Kathmandu.

The hijacking episode should have led to healthy introspection and corrective measures in both the countries, without affecting the relationship between them. The initial Nepalese reaction was indeed of shock and sympathy for India. This was, however, soon overtaken by resentment caused by the perception that India was deliberately casting disproportionate blame on Nepal.

Much pain was caused to the Nepalese pride, self-image, reputation and economy by India when it cancelled all flights to Nepal within hours of the hijacking. Nepal being caricatured as a favoured haven for terrorists in many quarters in India and the Indian government's incorrect identification of a Nepalese passenger among the hijackers also caused a lot of anguish in the Himalayan kingdom. Amidst this scenario, it was not difficult for vested interests to launch a propaganda offensive insinuating that India's hidden agenda was to exploit the hijacking in order to further its own security objectives.

For New Delhi, the hijacking incident (which was followed by another, involving the arrest and expulsion of a Pakistani diplomat implicated in a counterfeit currency racket) confirmed the view that Nepal's insensitivity to repeated requests for curbing ISI activities on its soil had resulted in a major threat to India's security.

A year after the hijacking, there was unprecedented anti-India street violence against India, in which New Delhi saw evidence of the ISI hand.

These incidents fuelled misunderstandings of a kind that had perhaps not manifested itself in the past, even in difficult moments of India-Nepal relations. The one durable asset in the bilateral relationship—trust and goodwill at the people-to-people level—seemed to be badly damaged.

The flights have since resumed, but Indian tourists have not returned.

Even before tragedy struck at Narayanhity Palace on the night of Friday, June 1 2001, Nepal was in the midst of a multiple crisis. This was created by the increasing disenchantment with multi-party democracy and chronic political instability, which had resulted in nearly a dozen changes of governments in the past few years. Other factors contributing to the disenchantment were the blatant politicisation of the bureaucracy for over a decade by successive governments, rampant corruption, the virtual collapse of governance in several districts and the growing reach and capacity of the Maoist insurgency.

In this situation, people were pinning their hopes on King Birendra to somehow find a way out. Cautious by nature, the king was resisting pressure from hardliners to take extra-constitutional initiatives to deal with the grave challenges facing the nation. His preference was to see a broad-based political consensus emerge, before taking any action. He was also hopeful that as and when he took an initiative, the international community, especially India, would give him its backing. His patience and evident reluctance to stage a palace coup had only added to his popularity, prestige and reputation as a democrat at heart.

It was in this volatile situation that Nepal suddenly lost its monarch and his entire family in a bizarre massacre by Crown Prince Dipendra. The latter was crowned king while he lay in coma, before succumbing to his injuries. He was succeeded by his uncle Gyanendra ('Three Kings in Four Days', as one Nepali newspaper disbelievingly put it).

Besides shock and grief, the scale of the tragedy, its mysterious circumstances and the way it was officially handled generated confusion, suspicion, anger and disbelief among the people. The immediate assessment was that it might take generations for the institution of monarchy to be restored to its earlier position as a revered symbol of Nepal's unity and national personality. And, that the combination of popular disenchantment with democracy and the vulnerability of the monarchy spelt serious danger for Nepal as the country the world recognises today.

King Gyanendra succeeded his brother in the most difficult of circumstances. After a shaky start, he has been discharging his constitutional responsibilities with impressive clarity of direction, firmness as well as finesse. He has made it clear that while the Constitution will be fully respected, and there is no question of turning the clock back as far as democracy is concerned, he will not be a passive spectator to the fast deteriorating situation in the country.

The image of the monarchy, and of King Gyanendra personally improved dramatically within a few months of the tragedy. In fact, his son Paras was anointed crown prince in October 2001 without riots breaking out in the streets—something that had seemed unimaginable only a few weeks earlier. The country has generally adjusted to the higher profile of the king. In the streets of Kathmandu, people may still find it hard to accept the official version of what happened to King Birendra on June 1, or are still to be fully reconciled to the present dispensation. But there is a sense of hope that the serious problems facing the country, especially the Maoist insurgency, will now receive the attention they deserve, thanks to a pragmatic and decisive monarch—even if this competes with apprehensions about the future of democracy if politicians do not get their act together fast.

There can be little doubt that the roots of the Maoist problem lie in the demonstrated inability of a decade of multi-party democracy to address the social and economic problems of the country. As elsewhere in the world, including India, such movements prosper when governance fails.

The Maoist movement was launched in February 1996. From a small group of a few hundred revolutionaries armed with khukris and crude pistols in three mid-western districts, the movement was able to grow in a dramatic fashion to its present day strength. Until the Emergency was declared in November 2001, the Maoists were in complete control in some 25 of Nepal's 75 districts extorting money and attacking targets at will. They were demonstrating the capacity to demoralise the police, bring down elected governments, and posed a serious political and ideological challenge to leftist parties. This clearly could not have happened if the various power centres—including the government of the day, the opposition, the palace, the business community, the media and the intelligentsia—had not acquiesced, if not connived in, the growth of Maoist power, in one way or another, during the past five years.

India, too, must accept its share of responsibility—it has been a passive spectator for far too long, despite the obvious dangers it poses to its own security. There is no excuse for the fact that despite frequent communications from the Nepalese side, Maoist leaders for the past few years have been moving freely across the border, holding meetings with senior Nepalese politicians on Indian soil, without Indian agencies apparently knowing about it. To plead that it is difficult to keep track of such activity because of an open border, is to give credibility to the same argument made by Nepal in defence of its inability to prevent cross-border traffic of criminals and terrorists. What is sauce for the goose must be sauce for the gander.

For the Maoists, the royal tragedy of June 1 was an unexpected opportunity and they seized it. They pronounced the monarchy dead, refused to recognise the new king and intensified their insurgency. The continuing internal dissent within the ruling Nepali Congress, the running confrontation between Prime Minister Koirala and the opposition, which had paralysed the Parliament for several months, as well as the poor chemistry between Koirala and the palace further strengthened them. After they had succeeded in forcing Koirala's resignation, they were quick to agree to a ceasefire and negotiations to end the insurgency, with the new government led by Sher Bahadur Deuba. The sense of relief and hope was, however, short-lived. In November 2001, the talks collapsed and, escalating their violence, the Maoists attacked army posts for the first time, causing serious casualties.

The declaration of National Emergency and the authorisation given by the king for the army's involvement in offensive action against the Maoists, who have been declared a terrorist group, has opened a completely new phase. The killing of hundreds of security personnel at the hands of the Maoists, and vice versa, has ended the army's logic, being projected for sometime, for being uninvolved—namely, that the Royal Nepalese Army could never be utilised in a battle against fellow Nepalese. This has huge and, at the moment, difficult-to-define implications for the future.

Thanks to the awareness of terrorism as a global threat created by the attacks in the US on 11 September 2001, the rest of the international community has unreservedly backed the government of Nepal. The government of India has extended its full cooperation to the Nepalese government. But it must contend with the fact that the major powers of the world are now increasingly involved, including in a direct military sense, in assisting Nepal to combat the Maoist threat—something which it would have energetically resisted until the other day, as a potential threat to its own security.

What does this spell for the 1950 Treaty?

For the time being, the main political parties, the palace and the army are on the same side, addressing the Maoist threat with a sense of urgency and direction. It is, however, too early to predict the success of the government. The unity and political will being presently displayed will come under increasing strain if there is a prolonged struggle and there are heavy civilian casualties.

The history of radical movements in other countries suggests that they cannot easily be extinguished by force, especially when the problems of poverty, governance, political participation and social disparities are as serious as they are in Nepal. The social and economic reforms demanded by the Maoists have tremendous appeal, especially for the rural poor and the marginalised sections of society. Thus, the trend towards radicalisation can be contained only if there is early success in the efforts of the army and the government to break the backbone of the movement, followed up with a credible and accelerated process of socio-economic reforms.

India and Nepal: The Elusive Search for Security

With its landlocked situation and the excessively intimate social, religious, cultural and economic ties with India, Nepal has always looked for a psychological counterweight to give it a sense of separateness and self-importance. Much of the history of Nepal's relations with China, Pakistan or indeed the rest of the world, has to do with this fundamental need.

India became free in 1947, but could not free itself from the British mindset. Nehru had a lofty vision of Nepal's isolation being ended, a democratic process being initiated and the economy being modernised. But India's security perspective was essentially a hand-me-down from British India. India expected that, given the age-old ties of history, culture and religion and the sheer facts of geography, Nepal's own self-interest would compel acceptance of the inextricable interlinkages between the security interests of the two countries. This was immediately challenged in Nepal. The imminent takeover of Tibet by China left India with no option but to formalise common security arrangements with Nepal as quickly as possible.

The Treaty of Peace and Friendship negotiated with the discredited and shaky Rana regime in 1950 was a straightforward imitation of the 1923 treaty. It became a subject of controversy in Nepal almost immediately, and has remained a rallying point for anti-India elements ever since.

India's role in ending the autocratic Rana regime, restoring the monarchy, brokering Nepal's first experiment with democracy, and financing Nepal's first two Five Year Plans won it considerable goodwill, but the seeds of anti-Indianism were planted with the formal assertion of the Himalayas as a common security perimeter. Subsequently, India's visibly overactive diplomatic involvement in Nepal's internal affairs, the establishment of the Indian Military Mission and the joint manning of posts on the Nepal-Tibet border only helped to fuel resentment and suspicion about Indian intentions vis-à-vis Nepal's aspirations for sovereign space. This was despite King Tribhuvan's personal support for the policy of alignment with India and a shared perception of the threat from China.

King Mahendra's accession to the throne in 1955, following King Tribhuvan's death, ushered in a phase of uneasiness in bilateral relations and uncertainty for the democratic process even as Sino-Indian relations deteriorated. Within five years, the democratic structure had been dismantled and Nepal was an absolute monarchy. Relations with China were established, and a conscious process of diversification of Nepal's political, trade and economic relations with the outside world was pursued.

The Sino-Indian war resulted in a huge setback to India's image in Nepal. In a bid to reassure King Mahendra about its intentions vis-a-vis the monarchy, New Delhi took the decision to discourage all activities of pro-democracy leaders on Indian soil. But the nationalistic tide in Nepal could not be stopped. By the end of the decade, Nepal had officially pronounced the 1950 Treaty as being outdated and non-operational. It declared the special relationship with India non-existent and the Arms Assistance Agreement of 1965 (under which the Indian government was to supply the entire requirement of the Royal Nepal Army) as annulled.

India's victory in the Indo-Pakistan War of 1971, and the limited help China was able to give to Pakistan restored India's position as the pre-eminent power in South Asia.

King Mahendra died in 1972. Birendra succeeded his father amid a sense of insecurity created by activities of Nepali Congress leaders exiled in India. Indira Gandhi's assurances of non-interference in Nepal's affairs did little to remove this apprehension. This inevitably translated itself into orchestrated anti-Indian activity on the part of the government, media, and intelligentsia.

The Zone of Peace proposal, a thinly disguised attempt to bury Nepal's security obligations to India under the 1950 Treaty, complicated matters further. When the democratic forces in Sikkim succeeded in removing the Chogyal and Sikkim merged with the Indian Union, the palace reaction was so adverse that it led to a crisis in bilateral ties.

The years that followed saw many wasted opportunities for expanding cooperation. Nepal's expensive forays into nationalistic campaigning were matched by India's overreactions. Leaders on both sides easily misjudged each other's intentions, duly encouraged by their over-zealous officials. Bilateral relations frequently came under strain, finally culminating in the trade embargo and Nepal's provocative purchase of anti-aircraft guns, medium range SSMs and assault rifles from China in 1988 in contravention of the 1950 Treaty.

Meanwhile, the domestic policies of the panchayat regime in areas like democratic reform, development, education and planning during the period also ran aground. It was the comprehensive failure of domestic and foreign policies that united political parties of the left and right in the successful mass movement for restoration of democracy of 1989-1990.

Encounters of the Democratic Kind

The ushering in of multi-party democracy in 1990 created high expectations of a more stable environment for developing Indo-Nepal relations on a long-term basis. As head of the interim coalition government of the Nepali Congress and United Left Front, Prime Minister K.P. Bhattarai visited India in June 1990. The 15-month diplomatic stalemate was resolved, mutual respect for each other's security concerns emphatically stated, trade and transit facilities to Nepal liberalised, and a forward-looking agenda for cooperation in water resources announced. Prime Minister G.P. Koirala paid a highly successful visit to India 18 months later during which the goodwill and cooperation in several important areas of bilateral cooperation were further enhanced.

The CPN (UML) was, however, able to whip up popular sentiment against Koirala's allegedly pro-India policies. They insisted that the 1950 Treaty should be abrogated as it was unequal and outdated. Thanks to poor official handling of the controversy over the Tanakpur barrage built by India, it soon became a major irritant in bilateral relations. The Tanakpur project did not involve consumptive use of water for generation of electricity, but it was necessary to tie the left afflux bund to the high ground on the left bank of the river on Nepalese soil. The opposition attacked the Koirala government for the lack of transparency surrounding the understanding reached between Nepal and India on the project. It claimed that Nepal had received less than its entitled share of free water and power in lieu of the land provided to India. The opposition also maintained that the agreement should have been ratified by a two-thirds majority of Parliament rather than simply presented to the country as a decision of the executive.

The Nepali Congress government fell under the weight of intra-party divisions. Koirala resigned and mid-term elections were held in November 1994 resulting in a hung parliament. A minority UML government led by Manmohan Adhikari, a veteran politician who had been jailed by the British for participating in the Quit India Movement during his student days in India, assumed power. It lost no time in distancing itself from its pre-election anti-India rhetoric. Intensive discussions were held between New Delhi and Kathmandu at the senior official level on the full spectrum of bilateral cooperation—political, trade, security, and water resources—following a visit by Deputy Prime Minister Madhav Nepal in February 1995. This was preparatory to the official visit of Prime Minister Manmohan Adhikari, which followed a few weeks thereafter.

There was no more talk by the UML of abrogation of the 1950 Treaty. The demand for additional concessions at Tanakpur was subsumed in a new proposal for integrated development of the Mahakali river. India would agree to enhance the water and power to be supplied to Nepal at Tanakpur. But this would be within the framework of a wider agreement to construct a multi-purpose dam further upstream at a border stretch of the Mahakali at Pancheshwar.

The UML sought to reassure India about its intentions by refusing to allow a UK-based parliamentary group to hold a conference on Kashmir with the participation of militant groups from both sides of the line of control, discouraging leaders of the Darjeeling-based movement for Greater Nepal from visiting Nepal and in other ways as well.

The Adhikari government fell after nine months in office. While rejecting the concept of a special relationship with India and raising 'national' issues—like the need for the 1950 Treaty to be updated, the Bhutanese refugee problem, etc.,—with greater persistence than its predecessor, the UML had given sufficient indication of its serious desire to strengthen relations with India on a long-term basis.

The following years saw political instability assume chronic dimensions. Prime ministers and governments changed with bewildering frequency. Every possible permutation and combination of political parties was forged through temporary alliances in their bid for power.

In September 1995, Sher Bahadur Deuba succeeded Adhikari as the head of a three-party coalition of Nepali Congress, Rashtriya Prajatantra Party (RPP) and National Sadbhavana Party (NSP). Lokendra Bahadur Chand, leading a coalition of the dissident group of the RPP, the UML and NSP, replaced him in February 1997. Surya Bahadur Thapa replaced him after six months at the head of an RPP-NC-NSP coalition. He was forced out by Koirala, who first formed a minority government, then a coalition with the breakaway CPN (ML) and finally with the main opposition CPN (UML) prior to the general elections of 1999.

In India, too, there was political uncertainty and change. Between 1996 and 1999, there were five changes of prime minister and three general elections.

Both countries paid a stiff price for this political turbulence, including in bilateral ties with each other. Yet they succeeded in maintaining a certain stability, continuity and direction which appeared to vindicate India's long-held conviction that multi-party democracy was not only good for Nepal but offered the best hope for developing bilateral cooperation on a long-term basis.

The experience of the Mahakali Treaty was particularly striking. The treaty was first proposed to the Narasimha Rao government by the UML in April 1995. The UML government fell before the proposal could be discussed. However, its successor, the NC-RPP-NSP coalition led by Sher Bahadur Deuba, picked up the threads of the same proposal in the hope that the UML, now the main opposition party, would find it difficult to oppose a draft initiated during its own administration. The treaty was finalised on the basis of a formal all-party consensus in Nepal and signed in New Delhi by Prime Ministers Sher Bahadur Deuba and Narasimha Rao during the former's New Delhi visit in March 1996.

By the time the treaty was placed before the Nepalese Parliament for ratification, the Gujral government was in office in India. The Nepalese Parliament ratified the treaty with the requisite two-thirds majority after a thorough, and occasionally, divisive national debate.

The Deuba government fell soon thereafter. Its successor was a coalition led by anti-Mahakali dissidents in the RPP and CPN (UML), Prime Minister Lokendra Bahadur Chand and Deputy

PM Bamdev Gautam. The new government opted to honour past international commitments and the instruments of ratification of the treaty were exchanged during Prime Minister Gujral's official visit to Kathmandu in July 1997.

The Mahakali treaty attracted attention in a number of countries as an important indication of the ability of two multi-party democracies to reach an agreement on cooperation in water resources on the basis of equality, transparency and equitable sharing of costs and benefits.

The Nepalese Constitution requires ratification by two-thirds parliamentary majority for any agreement affecting the country 'extensively, seriously or in the long term'. Many had thought that with such a provision, Nepal and India would never be able to reach an understanding on cooperation in such a sensitive area as water, since ratification by Parliament would be next to impossible, given the quality of politics in the subcontinent.

Nepal has some 83,000MW of hydropower potential, half of which is feasible for development. It presently has a demand of only 270MW. With India's energy deficit projected to reach 20,000MW by 2010, the compelling logic of economic complementarity is all too obvious. Also, large-scale export of hydropower is perhaps the only way Nepal can hope to achieve speedy growth and remove poverty within a decade. The only other resource it has is tourism, which has its limitations.

Thus, the fact that despite a hung parliament and considerable political uncertainty, Nepal's main parties could unite to the extent of securing parliamentary ratification for the treaty was hailed in many quarters as an impressive demonstration of the maturity of its democracy and the promising prospects now available for investment in the power sector.

That a power trade agreement had already been signed between the two countries during Deuba's visit to India—providing in principle for private sector investment in hydropower projects in Nepal for export to private sector consumers in India—further encouraged interest from prospective investors worldwide. In fact, within weeks of this development, Enron announced plans to invest in a 10,800 MW project at Karnali Chisapani. Thanks to the Mahakali treaty, Nepal seemed truly on the path to economic growth and prosperity.

It is unfortunate that the treaty—the only possibility that exists at the moment for the two countries to harness water resources in a major way, since it has been ratified by the Nepalese Parliament—is being implemented at such a slow pace. The two main reasons for this are: the inability of the political community in Nepal to resist the temptation to politicise the treaty every now and then; and the inability of the Indian side at operational levels to sustain the vision behind the treaty, resulting in compartmentalised, overly-technical, poorly coordinated approaches to issues which demand understanding and respect for the total picture. There is also the failure to understand the tremendous mutual benefit of executing a major project such as this on the basis of equal partnership and transparency.

Similarly, a far-reaching trade treaty was signed in December 1996, providing for duty-free access to the Indian market for all goods manufactured in Nepal, irrespective of labour and material content. The idea was to stimulate Indian investment in export-oriented manufacturing activity in Nepal, and, thus expand the basket of exportable commodities from Nepal to India—the only way to address Kathmandu's long-standing grievance of a huge trade deficit and the huge potential for Indian investment in Nepal, which had been largely untapped for decades.

The treaty began to show results almost immediately. In the next five years, Nepalese exports to India increased at the rate of 57 per cent per annum, and India's at 14 per cent. Besides, a number of Indian companies including Hindustan Lever, Dabur, and Colgate invested in joint ventures on the Nepalese side of the border for export to India and third countries.

In 1997, Prime Minister Gujral paid an important visit to Nepal at the invitation of his counterpart, Lokendra Bahadur Chand. Apart from other agreements signed, Gujral overruled objections from his bureaucrats and agreed to a long time Nepalese request for an alternative transit route to and through Bangladesh (the so-called Phulbari Route).

In order to address the special security concerns posed by the fact that the route passes through the sensitive 'Chicken's Neck' area of West Bengal, it was decided to provide escort for the Nepal-bound and Nepal-origin cargo by Indian security personnel—perhaps the most striking example of going the extra mile in accommodating a landlocked neighbour's aspirations in the history of transit agreements. The fact that this exceptional gesture was being made with a coalition government led by individuals who did not have a particularly 'pro-India' complexion, did not go unnoticed.

The message to Nepal was that India's policies would not be influenced by the political orientation of the government in power. It was further reinforced by Prime Minister Vajpayee when the Indo-Nepal transit treaty came up for renewal. In what was possibly a unique concession to a landlocked neighbour, the treaty was made automatically renewable every seven years, unless either country gave notice to the contrary before its expiry. In other words, Nepal's access to the sea was in principle granted in perpetuity, not something to be renegotiated and renewed every seven years.

During this period, King Birendra shed his reserve vis-à-vis India. In various ways he sent out signals to India, as well as his own people, that the misunderstandings and bitterness of the eighties should be put behind both countries and that he was personally strongly supportive of closer India-Nepal relations.

He maintained regular contact with the Indian leadership on all matters of mutual interest so that, to the extent possible, neither country was taken by surprise by developments in the other. He regularly graced private and public functions at India House after more than 20 years of avoiding them and made unusual departures from protocol in dealing with the Indian Embassy or visiting Indian dignitaries. The monarch also paid several private as well as official visits to India, including a pilgrimage to Hardwar, Kedarnath, Badrinath and Dwarika. He warmly received President Narayanan on an official visit and was himself invited to visit India as Chief Guest on Republic Day, 1999—the first time a king of Nepal had been accorded this honor in 50 years.

Mutual goodwill and the momentum for strengthening cooperation appeared to have reached unprecedented levels. Speaking in Parliament in reply to a no-confidence motion shortly after the king's visit as Chief Guest on Republic Day, Prime Minister Vajpayee defended his government's foreign policy achievements by citing Nepal as an example. He said that an election campaign was in progress there but there was not a hint of anti-Indianism in the air!

Indeed, unlike in previous elections, India-related issues like the 1950 treaty, Mahakali Treaty or Kalapani border dispute did not figure in the campaign. Tanakpur, which had brought the Koirala government down in 1994 and had once seemed such an intractable issue, was not mentioned even once.

The results of the general elections in May 1999 were also encouraging. The Nepalese electorate ignored threats from the Maoists against participation or voting in the elections and cast their ballot for stability, development and apparently also for good relations with India. Parties and individuals professing a commitment to the politics of the far left as well as the extreme right were categorically rejected.

Unfortunately, a number of factors, notably political instability and problems of governance, the activities of forces hostile to India and to India-Nepal relations and the inability of both sides to sustain a vision of long-term cooperation especially at the operational levels rudely disrupted these promising trends. As in the past, India's security concerns and Nepal's inability to satisfy them became the driving force in the relationship, especially after the hijacking episode.

Both China and Pakistan have in the past deliberately stoked Nepal's yearning to over-assert its nationalism vis-à-vis India, knowing that this would drive a wedge between the two close neighbours. This was very evident, for example, when King Birendra invested his personal prestige in securing international support for his Zone of Peace proposal, which was a thinly disguised attempt to neutralise Nepal's obligations under the 1950 treaty. Similarly, statements by Pakistani and Chinese leaders during the trade dispute between India and Nepal in the late 1980s fuelled tensions between the two countries.

The success of the movement in April 1990 was a major diplomatic setback for China, which had encouraged Birendra to 'stand up' to India. China was forced to acknowledge that it was in no position to come to Nepal's rescue if there was a total breakdown in India-Nepal relations.

Since then, China seems to have withdrawn into a more passive mode, concentrating on furthering its economic interests rather than actively engaging in partisan politics in the new multi-party system or engaging in activities which would be seen as hostile to India's interests. Its public position on issues like Kalapani has been neutral. The Maoist insurgency is overtly pro-China and anti-India; there is, however, no reliable evidence of Chinese support to their activities.

At the same time, China has, in recent years (especially after India's Pokhran nuclear tests in May 1998), visibly stepped up its political interactions with different power centers—the monarchy, the leftist parties, parliamentarians, academia, the business community, and the Buddhist groups. It should be mentioned that Chinese have their own security concerns. For example, the Karmappa episode has heightened Chinese apprehensions of threats to its security arising from political instability and the lax and permissive environment of Nepal. While the Chinese public posture has been tactful so as not to offend Nepalese sensitivities, there can be no doubt about the seriousness with which China views this development.

To sum up, Chinese actions in Nepal bear constant

monitoring, but judgement must be reserved about the extent to which they are aimed at undermining India's vital interests. A strong India-Nepal relationship based on mutual trust and confidence as well as strong inter-dependent trade and economic linkages; a self-confident India which does not panic each time there is a high-level contact or a substantial commercial contract between Nepal and China; and a stable understanding between India and China that Nepal would not be used by either country for any activity which would have adverse security implications for the other may together provide the best recipe for a stable security environment for the three countries. Given Chinese sensitivities with regard to Tibet, and Indian anxieties about activities close to the India-Nepal border, a tacit India-China understanding may not be impossible to achieve.

Pakistan established diplomatic relations with Nepal in 1961. Until today the bilateral content of ties between Pakistan and Nepal is very modest. Pakistan's main interest has been to utilise its Kathmandu mission for anti-India activities. During the years of absolute monarchy, there was ample opportunity to cause India embarrassment by its high-profile support of Nepal's moves to assert itself against India. After 1990, a democratic set-up offered a wider playing field for fulfilling its objectives.

Over the years, the Pakistani Embassy in Kathmandu has become a major centre for ISI and other anti-India activities. It is known that the majority of the embassy staff are not professional diplomats from Pakistan's foreign ministry but ISI agents. The diplomatic bag is almost certainly used for transporting not only counterfeit Indian currency, which can be smuggled to India, but possibly drugs and RDX as well. Pakistani diplomats have been caught red-handed in operations involving counterfeit currency as well as RDX. In two cases, they have been expelled. Islamic fundamentalist influences and smuggling syndicates have also steadily developed bases in Nepal for over a decade.

The implications for India have been more serious than Nepalese political leaders were willing to concede until recently. Pakistan has traditionally relied heavily on unconventional or proxy military engagement to further its interests in Jammu and Kashmir and elsewhere in India. Its strategy of creating and perpetuating a Kashmir crisis for India required an ability to send across to the Indian side a steady flow of intelligence agents, drugs, arms and money. The 1700 km Nepal-India open border offered valuable opportunities to launch such operations because of India's success in containing militancy in Punjab and its substantially increased vigil to counter infiltration across the LOC in Kashmir.

Anyone vaguely resembling an Indian or a Nepali can cross through any of the check posts on the long border without documents or verification of any sort. The posts are inadequately manned and poorly supervised. The local situation, especially on the Indian side, in terms of roads, infrastructural facilities, effective police presence and administration morale has been traditionally unsatisfactory.

In addition, there are vast stretches of the border through open farmland, villages straddling a largely undefined border on rivers frequently changing course and tracts of forest land which make it possible for criminals and terrorists to cross from one side to the other with impunity. They have been encouraged by the fact that the security and immigration checks at Kathmandu's Tribhuvan International Airport have been notoriously lax for a long time (these are reported to have been strengthened after the hijacking).

The post-Ayodhya tensions also created an opportunity for Pakistan to strengthen an anti-India base close to the border in the Terai, with considerable assistance, not necessarily always official, from certain Islamic countries. The entire Nepalese Terai is now dotted with hundreds of mosques and madarsas, matching the proliferation on the Indian side. There are dozens of Muslim organisations, some of which are known to have close contacts with the ISI and the Pakistan-based Islamic fundamentalist groups. The size of the Nepalese Muslim community is reported to have grown from 2 per cent of the local population in 1981 to 5 per cent (about 10 lakh) at the turn of the century. Successive governments in Nepal have had to weigh the impact on their vote-banks when considering action to control anti-India activities inside mosques and madrasas instigated by the ISI.

The cooperation extended by successive Nepal governments on our security concerns cannot be said to be unsatisfactory. Contacts between the concerned agencies of the two countries have been excellent, often leading to major successes in terms of seizures of RDX or counterfeit currency or arrests of terrorists and Pakistani agents. It is interesting that this cooperation has continued even when governments in Nepal, which were not considered to be particularly close to India, have been in power.

Nepal realises that anti-India activities from its soil pose a serious threat to its own well-being and security and that cooperation with India is essential in its own interests. It would help, however, if there was more public acknowledgement about the seriousness and scale of such activities by the Nepalese political community. Without this, public opinion in Nepal will continue to underestimate them. And, the real objective of cooperation in security—which should be to prevent terrorist activities and not act against those involved after the event—will not be accomplished.

In the post September 11 situation, Pakistan itself is under increasing international pressure to withdraw support to jehadi groups on its soil, engaging in terrorist activities in Jammu and Kashmir, and elsewhere. The ISI has, however, invested heavily over the years in Nepal. The narco-terrorist nexus is a flourishing industry with powerful vested interests on both sides of the border that will resist any attempt to curb it. The dangers to India's security will probably remain, even if Pakistan dismantles bases within its borders and inside POK.

Apart from more effective joint management of the border

and improving the infrastructural arrangements, the core issue of improvement of the quality of governance on both sides of the border will have to be tackled with a sense of urgency. Without this, threats to India as well as to Nepal, whether from unfriendly third countries or the Maoist insurgency or the drugs-and-arms smuggling network, will continue.

Indian agencies and the media must also appreciate that the public admonishing, which is periodically administered by whipping Nepal for being a base for ISI activities, is severely counterproductive. With the Emergency declared in Nepal against the Maoist insurgency and the new awareness of the fact that terrorists do not respect borders, this is a shared concern and can only be addressed jointly in a cooperative rather than accusatory environment.

It is now more than five decades since the controversial Treaty of Peace and Friendship was signed between India's ambassador to Nepal, C.P.N. Singh and Prime Minister Mohun Shamsher Jang Bahadur Rana. Most Nepalese consider the content of the treaty to be an affront to their sense of sovereignty and the levels at which the two governments were represented as 'unequal'. They also feel that the treaty was forced upon an unrepresentative Rana regime when it was on its last legs, thus denying it any kind of legitimacy or credibility.

Indian diplomats and political leaders have, for years, been saying with a straight face that the treaty is an understanding between two sovereign governments; that there is nothing unequal about it; that it is a reflection of the special relationship that has existed between the two countries for centuries rather than the reason for it. And that, in any case, the treaty does not provide for any amendment.

The subtext in all this is that Nepal cannot expect to have its cake and eat it too. The treaty imposes certain security obligations on Nepal in exchange for important economic benefits. Nepal would dearly wish to retain the economic baby and throw out the security bathwater. India insists that both remain together.

King Birendra's tentative effort to pressurise Rajiv Gandhi on the treaty was promptly given up when the adverse implications for Nepal were communicated to him. The CPN (UML), which had made abrogation of the treaty a central plank of its successful election campaign in 1994, scaled down its request to an open-ended 'review' at the official level. Encouraged by the positive indications given by Prime Minister Gujral that India was at last sensitive to Nepal's psyche, Foreign Minister Kamal Thapa brought a non-paper to New Delhi in 1997 as a basis for discussion on a new treaty. However, he had to go back empty-handed (the non-paper itself has been disowned by successor governments as representing the Nepalese position).

The fact of the matter is that neither country today fulfills its obligations under the treaty, either in letter or spirit. Nepal freely discriminates against Indian nationals in that country, without too much protest from India.

Technical violations of the treaty, including in the military sphere, are also fairly routine. There has been no consultation worth the name by India with Nepal in regard to the conflict situations in which it has been involved, as required under the treaty.

Nepalese nationals in India no longer find it as easy to carry on their business, buy property or secure employment as they used to. India's security perimeter itself has shifted from the Himalayas to the open border in the plains. Moreover, the main threat through Nepal is from the ISI and the drug-and-terrorism nexus rather than China.

Thus, we have the piquant situation that the treaty has lost much of its relevance in the security context. It is increasingly implemented more in the breach than in observance by both countries; it has a poor imperialist odour to it, which is not quite compatible with the engagement to define a forward-looking relationship. India gets hardly any benefit under the treaty, but is unable to adjust to the idea of its revision. And, Nepal finds the treaty to be a major psychological irritant, but desperately wants to continue to retain the dwindling benefits from it.

India has left it to Nepal to come up with concrete suggestions on what it wants. The impasse is, however, likely to continue unless India comes forward with positive proposals of its own. An amicable solution should be possible. This should ensure respect for Nepal's sense of sovereign pride, cooperation on matters of mutual security concern, the entitlement of either country to apply its laws and regulations to nationals of the other (a consultative mechanism could be envisaged to deal with major adverse implications if any) and suitable consideration by India to Nepal's vulnerability because of its size and state of economic development.

The people of Nepal had invented the concept of non-reciprocity in their dealings with India long before Gujral articulated it as a doctrine in his famous Chatham House speech. Indeed, successive governments in India before and after the Gujral government have, in fact, been implementing this principle in its spirit. But the writing on the wall is that a special relationship—one in which Nepal obtains economic advantages in exchange for dilution of its sovereign space—is as good as dead. The sooner India adjusts to this fact, the better it will be for the future prospects for India-Nepal relations.

In the search for satisfaction with its security concerns and stability in the long-term relationship, India has, in a sense, come full circle. In the early fifties, it sought an understanding with the autocratic and unpopular Ranas, then pursued the effort with the monarchy and a democratic set-up, which it helped to install.

In the subsequent decades, it switched between active support for friendly democratic forces and a none-too-friendly, not particularly popular monarchy in the hope of securing at least tactical adjustments from the latter while not abandoning principled support for the former.

By the end of the eighties, it was pitching in whole-heartedly with the democratic forces while maintaining a cold and formal relationship with the king, foreseeing a popular tide in favour of pro-India groups in any free and fair election.

The first half of the nineties saw bold steps being taken between the NC government and India in strengthening ties. These were, however, undermined by the widespread and largely unfair perception that Nepal's traditional nationalistic sentiments were not being sufficiently respected, and that India was putting all its eggs in one 'pro-India' political basket in Nepal in order to promote its own interests.

In the last five years of the twentieth century, India, under four different prime ministers and perhaps for the first time, was addressing Nepal's national aspirations with a sense of objectivity as well as magnanimity. This was done irrespective of which government was in power in Nepal. A conscious effort was made to create greater trust and confidence in India's long-term intentions among all the power centres, including the major political parties and the palace. There was a tantalising glimpse of a brighter future for peoples on both sides of the border as a series of milestone agreements were reached, but political instability ultimately undermined these positive trends.

The hijacking episode and its aftermath have now transformed the entire environment to such a degree that both countries need to think afresh about the future course of their relationship.

Nepal today faces the daunting task of coping with serious challenges on several fronts, with its faith in multi-party democracy eroded, and the institution of monarchy wounded. How India decides to move in this complicated situation, especially in its perennial search for greater security, would undoubtedly have a bearing on the future course of events in the Himalayan Kingdom

What is certain is that muddling through is no longer an option for India.

China

C.V. Ranganathan

The record of over five decades since India's Independence and China's 'liberation' shows that the Indians and Chinese need to break out of a historical pattern—in which they have unilaterally projected their best hopes and their worst fears upon the mixed realities of the two countries.

Multiple confusing images of the 'other', present in each country, need to be dealt with if the India-China relationship is to become more substantive and meaningful than the present levels achieved. On the Chinese side, there is a lack of sensitivity in appreciating that the needs of Indian geography dictate non-hegemonistic Indian interests from a wide arc—stretching from West Asia to Central, South and South East Asia. There is also a need to understand the dynamics, compulsions and constraints that guide the working of the plural polity that is India.

In the evolving international situation after 11 September 2001, culture matters more than ever before. The values embedded in this culture will shape socio-economic, political and technological futures.

As cradles of human civilisation, India and China have impacted each other from ancient to modern times. Visions that such a glorious past could provide the basis for Sino-Indian solidarity and exemplary coexistence, however, proved short-lived and tapered off in the decade from 1949 onwards. After that, misunderstandings and mutual misperceptions over the domestic and external priorities of each country, compounded by the interplay of two Cold Wars, the US-Soviet and the Soviet-China tensions and territorial disputes led to bitterness and even armed conflict. This was followed by over two decades of minimal, indifferent and hostile relations. The distant peregrinations of their ancestors then became a diminishing preoccupation of just a few scholars in each country.

Neither side refrained from invoking subliminal and contemporary negative memories of the other either to rationalise controversial actions or to react to these. On the occasion of India's nuclear tests in 1998, the nuclear weapon capabilities of China and its assistance in the non-conventional fields to Pakistan were cited among the reasons for India exercising its long-delayed nuclear option. Intemperate statements were made in India about China being a threat, a rival, even an enemy.

On the other side, a litany of complaints about India using China as a pretext to conduct the tests and about India's 'hegemonistic' designs in the neighbourhood was revived. That all this came ten years after a brisk exchange of visits at the highest levels of leadership from 1988 onwards showed the fragile basis of the otherwise constructive high-level dialogues. It took a whole year of diplomatic efforts to assuage hurt feelings and restore normalcy. Public affirmations by leaders of both sides—that no country views the other as a threat—followed and comfort levels were restored to the relationship.

China's success in translating its rapid economic growth into international prestige and status is an object of admiration as well as envy in India. The strides taken to keep itself abreast of the revolution in military affairs is watched with a measure of apprehension by India.

But, more than China posing a military threat—now moderated by political exigencies—it is its perception as an economic threat that prevails in Indian business circles. A rapidly rising curve of two-way trade, consisting of raw materials and manufactures, followed by some mutual investments are welcome signs of complementarities present in the economic relationship. However, for the further potential in this relationship to be realised, businessmen from both sides need to put in far greater intellectual efforts and material commitments than are visible at present. The opportunities provided by China's entry to the World Trade Organisation (WTO), and the challenges this can pose need close professional monitoring.

Some Indian perceptions of China are more subjective than real. On account of its economic growth and dense relationships with the advanced countries, there are some people who feel that China does not attach priority to its relation with India, or worse still, does not respect it. One has only to see the impressive list of very high-level Chinese politicians who have visited India in the last few years to understand that the Chinese do attach importance to India. Chinese foreign policy towards South Asia has been predicated in recent times on India being the dominant South Asian power.

Although China's economy has far outstripped India's, Chinese have high respect for India's soft power in fields related to information technology, pharmaceuticals, education and even entertainment, to name a few areas. As competent and well-qualified managers, Indians are the preferred nationality to man foreign invested and international institutions in China. Indian positions, which are articulated in international negotiating fora, are followed closely by China as approximations to its interests. No casual Indian visitor to China fails to be affected by the goodwill shown to him or her.

The mixed images referred to above do not capture the whole picture. As guides to policies that would advance Indian interests they are totally inadequate, misleading and counter-productive. Media presentations of these and similar perceptions in both countries only increase the gaps in mutual understanding. Thus, till the Sino-Indian relationship acquires an all-round depth and breadth, a mediatory role from both governments to help steer a steady course would be necessary.

At the same time, it is essential for non-governmental institutions, business and other circles to contribute to the building of deeper linkages than the two countries enjoy at present. Only a combination of the two would establish vested interests that would immunise the relationship from political vicissitudes. Such a situation exists in the case of China's relations with the US, countries of the European Union and Japan. There are dangers in seeking to encapsulate Sino-Indian relations in catchall phrases meant to serve as over-arching guidelines to their conduct.

The utilisation of external circumstances to benefit domestic social and economic growth was China's consistent strategy from the 80s. In turn, its domestic economic growth has been a major cause contributing to the vast changes in international relations.

Standing the doctrine of Mao Zedong—on the symbiotic relationship between domestic and external policies—on its head, Deng Xiaoping showed immense pragmatism, flexibility and manouevrability in shaping China's economic reforms at home while readjusting Chinese policies to the changing environment abroad.

By September 1982, about five years after his second resurrection to power, Deng had removed the worst evils of the Great Proletarian Cultural Revolution, which lasted for 10 catastrophic years from 1966, purged the evil 'Gang of Four' and most of their remnants and, for the most part, stabilised the top level of political leadership after the death of Mao Zedong in 1976.

Outlining that the three major tasks for the Chinese people in the beginning of the reform era were to intensify efforts at modernisation; reunify the motherland (referring to Taiwan, Hong Kong and Macao) and oppose 'hegemonies', he emphasised that 'of the three tasks, economic construction is the core and constitutes the basis for solving both international and domestic problems'. (Opening remarks at the Plenum of the 12th Party Congress of the Chinese Communist Party).

Mikhail Gorbachev came to power in Moscow in 1985 as general secretary of the Communist Party of Soviet Union and gave indications of a radically altered set of domestic and external priorities for his country. China was not slow to see that the international situation would change drastically. Some specific actions or initiatives by Gorbachev convinced Deng that it was time to bury the hatchet between Beijing and Moscow—these were the announced departure of Soviet troops from Afghanistan, former Soviet Union's lessening of commitments to Vietnam's occupation of Cambodia, the formula for seeking solutions to the territorial dispute and the validation of the economic reforms introduced in China as 'socialist'.

Negotiating mechanisms were rapidly put in place to resolve long-standing problems between the parties and states of the erstwhile Soviet Union and China. As president of the Union and general secretary of its ruling party, Gorbachev's visit to China in 1989 marked the complete normalisation of relations between the two countries. Although that visit was overshadowed by the Tienanmen Square incidents, it marked a decisive turning point in a relationship characterised by bitter hostility and, at times, armed conflict spread over three decades.

The Chinese were as shocked as anyone else with the collapse of the Soviet Union in 1991 and of Communist parties almost everywhere either just before or after that epochal event. Coming not long after China's domestic turmoils and still facing opposition from his conservative peers of the early revolutionary years, Deng drew the only practical lesson that was relevant if the Chinese Communist Party was to survive—

that it would lose credibility, even legitimacy, unless it made possible the well-being of a majority of the Chinese masses and raised their living and consumer standards.

Yet, he was convinced that liberalisation of the economy should not lead to false anticipation of any loosening of the grip of the mono-party-state, which in Deng's reading, was the cause of the collapse of the erstwhile ruling Communist parties. Economic performance, rather than any other criterion, would be the sole yardstick. There was also strong re-emphasis on the importance of adhering to the 'four basic principles' that reform could not challenge—socialism, dictatorship of the proletariat, Marxist-Leninist-Maoist thought and leadership by the Chinese Communist Party.

But emphasis on these tough political parameters were balanced by Deng staking his personal reputation on the most international aspects of China's reform era, namely the 'open door' policy of attracting foreign direct investments and pushing the Chinese entrepreneurs to seek markets abroad. He personally made a tour to southern China in 1992 to Special Economic Zones adjoining Hong Kong and to other coastal growth areas. In affirming their great contributions and calling for their emulation, Deng gave a further impetus to opening the Chinese door wider for foreign engagements, and encouraged private entrepreneurship.

During the period from the early 80s to the mid and late 90s, China engaged in active diplomacy to solve problems inherited from the Maoist era with its major South East Asian neighbours. The signing of the Paris Agreement in 1991 on Kampuchea, which heralded the withdrawal of Vietnamese presence from that country, marked a turning point in Sino-Vietnamese relations. The post-Soviet Russian regime under Yeltsin persisted in strengthening Sino-Russian relations. China also took early steps to deal with the new independent states of Central Asia to remove the Soviet era legacy of border disputes. Western countries led by the US and Japan gradually changed their policy of protest over the Tienanmen incidents of 1989—

once they realised that the conservatives in the Chinese Party, who backed the violent suppression of demonstrators, were losing ground and that China's 'open door' policy was reaffirmed by Deng in 1992.

Except for some continuing sanctions on technology imports by China, investors and businessmen from these countries flocked back to China. Negotiations on the handing over of Hong Kong to the Chinese were completed by the British in 1997, and by the Portuguese, of Macao, in 2000. By the closing years of the century, China was ensured the largest possible environment of peace in its extended neighbourhood by its domestic economic and proactive foreign policies. This, in turn, helped China to concentrate on speeding its growth. By the end of the last century, China had come to enjoy unprecedented peace and security as well as economic well-being for the majority of its people. India also benefited from this turn of events through the 80s and 90s.

Sustaining economic growth continues to remain the raison d'état in the beginning of this millennium as in the last decades of the previous century. As a compliment to this, peaceful external conditions continue to remain the prerequisites for the maintenance of stability at home and on China's borders. Ensuring state security and shouldering international responsibilities, as would suit its self-image as a great power, are the other features of China's external strategies.

Not surprisingly, it is China's relationship with the US that dominates China's strategic thinking (as indeed it has come to dominate Indian thinking too). The US is the only power, which can thwart, or ironically, assist China's future aspirations. The most realistic assessment of Sino-American relations would be to view these as one of cooperation where their interests coincide, combined with competition where they do not, irrespective of changes of presidents in the US. The relationship would defy categorisations, which American and Chinese intellectuals are prone to make in their analyses. Brinkmanship, followed by conciliation over issues that affect them directly and those that have a bearing on broader global developments, would continue to characterise this relationship.

The evolving situation in Taiwan is one glaring example of this. Current American interest is the stable continuation of the present *status quo*. The American commitment to 'one China', which became the foundation stone for the establishment of Sino-American ties, has one implicit assumption—that China would not use force to reunify Taiwan and that Taiwan would not provoke China by attempting to become an independent sovereign entity.

The social and economic integration of Taiwan with China is moving ahead rapidly, with the regime in Taipei progressively lifting the limitations on investments in the mainland, increasing trade and the development of close social and family networks on both sides. How these ground realities would affect the highly sensitive and political issue of reunification of Taiwan with the mainland remains to be seen. The issue needs to be worked out by the leaders and peoples on both sides of the Straits alone.

With the rapid democratisation of Taiwan and the emergence of a plural society, there are other challenges that China needs to face. Chinese impatience and pressure exerted on Taiwan to negotiate reunification makes the US more receptive to pleas of enhancing the quantity and quality of military aid to Taiwan. The Bush Administration, in fact, has been more affirmative than past administrations about America's strategic interest in Taiwan. It is in this context that Beijing views with apprehension the commitments to go ahead with the American national missile defence (NMD) schemes and the possible deployment of theatre missile defence (TMD) systems in China's neighbourhood.

The American deputy defence secretary, Paul Wolfowitz, reputedly one of the hardliners in the administration, was quoted as saying: 'September 11 changed everything. People now see the value of having a strategic dialogue with China.' Like most countries, India included, China took this tragedy as an occasion to draw international focus on its domestic problems posed by terrorism and to enlarge, to the extent possible, practical ways and means of cooperating with the US. Still unprepared to come to definitive conclusions on whether international terrorism has changed the nature of the international system, the Chinese have used September 11 to alert the international community to the threats to domestic security from the plural sources of terrorism. The dangers of weapons of mass destruction falling into wrong hands also makes China support the coalition against international terrorism.

China quickly extended sympathy to President Bush after 11 September. It agreed on intelligence sharing and supported the Security Council resolution that heralded intrusive interventions to de-Talibanise Afghanistan. Chinese cooperation with the US on the issue of international terrorism also marked the resumption of high-level military exchanges after the previous setback in relations following the spy plane incident.

President Bush's repudiation of the Bill Clinton administration's policy on North Korea puts China in a difficult spot. It had won the goodwill of previous administrations for its cooperation in influencing the North Koreans to maintain stability in the troubled Korean Peninsula. Prospects of normalisation opened up through the fitful four-party dialogue of North and South Koreans, the US and China. South Korea's sensitive policy of intensifying dialogue and exchanges with the North was, however, discouraged by the Bush Administration. At this point, it is unclear how the US's Korean policy will shape up. The greater American emphasis put on North Korea as a regime, which supports terrorism, and the possible acquisition of weapons of mass destruction by it, could also complicate Sino-American relations.

Thus, there is a conflict of interests between China and the US over some critical issues. But the deeper integration of the Chinese economy into the global economy requires trade, investments and technologies from the US and other advanced countries. Common issues of a global nature make for mutually beneficial intersections of American and Chinese interests. All this would dictate a non-confrontational approach to the US that China seems to be presently adopting.

Both India and China realise that maintaining the best relations with the US is of special advantage to each of them. But each views with suspicion the efforts made by the other to establish closer relations with the US. For India, the clear benefits of having excellent relations with the US are self-evident, given the developments following the chain of events in the region after 11 September 2001. For China, the peace and stability it seeks in East Asia would be impossible to achieve unless it has good relations with the US. The geopolitical interests of each country are best realised not in separate or joint confrontation with the US. This context should inform the management of India-China relations at present and in the future.

This does not mean that American global domination will go uncontested by China and Russia. The increasing Sino-Russian closeness in a wide variety of fields reflects China and post-Putin Russia's common concern about the expansion of American-led Western influence in Eurasia. Leaders of both countries proudly announce the Sino-Russian relationship as one of 'strategic partnership'.

Agreements on the 4,000 km long boundary, confidence-building measures in the military field, exchanges at high government and other functional governmental and non-governmental levels, and increasing trade in military and civil goods have cumulatively contributed to a growing relationship with solid substance. The sophistication of military hardware and technology from Russia to China makes up for big gaps in China's defence preparedness. It is expected that in 2001, the figure of two-way trade between China and Russia would exceed US $10 billion.

Certain geo-economic imperatives also drive Sino-Russian

relations. Russia's efforts for the development of Siberia and the Far East complement China's plans to bridge the gap between its own developed and less developed regions. Some big infrastructural projects to provide better connectivities between China's north east and the Russian far east through highways, improved railways, bridges across the border rivers, gas and oil pipelines, are being planned.

In another vast region—comprising Russia, China and four Central Asian States—Uzbekistan, Kazakhstan, Tadzkhistan, and Krygyzsthan—geopolitical and economic requirements have contributed towards the formation of the Shanghai Cooperative Organization (SCO) in July 2001.

For some time before 11 September, five of these partners, later joined by Uzbekistan, joined hands to combat the three 'evils' of religious fundamentalism, secessionism and international terrorism. The formation of the SCO formalises this political objective to face a common threat to Russia (at Chechnya and other places), China (at Xinjiang which has common borders with three of the Central Asian States), to Uzbekistan and Tadzhikhistan. An institution that would coordinate intelligence, military and diplomatic actions between the six, has been set up at Bishkek, Krygyzsthan.

The SCO also aims at expansion of political, economic, social and cultural relations between the six. Frequent meetings at the summit level and at the level of foreign ministers and officials have taken place and are envisaged as routine. Not viewed as a military alliance, the SCO has interestingly adopted as its foundational norms the three 'nons'—non-alignment, non-direction against third parties and non-confrontation (*sic* against the US) in addition to the traditional five principles.

The SCO is seen by its members as a new type of regional organisation for political, economic, scientific and cultural cooperation. Its objectives are in accordance with Indian interests and need to be encouraged by New Delhi.

Putin's rise to power in Russia has marked steady consolidation of the economy and a reversal of the country's sliding standing in the international community that happened in the Yeltsin years. Putin has adopted a pro-active approach to the European Union and its major countries, necessitated by strong political concerns over the eastward expansion of NATO and by economic requirements.

The Bush Administration's unilateralism over a variety of issues—such as repudiation of the ABM Treaty, determination to pursue the NMD programme, abandonment of the Comprehensive Test Ban Treaty, rejection of the Kyoto Protocol on global warming and sanctions against Iran, Iraq, Cuba, Yugoslavia and North Korea—have generated grave misgivings in Europe. Russia shares these misgivings. And, to the extent that the unilateral drift in the Bush Administration's rollbacks affects China's security and other interests, so does China.

Post 11 September, the certainty of continued American ground presence in a wide arc—from West Asia, Pakistan, Afghanistan and some Central Asian states to South East Asia and East Asia—would need delicate management by the Russians and Chinese. Joint confrontation versus the US is not an option. In the vague coalition against international terrorism, some of the host countries involved such as Pakistan, Afghanistan, Uzbekistan and others are good friends of either Russia or China. But they have exercised their sovereign and autonomous judgements in inviting added American military presence in their countries.

Both Russia and China have to reckon with American political and military predominance and also their dependence on the US for trade, investments and technology flows. The best outcome for the international community and India is that growing American influence, military and economic weight is exercised in a manner that should not harm their collective and separate interests. It is, of course, a bit early to speculate whether this would indeed be the case in what is still an evolving situation.

China has watched with some concern the quickness with

which Japan seized the opportunity of the US-led war against terrorism to enlarge the scope of the activities of its self defence forces (SDF), and the despatch of three warships to the Indian Ocean. Taiwan is also a major issue in Sino-Japanese relations. Japan cannot be expected to promote the reunification of Taiwan with China on terms with which neither Tokyo nor Taipei is comfortable.

The self-perpetuating, indeed even strengthening, role of the American forces in Japan under the revised US-Japan Defence Guidelines is viewed with much ambivalence by China. The Chinese harbour reservations about a politically assertive Japan, particularly given their historical memories of Japanese atrocities in their country during the 30s and 40s. All this is balanced by China's pragmatic need for a multifaceted relationship with Japan, commensurate with the latter's economic and technological capabilities.

Apart from managing the high quality of bilateral relations with Tokyo for trade, investment and cultural reasons, there is the larger and important regional setting where China needs to interact with Japan. This has acquired importance after the Asian economic crisis of 1997. Both have a deep interest in contributing to stability in the Korean Peninsula.

The five original members of the Association of South East Asian Nations (ASEAN) formed the group in 1967 under the impetus of the then perceived revolutionary expansionism of China. ASEAN's growth over the years, to include the three Indo-China states, Brunei and Myanmar, symbolises one of the major changes in the geo-political situation in South East Asia. China's growing economic weight and its active participation in ASEAN fora in recent years marks another major change. China and Japan need to cooperate, not work in opposition to the institution's goals, vis-à-vis ASEAN.

China has to accommodate some of the ASEAN countries' decisions to rely on countervailing American and Australian military presence in the region both as insurance and to sustain Western interest in the area. China's extensive claims over the waters, islands and reefs in the South China Seas have the potential to bring it in direct conflict with Philippines, Brunei, Malaysia, Vietnam (and Taiwan). Vigorous diplomatic and economic moves by China, through intensifying bilateral trade, investment and leadership exchanges with each of the major members of the ASEAN, support to the association's political cohesion and active participation in the various fora offered by it, are the instruments adopted by China to ease apprehensions.

By attempting to mesh China in the ASEAN Regional Forum (ARF) and the 10 + 3 informal meeting between China, Japan and RoK and the 10 + 1, ASEAN-China meeting, the ASEAN engages China collectively to ensure that tensions over territorial claims are contained. Work on a draft 'Code of Conduct' to guide relations between China and ASEAN is proceeding slowly.

So far, there is not much evidence of the proposed joint exploitation of the resources of the South China Seas. China took a major political initiative at the November 2001 ASEAN Summit in Brunei when it proposed the establishment of an ASEAN-China Free Trade Area in a decade. In thus offering to open wide its markets to ASEAN countries, China has taken an imaginative step towards regional economic integration at a time when ASEAN's export-centred economies are facing a global slowdown. In Central and South East Asia, it is evident that Indian and Chinese interests intersect and can be worked to mutual benefit.[1]

When Deng Xiaoping met former Prime Minister Rajiv Gandhi in 1988 in Beijing, he referred to Western comments that the twenty-first century would be an Asian-Pacific century. He went on to add that if India and China did not achieve economic growth and provide for the well-being of their people, there could be no talk of an Asian-Pacific century.

Fourteen years later, when Chinese Premier Zhu Rongji visited India, he declared in the banquet held in honour by Prime Minister Vajpayee on 14 January, 2002: 'As two largest developing countries in the world, China and India have on their shoulders important responsibilities for maintaining peace, stability and prosperity in Asia.' Media commentators in India interpreted this statement as a sign that China had belatedly acknowledged India's importance in Asia, ignoring the deeper significance of the commonalities between the two countries that the Chinese premier had in mind.

11 September marked not just understandable American unilateralism in dealing with the worst manifestations of transnational terrorism but also the linear spread of American military presence in Asia and the Pacific. The Chinese could argue that they fear a greater degree of encirclement from the US and its allies than earlier. For India, the added American presence in regions close to it should work to its advantage, and should not compromise Indian interests. Growing Indo-American military links should not be perceived as being aimed against China. It is in the interests of India and China if the use of the term axis of evil—referring to Iraq, Iran and North Korea—remains just rhetoric.

While both would welcome the de-Talibanisation of Afghanistan and the transition to normalcy there, they need to take special care to see that their 'partnership' in the international coalition against terrorism is not perceived as anti-Islamic. For India, with its large Muslim population and its good relations with Islamic countries, this is vital for domestic harmony. For China, too, this is not an unimportant matter. At the same time, neither India nor China can ignore the fact that their policies in dealing with the areas populated by Muslim majorities (Kashmir and Xinjiang respectively) would be subjected to scrutiny by human rights lobbies at home and abroad. In this respect, as a democracy, India is subjected to sharper watch than China. But the Chinese need to be conscious of the fact that violations of human rights in Xinjiang and elsewhere cannot be condoned under the rubric of the fight against terrorism.

For both countries, the security of supplies of imported energy is important, as both are large importers. Peace in West

Asia and stability of returns on their foreign investments in energy exploration, exploitation and transportation is a must. They must cooperate in the democratisation of international institutions if their moral leadership of the developing world is to be credibly sustained. Finally, it is in their interests that the rights and obligations of membership of the World Trade Organisation (WTO) are equitably exercised.

The common domestic problems which China and India face, are well known—public sector reform, financial institutions' restructuring, development of the non-state sector, encouragement to greater economic competitivity and efficiency to face globalisation, increasing productivity in agriculture, finding employment for growing numbers in rural areas, minimising regional disparities, fighting endemic corruption in both societies and regenerating the degraded environment . . . The list is endless.

For all the systemic differences inherent in the Indian democracy and China's mono-party rule, there are striking parallels, even convergences, as the two countries carve out their future domestic political agendas. India needs to accommodate the political demands generated by social changes and its numerous revolutions. The instruments of a democratic polity have to be used to lessen the ill effects of a hierarchical society and traditional inequalities in India. No one can gainsay that there has been a measure of success.

Social turmoil in China preceded its economic reform. Chinese leaders have focussed on growth, since economic stagnation would have brought fearful consequences for them. In this, they have achieved great success. However, the vast majority of the public in both countries are losing faith in the ability of their governments to provide corruption-free and accountable governance despite economic growth.

The future Chinese leadership from 2002 and 2003 would need to focus on managing gaps between political and economic development and find ways to accommodate power-sharing while maintaining overall social stability. The only measure of acceptance for Indian parties, who wish either to maintain or seize power, is their ability to effectively implement policies that would raise living standards in an atmosphere of political stability. How to build social welfare to facilitate difficult transitions to a more marketised economy is a challenge both sides will face. Enduring reform in both countries will have to be driven from the bottom, from provincial and state governments and the growing non-state sectors.

There will be a shift in China from the current generation of leaders in their seventies to new ones in their fifties, who were raised in the reform era. They will be modernisers in their own rights and well-educated technocrats, exposed to the world. In India, there are examples of central and state-level leaders who have little sympathy for statist pre-reform policies. They may facilitate faster social and economic modernisation. In both countries, governments would continue to play crucial roles in mediating between different vested interests and looking after crucial areas of infrastructure, education and health. The new leaders of India and China could profit much from sharing experiences.

The vast neighbourhood which they share, the domestic and external circumstances which surround them and the fact that India and China are the two fastest growing economies in the world lead to the conclusion that it is in their best interests to make their relationship more substantive and relevant to contemporary times. Political leaders of both countries, their advisers and opinion makers need to bring fresh perspectives on existing problems such as the boundary dispute. Simultaneously, they should boldly fashion a broader agenda for constructive cooperation. On the boundary dispute, both India and China would have to give up the high degree of self-righteousness that has marked the attitudes of both sides when they first confronted their differences in the late 50s of the last century.

Unilateralism, mutual misunderstandings and misperceptions, counterproductive actions and overreactions to these have been the unfortunate legacies of the 50s and 60s. Since the path-breaking visit of Rajiv Gandhi to China in 1988—which was followed by other subsequent high-level exchanges—these features have lessened. In the overwhelmingly vast sections of the public, in both countries the unresolved boundary dispute does not evoke the same degree of strong emotions that it did in the past.

To recall briefly the unhappy past, India's unilateralism consisted of firming up boundary lines with the Xiṇjiang province of China and Kashmir (including POK) inherited from the British with one major difference—the British showed these borders with symbols which indicated that these borders were undefined in the sense that there were no agreements or treaties with successive Imperial or Republican governments of China relating to these borders.

To the east of India, the international boundary adopted between present-day Arunachal Pradesh and Tibet by the government of India was the MacMahon Line, which was negotiated in 1914 by Chinese and Tibetan representatives in Shimla with British-Indian representatives. But the agreement, which incorporated it along with maps on a small scale, was not ratified either by the Tibetan or Central Chinese Governments.

Both India and China had contrasting approaches towards the boundary after Indian Independence in 1947 and China's liberation in 1949. The essence of the Indian stand was that there had always existed a well-defined customary and traditional boundary between India and China. This was marked by the world's most impressive geographical features, delimited in major portion by historical agreements or treaties and controlled on its side by administrative jurisdiction as appropriate to the remote conditions of the peripheries.

The Indian view of historic borders was in contrast to the Chinese strategic view of its borders. While the Chinese were prepared to use diplomatic, and where necessary military, methods in pursuit of their concept, the Indian approach from

1950 was primarily declaratory, unilateral and ineffectively military. In the correspondence initiated between the prime ministers of India and China between 1958 and 1959, the wide gaps in the positions of the two sides were made public. The Chinese categorically rejected India's version of the depiction of the boundary by affirming what was shown on their maps. The claims were to 50,000 square miles (128,000 square kilometres) in Ladakh and Arunachal Pradesh.

The claims, however, did not imply that the Chinese were not prepared to negotiate the boundary with India. By the mid-'50s, their negotiating stance was prepared not just vis-à-vis India but with reference to the borders of all countries neighbouring China.

This consisted of the following—public affirmation by the two parties across the borders that there was indeed a dispute for which the newly independent countries were not responsible, as boundary lines were drawn in colonial or feudal times where China was concerned. Old maps would be revised only in accordance with the sovereign decisions of the newly liberated governments. Once this was acknowledged, the basis suggested was mutual understanding, mutual accommodation and mutual adjustments. 'Understanding' meant that China would not accept the legality of territorial settlements imposed on a 'weak' China by the British, French or the Tsars. However, China would respect the administrative jurisdiction created by such settlements. Examples of these are the MacMahon Line and the 'unequal' treaties between the former Soviet Union and China.

Mutual accommodation referred to actual territorial exchanges where each side could be compensated through negotiations for agreeing to permanent alienation of territory. Specific border conditions such as strategic and other considerations would apply. Following the acceptance of these principles, officials would meet, discuss, conduct surveys and facilitate decisions to be taken at the political levels.

Variants or combinations of the approach have led to

boundary agreements between China and Myanmar, Nepal, Afghanistan, Mongolia, Laos, Pakistan (with respect to POK) in the 60s, with Russia and Central Asian States in the '90s and with Vietnam in 2000. In the course of meetings between Indian and Chinese leaders, and in the voluminous correspondence available in the public domain, the same positions were adopted.

In the Arunachal Pradesh sector, although no previous Chinese government had accepted the legality of the MacMahon Line and claims were made to most areas to its south, the Chinese were willing to accept the line as marking India's administrative control. In the Ladakh sector, the Chinese claimed a boundary approximately along the Karakoram Ranges far to the west of the Kuen Lun Ranges that India claimed. The Indian treaty basis to this claim was disputed by the Chinese as indeed by Western and reputed Indian scholars. India's administrative jurisdiction did not extend in the 50s to the remote areas of Ladakh as was shown when the Chinese cleared a road through the Aksai Chin area to connect Xinjiang and Western Tibet in 1957. Until September 1959, even Nehru made public his uncertainty over India's claims to Aksai Chin.

Premier Chou Enlai's visit to India in April 1960 was an opportunity lost for the settlement of the boundary. He hinted at a boundary alignment along the lines of China recognising the MacMahon Line in the east with adjustments in return for India's acceptance of the Chinese claims in Ladakh. Nehru turned this down on the grounds that there could be no barter of Indian territory. One suspects that in coming to this categoric position, he was egged on by some hard-line cabinet colleagues and some vocal right wing political parties.

Some unilateral actions taken by the Chinese in the period when the border dispute was germinating need to be noted. The completion of the road through Aksai Chin came after India's affirmation of its territorial extent in that area became known to the Chinese. One could speculate that had the Chinese brought the requirement to link their remote regions to India's notice before the friendship soured, India may have been more accommodating. Opportunities were provided for this in 1956 and 1957 when Premier Chou Enlai met Nehru in India. The other unilateral action was Chinese advances in Ladakh in areas far to the west of the road. These actions were weakly resisted by badly manned and poorly equipped Indian posts. This was followed by Indian troops advancing to the limits of a unilateral interpretation of the MacMahon Line in its northwest corner.

The chain of these actions and reactions inevitably led to the 1962 armed conflict. Exhaustive post mortems exist on the Indian military, its conduct and administrative failures in the days leading up to the conflict. Suffice it to say that India was left with deep feelings of humiliation, betrayal and enhanced wariness of China. The complete withdrawal of Chinese troops from Arunachal Pradesh in 1963 and the return of captured Indian soldiers and military equipment did not fully assuage these feelings for several decades after the war.

Mutual misunderstandings and misperceptions over a much wider spectrum than the territorial dispute became a feature of Sino-Indian relations from 1959 onwards. This lasted till 1976. The Dalai Lama's escape to India in 1959 revived strong criticism of Nehru who was accused of appeasing China ever since Chinese troops entered Tibet in 1950. He was also under pressure for not taking a stronger stand on the boundary dispute, brought out in the open through the White Papers released in Parliament in 1959.

Nehru tried to moderate public opinion in his own observations about Tibet and the boundary dispute. He expressed strong sympathy for the people of Tibet but refused to allow the tragic events there to dim his faith in the essential rationale of recognising it as an autonomous region of China and did not disrupt India-China relations on account of it. The year was also marked by a bloody incident in Kongka Pass in Ladakh with loss of life. Events in Tibet, the public acknowledgement of the boundary dispute and bloodshed in disputed areas cumulatively inflamed Indian public opinion against China. The Jan Sangh party and those allied to it in Parliament and outside were particularly vocal critical of Nehru.

From the Chinese side, there was stereotypical Marxist-Leninist-Maoist vitriol poured against Nehru, the Congress party and the critics of China. The Indian political elite as a group was caricatured as pro-West bourgeoisie, who did not represent the masses of the Indian people. Articles in the Chinese press following the Dalai Lama's asylum in India, at least one of which was said to have been vetted by Mao Zedong, showed no understanding of the Indian parliamentary system or its free press, and no sensitivity to the fact that Nehru's was the most moderate voice in a plural society.

Domestic politics in China and the onset of a bitter feud with the former Soviet Union from the late 50s also affected Chinese perception of India when India-China relations started deteriorating. In a 1959 Krushchev-Mao meeting at Beijing, the former made it clear that for the former Soviet Union, better relations with the US had become a priority in the nuclear age. And, that peaceful coexistence with it was in the best interests of the Socialist Camp led by Soviet Union. Thereafter, there were deep manifestations of ideological and state-level disputes between China and the Soviet Union.

For Khrushchev and the Soviet leaders, Nehru was a progressive leader and India's non-alignment was an asset to the socialist camp in the Cold War. Improving relations between the Soviet Union and India, however, symbolised for Mao Zedong all that was wrong with it. Specifically on the boundary dispute with India, Mao could not forgive Krushchev for adopting a neutral posture, without blaming India and calling for peaceful negotiations between India and China to resolve it. Some Western scholars came to the conclusion that the brief punitive mission in 1962 was as much aimed at the Soviet Union as it was directed against India. Thus, the prevalence of two Cold Wars, the one between China and the US, and the one between former Soviet Union and China had a baneful effect on Sino-Indian relations between 1959-62.

Thereafter, particularly after 1966—when the Great Proletarian Cultural Revolution was unleashed by Mao Zedong to rid the Communist Party of China of 'capitalist roaders' and 'revisionists' (those who advocated lessening of hostility vis-à-vis Soviet Union and were seen to oppose the domestic policies of Mao)—relations with India got worse. It was not till 1976, when former Prime Minister Mrs. Indira Gandhi took the decision to reassign an Indian ambassador to China, (K.R. Narayanan), that normalcy was restored to relations with China.

A *status quo* by which India is in complete control of areas south of the MacMahon line in Arunachal Pradesh and the Chinese are in control of all the areas claimed by it in Ladakh, marked by a notional Line of Actual Control all along the boundary, prevails to this day. In 1979, when A.B. Vajpayee visited China as External Affairs minister, India gave up the unviable stand that there could be no negotiations with China on the substance of the boundary dispute, and that there were only minor differences to be negotiated. During that visit when he met Deng Xiaoping, the latter repeated in broad terms what Chou Enlai offered in 1960, calling it a package solution to the boundary dispute. This remains the broad Chinese approach, though neither side has moved to negotiating details.

After 1981, officials of the two sides met annually to discuss the boundary and to take concrete steps to improve all round relations. From 1989, following the agreements reached when Rajiv Gandhi visited China in 1988, a joint working group assisted by a sub-group of border, military and diplomatic experts have been working on practical steps to maintain peace and tranquillity on the border, conduct reviews of the international and regional situations, raise matters of concern to each side and suggest practical exchanges to improve relations. In 1993 and 1996, two major agreements of political and military significance were signed when former Prime

Minister Rao visited China and when President Jiang Zemin visited India.

These two agreements have far reaching implications for restoring confidence and trust to the relationship, particularly in those sections of the military leadership in both countries where it is most needed. When implemented, they would have a beneficial fallout on political and public opinion.

Centred around mutual agreement on the delineation of the Line of Actual Control, which separates the armed forces of both countries, there is a wide array of articles dealing with mutual withdrawals of troops and equipment, disengagement in agreed geographical zones, conduct of ground and aerial exercises, and a series of confidence-building measures. Exchanges of official maps on large scales, an exercise which has already commenced, would help each side understand better the perceptions of the other side, of the alignment of the Line of Actual Control.

De facto peace and tranquillity has prevailed along the India-China boundary over more than two decades where not a shot has been fired in anger. When Indian troops were engaged in Kargil in 1999 or mobilised in 2001 across the Pakistan borders, no diversionary Chinese troop movements across Arunachal Pradesh or Ladakh, which would cause concern, were reported. An imaginative use of the provisions of the two agreements of 1993 and 1996 would ensure that Indian and Chinese forces guard the borders in a non-violent and non-provocative manner. The exercise of implementing the two agreements on the ground is without prejudice to the position of both countries on the substance of the boundary dispute. This should remove suspicions that the Line of Actual Control would eventually congeal into a permanent boundary agreement to the disadvantage of either side.

Given the fact that neither side has undertaken the important task of preparing public opinion for alienation of territory, a permanent boundary agreement between India and China is still a distant prospect. Exaggerated worries about the electoral prospect of political parties in India seem to be inhibiting factors for both ruling parties or coalitions to squarely face the issue. On the Chinese side, there seems to be a preoccupation with domestic matters and concerns about Tibetan reactions over deals involving original Tibetan claims to places in Arunachal Pradesh.

Without the exercise of the necessary political will in both countries and the build-up of a perception of mutual gains from a more vibrant overall relationship between India and China, the resolution of the boundary dispute would not be possible. But the maintenance of a tension-free environment surrounding the boundary is a welcome sign that the relationship has acquired more maturity.[2]

On the basis that the government of India recognises Tibet to be an autonomous region of China, and that anti-China political activities by Tibetans in India are not permitted in Indian soil, there has been a *modus vivendi* between the two countries which has endured. That the Dalai Lama has become an international icon is a post Cold War phenomenon. Western countries brought along their external agendas, promotion of democracy and respect for human rights with special focus on mono-party states. Humanitarian instincts, backed by the people, as well as realpolitik approaches determine Western approaches to the Chinese-Tibetan problem. India is not responsible for the fact that the Dalai Lama, and Lamaism as a spiritual practice have been widely accepted globally. Tibetan institutions are well funded, they operate internationally, and these are factors to be reckoned with.

Growing prosperity for sections of the native population in Tibet, the spread of education there and the eradication of the worst features of pre-Communist Tibet have not diminished the deep attachment to the Dalai Lama. He symbolises Tibetan identity, culture, faith and reverence for a way of life that economic and social development alone have not fully displaced. In this respect, Tibetans are not very different from ethnic minorities elsewhere.

Over recent years, the acceptance by the Chinese that New Delhi does not seek to play a Tibetan card from India to destabilise Tibet has contributed to a lessening of the Tibetan factor in India-China relations. From India's point of view, the ideal solution to the Sino-Tibetan issue would be if constructive dialogue takes place between the representatives of the Dalai Lama and the Chinese, leading eventually to his return to Tibet along with his followers to a life of dignity, safety, religious and cultural freedom. And, with the Dalai Lama enjoying the status and respect that are his due. A cynical approach such as waiting-out his lifetime may be counter-productive.

There have been intermittent talks between the representatives of the Dalai Lama and the Chinese over the years. According to what is available in the public domain, the Chinese conditions for reconciliation are that the Dalai Lama should accept the concept of the great unity of China, meaning no independence for Tibet. Secondly, and after the Dalai Lama established contacts with Taiwan and paid a visit there, that he should accept that there is only one China, that Taiwan is part of it and that the PRC government is the only legitimate government for the whole of China. These are conditions from which the Chinese can never be expected to resile. Everything else they say is negotiable.

Some conditions put forward by Tibetan representatives are that the 'one country, two systems' principle be applied to Tibet. This was the principle applied to the reintegration of Hong Kong and Macao and is still open for Taiwan to accept. The Chinese have turned this down because of the separate histories of these places. The other is that an enlarged Tibetan entity should include areas adjoining Tibet in Sichuan, Quinghai, Gansu and Yunnan provinces of west China where Tibetans reside. The Chinese argue that these areas have never come under the administrative jurisdiction of Tibet.

Thus, both sides are backward rather than forward looking in their present approaches to the dialogue. It is for the Chinese to create the environment for constructive dialogue with the

Tibetans. And, it is for the Tibetans to be moderate in stipulating conditions for their return. In the overall context of an improved India-China relationship, India can, at best, encourage a direct Sino-Tibetan dialogue.

11 September has provided a sobering opportunity for India and China to carefully examine how the Pakistan factor in the India-China-Pakistan triangle can be dealt with. This may seem difficult to envisage in a situation where relations between India and Pakistan reached a nadir by early 2002. However, with some exceptions, contemporary Chinese behaviour on some issues that bedevil Indo-Pakistan relations, provides room for optimism that the future evolution of the triangle could be beneficial to the region. From the '80s, when prospects of Sino-Indian relations improved, China's position on Kashmir, which is seen as one of the litmus tests by both India and Pakistan of their relations with China, has become very nuanced. This must belie unreal Pakistani expectations that do not take into account the realpolitik behind China's readjustments of policies towards the sub-continent.

A summary of the present Chinese position on Kashmir from the spate of pronouncements made on occasions of high-level exchanges of visits between Islamabad and Beijing would consist of four propositions: one, that the Kashmir problem is a leftover from history for which the present governments are not responsible; two, that it is a sensitive issue concerning territory, ethnic compositions of peoples and religions and as such not amenable to early resolutions; three, that it should be settled by peaceful negotiations by India and Pakistan, that is bilaterally, and not through international intervention including Chinese; four, that if the problem cannot be solved for the time being, it should be shelved in favour of the development of all round relations between India and Pakistan with emphasis on economic aspects such as would benefit their peoples and the region as a whole.

During the Kargil conflict in 1999, the spokesman of the Chinese foreign office expressed the hope that 'both India and

Pakistan can earnestly respect the Line of Actual Control in Kashmir'. Other Chinese formulations on Kashmir make references to a settlement being in accordance with the wishes of the people of Kashmir and, on occasions, exhorting India and Pakistan to resume dialogues. This is how most Western and other countries view things.

The readjustment of China's relations in the India-Pakistan context and towards other countries in the South Asian neighbourhood is not based merely on the shifting contours of post Cold War geopolitics. The acknowledgement that India is the predominant power in the region is recognition of a reality that has existed for long. No outside power can displace India for its obvious impact on its neighbourhood nor displace the interdependence within the region that geography compels.

China's support to the consolidation of the development of regional cooperation through the South Asian Association for Regional Cooperation (SAARC) is in keeping with its policies in South East Asia and elsewhere. Multipolarity in the international order, which China desires as an alternative to the dominance of single powers could be achieved, through the emergence of autonomous regional groupings working together to realise common developmental objectives and through multilateralism.

An important statement made in the Pakistan Senate by President Jiang Zemin in 1996 emphasised the importance attached by China to the success of SAARC for peace and development in the region. Then, he went on to add: 'If certain issues cannot be resolved for the time being, they may be shelved temporarily so that they will not affect the normal state-to-state relations.' His audience in Pakistan may not have relished the statement.

11 September gave the Chinese an opportunity to provide a detailed official statement about the various pan-Turkic organisations which were indulging in terrorism, subversion, sabotage and fomenting internal dissensions within Xinjiang in recent times. In a lengthy article prepared by the information

office of the State Council in January 2002, the ultimate aim of these organisations was seen as the formation of a state of 'East Turkistan' composed by those Muslim minorities who speak the Turkic language and are spread across borders shared by Xinjiang and some Central Asian states. The historical precedent of a short-lived East Turkistan Islamic state, set up in November 1933 in Kashgar in Xinjiang, was recalled as an example of local extremists colluding with foreign forces to split Xinjiang from China in the colonial era.

Detailing the names of the various organisations and their anti-China activities, the article seeks to prove that China is also a victim of international terrorism. One organisation in particular, the East Turkistan Islamic Movement, whose aim is the setting up of a theocratic Islamic state in Xinjiang, has been seen as directly supported by Osama Bin Laden. He is reported as having advised the movement to link up with the Uzbekistan Islamic Liberation Movement and the Taliban in Afghanistan and as having provided financial and arms assistance to it. All this provides the rationale for supporting the international coalition against terrorism and the intelligence assistance provided by China to the US.

What should be of interest to India is that the article clearly acknowledges that the anti-Xinjiang terrorists based in Afghanistan and other areas on China's periphery have made a 'strategic shift' by evacuating its members from these places to South Asia (Pakistan is not named) and other Central and West Asian regions after the military interventions in Afghanistan. The threat of their regrouping and continuing activities aimed at China is acknowledged. The more open, albeit indirect, admission that the Taliban in Afghanistan and its southern base could continue to pose threats, is a common concern which India and China share.

If China is to be a constructive partner in the loose international coalition against terrorism, then the coyness with which it dealt with officially supported terrorism of the Taliban-type by Pakistan and other Gulf states needs to be given up vis-à-vis India. For some years before 11 September, China was a victim of externally sponsored terrorist activities but its attempts at curbing such activities, through quiet diplomacy with Pakistan and direct engagement of the Taliban regime, did not produce satisfactory results for China.

The agreement during Premier Zhu Rongji's visit to India in January 2002 to set up a mechanism to exchange views on terrorism is therefore a welcome development. Sino-Indian cooperation in this field has a much wider spatial significance for Asia than the subcontinent. With their growing economies, incomplete control over their peripheries, not fully developed financial and legal systems, both India and China must frankly deal with various complexities.

Effective cooperation to diminish, if not eliminate, the opaque nexus of international finance with trans-border crimes, the spread of drugs, terrorism and other ills, requires better domestic systems of governance than they presently have. Frank recognition of these aspects should inform their separate and combined actions in combating international terrorism even as they build up the confidence to cooperate with each other.

The emergence of a stable, modernising, self-assured and moderate Pakistan is clearly in the interest of both India and China. Both have welcomed President Musharraf's address to the nation on 12 January 2002 in this context. It would be churlish for Indians to be dismissive about Chinese claims that policies towards Pakistan have been readjusted. The Chinese posture that yet they seek to establish good relations with India without jeopardising their long established friendly relations with Pakistan, is not mere semantics. For a variety of reasons, including the fear that American and Western influence would become entrenched in Pakistan to China's detriment, Chinese policies would continue to be oriented towards the maintenance of friendship with Pakistan.

How China squares the circle of seeking an improved relationship with India while assisting Pakistan strengthen itself in the conventional and non-conventional military fields, remains a conundrum. Such assistance, it may be argued, minimised the strategic superiority of India vis-à-vis Pakistan. The contradictory strands of the Chinese approach have perhaps drawn more emotive reactions in India than the unresolved boundary dispute. The Pakistan card in Chinese hands is seen by some in India as a deliberate attempt to restrict Indian energies to the subcontinent. Such thinking may overstate the realities. But they do draw attention to the need to find a proper equilibrium in the India-China-Pakistan triangular relationship with which all three can be comfortable.

On China's assistance to Pakistan in the nuclear and missile fields, India has no direct leverages to exert vis-à-vis China. India cannot accept at face value the bland assertions by China that it abides by international norms and non-proliferation rules after her accession to the Non-Proliferation Treaty. However, after 11 September, the situation has changed dramatically within Pakistan, which could work to India's advantage.

China's own fears about weapons of mass destruction falling into irresponsible and wrong hands create some convergences with American positions on the subject. While the US-Chinese dialogue on the subject of China's proliferation has not satisfied the Americans that the Chinese are prepared to make firm commitments, there could be limited region-specific agreements, with respect to those regions which are proven terrorist havens. Further American ground presence in Pakistan enhances surveillance over clandestine or official transfers of material and technologies, which go towards development of non-conventional weapons of mass destruction. The confidence and trust in China's intentions for the further improvement of Sino-Indian relations, to which leaders of the two countries have committed themselves, would be severely affected if continuing evidence of Chinese assistance to Pakistan in the non-conventional fields surfaces as often as it does.

Over several decades, diverse pro-Pakistan lobbies have been built up in decision-making circles within the armed forces and other establishments in China. In its academic and public opinion making circles, there exists a lack of candour in dealing openly with the several fault lines in the governance of Pakistan. The quality of loyalty to friends who have helped China in its bad times, ensures that they will not be forgotten in better times.

In seeking improved ties with China, which is in India's self-interest, there should be clarity that China will never abandon Pakistan for the sake of good relations with India. Neither will it serve the pursuit of Indian interests if all Chinese actions vis-à-vis Pakistan are seen as inevitably causing damage to Indian interests. The development of Sino-Pakistan ties over the years shows the great determination with which China pursues its interests. Their closeness, for which hostile relations with India through the 60s provided the main rationale, is giving way in a different era, to a greater degree of realism in China's policies in a dramatically altered international environment.

Myanmar's admission into ASEAN some years back, has made the ASEAN an immediate neighbour of India. Realising that complementarities between Myanmar have to be exploited to the benefit of populations in the northeast, India has made modest investments in building road links to connect Indian states to western parts of Myanmar. Cooperation with Myanmar in coping with insurgency and drug smuggling is of vital importance to India. Promotion of Indian investments in infrastructure and industrial projects there, needs to be enhanced. The Hanoi Declaration of ASEAN in July 2001 adopted the Initiative for ASEAN Integration (IAI), a bold plan for the integration of the markets of Cambodia, Laos, Myanmar, and Vietnam. India would do well to participate actively in this initiative.

Three rounds of academic level discussions have focussed on possible multimodal land connectivities, cross-border trade and investments and cultural exchanges involving Bangladesh, India, Myanmar and Yunnan province in China. These discussions were initiated in Kuming, capital of Yunnan, in 1999.

The diverse ethnic populations of northeast India and Bangladesh have been cut off from mainstream developments on account of their geographical isolation and remoteness. Cross-border exchanges can go a long way in supplementing developmental plans to improve the economic well-being of populations in the peripheries. China's future plans involve massive infrastructural investments in Tibet, Yunnan, Sichuan, Xinjiang and other south western provinces to redress the serious regional imbalances which have cropped up after economic reforms. These areas are not distant neighbours of India. And, Chinese investments to develop its neglected western region would have an impact on India in this ever-shrinking world.

For the academic initiatives mentioned above to bear fruit, governments have to either support or involve themselves in the exercise. Numerous areas such as effective border and security management, provision of infrastructure in roads and navigation links, facilities for cross-border trade, banking and other amenities need to be attended to. In this, as in other areas, the required political will for sub-regional cooperation and imaginative approaches are required. If substance is to be added to the frequent-announced intention of 'looking east' in India's foreign policy, a beginning needs to be made with our immediate eastern neighbourhood before we look further afield. The active participation of Chinese and Myanmarese delegations in these initiatives would show that neither does Myanmar see itself as an exclusive area of Chinese involvement, nor does China exclude India and Bangladesh from expanding Myanmar's western links.

A complimentary vision needs to inform India's approach to its northern neighbours, commencing with Afghanistan. Fortuitous circumstances post 11 September, have led to the emergence of a commonality of interests between Russia, China and India in the vast Central Asian Region, which is resource-rich on the one hand but instability-prone on the other. We have seen how the Chinese and the Russians are seeking to promote stability through a new regional grouping with six member states under the aegis of the Shanghai Cooperative Organisation (SCO). It would serve Indian interests best if India became formally associated with the SCO in the capacity that its member states decide upon, when they finalise criteria for the participation of non-regional member states.

There is also a need to encourage a trilateral dialogue between the large continental-sized, civilisational states, Russia, China and India. This is a subject to which the Chinese and Russian foreign offices attach importance as do academic circles in India. In the first round of the dialogue held in September 2001, it became clear that none of the three parties would wish to confront the US and Western countries as each of the partners enjoys relations with the US which none would wish to compromise. But each has an interest in the stable development of the vast Eurasian Region. September 11 has shown that international terrorism and trans-border criminality are not confined to territorial limits. The three would benefit from exchanging experience in coping with problems of transitional economies and enhancing cooperation in various fields. Mutual sets of bilateral relations involving the three countries provide the basis for discussions on a more ambitious scale to optimise possible areas of cooperation where all three can contribute their human and material resources.

The entry of China into the World Trade Organisation (WTO) in November 1999 had increasingly become a necessity as much for reasons of pushing through a series of reforms in the economic, legal, social and other sectors as for political and psychological reasons of international acceptance of China as a great power.

If implemented fully, entry into the WTO will have a significant impact on China's deeper integration with the world economy. Prohibited sectors for foreign investment and participation such as telecommunications, provision of internet services, trading rights and distribution services for manufactures and agricultural products, banking and insurance have been opened up within differing time frames.

China has to reduce tariffs across the board. As per the Information Technology Agreement, all tariffs on items such as computers, semiconductors would be eliminated. Given the predominant role of State Owned Enterprises (SOE) in China in the overall economy, it has also agreed that such enterprises would make purchases and sales based solely on commercial criteria. Foreign companies would be able to compete in the domestic market on non-discriminatory terms and conditions.

China has agreed to a series of measures to deal with problems of dumping, export surges and subsidies to the SOEs. The range of these concessions—to level the playing field within China and to open up the economy even wider for foreigners so that they can directly play a bigger role in domestic sales and investments partnering private entrepreneurs—were extracted by the US and other advanced countries in long drawn out negotiations. They are of benefit to developing countries as well.

Lastly, given the absence of a legal framework that led to the absence of transparency and safeguards for foreigners, China has embarked on an impressively large agenda of legislation, in an attempt to introduce a rule by law to replace the rule by discretion that prevailed over the decades. Importantly, WTO membership provides the leadership the required external support for its oft-stated desire to move towards a market economy rather than to carry on with a hybrid system that had outlived China's growing needs for a more competitive and efficient one.

Anticipation of specific economic benefits to China from WTO membership is, of course, one of the primary drivers that motivated the concessions to the US and others. A number of Chinese economists have suggested that entry into the WTO could add up to 3 per cent growth, thus providing additional jobs, an important requirement at a time when the restructuring of loss-making SOEs is resulting in unacceptable levels of unemployment.

The entry would improve market access for Chinese goods to major markets in Europe, Japan and the US especially for textiles, fashion apparel and telecommunication equipment. It is also seen as a way to boost foreign direct investments from the US and Europe to supplement the traditional Hong Kong capital. China also wishes to direct investment from abroad in the service sector that needs to significantly expand to absorb surplus urban and rural labour.

China's admission to the WTO would significantly increase the competitive pressures on Indian exporters and manufacturers. However, the various openings consequent to WTO membership, referred to above, provide conditions for a more vigorous participation in China's economy for Indian businessmen. In a bilateral agreement with India prior to its WTO entry, adequate safeguards for various commodities in the agricultural and industrial fields of consequence to Sino-Indian trade have been given by China. Two-way trade between India and China in 2001 amounted to over US $3 billion. Trade with Hong Kong also stands at over US $3 billion. Together, although small by Chinese standards, this figure is a sizeable chunk of India's external trade. Investment fields of interest to India are pharmaceuticals, software, education, metallurgy, automotive components and refractories. The gradual build up of economic stakes in the relationship could provide an impetus to the overall relationship.

To conclude, over a wide arc from Central to South and South East Asia, Chinese and Indian interests are not conflictual. Rather, cooperation between India and China could contribute to the stability and development of these regions that are close to them. These regions could provide the resources for their growth as they could also be the sources of problems for them.

Nearer home, the emergence of modernising societies that eschew ideological extremes is in their mutual interest. Their geographical neighbourhood needs to be exploited to the north and east of India through envisaging land bridges and connectivities. That these are possible was shown from ancient times through the silk and spice routes. China's support to the processes of regional, sub-regional or multilateral cooperation with all countries in its neighbourhood, has advanced its interests. The example of China in this regard is very relevant to India.

On bilateral matters, both India and China can do no better than follow the advice of a veteran Chinese diplomat with much experience of handling India-China relations. In a recent article, he said: 'In order to reduce the possibility of any setback in the relations, legitimate interests and concerns of either side needs to be kept in mind when the other side takes important steps on sensitive questions.'[3]

---

1. The author wishes to thank Ambassador V.C. Khanna for allowing him to see his unpublished paper on 'China's Strategic Perception' (2002). He also wishes to thank his colleagues in the Institute of Chinese Studies, Delhi for several lively discussions on China and in particular Mrs. Meera Sinha Bhattacharjea for her published works on China's negotiating strategies on boundary questions.
2. For a more detailed study of the India-China boundary dispute and the impact of the Sino-Soviet dispute on India-China relations, see book by Ambassador V.C. Khanna and C.V. Ranganathan entitled *India and China—The Way Ahead* published by Har Anand Publishers, in January 2000.
3. Article by Cheng Ruisheng in *World Affairs*, vol. 5, no. 4, October-December 2001 (p. 26).

Afghanistan

M.H. Ansari

'My friend! The relations of this Government are with the actual Rulers of Afghanistan.'

Viceroy of India to the
Wali of Kabul, 11 July 1866

'As between Afghanistan and India, I cannot remember any point of real difference, and they take each other for granted.'

Jawaharlal Nehru
5 February 1959

The state of Afghanistan came into existence in the middle of the eighteenth century. Its territory included some of the provinces of the Mughal and the Safavi Empires, and the population lacked ethnic, religious and political unity. Before Amir Abdur Rahman Khan established control over the whole country in 1896 and accepted the title *'Siraj-al-Millat Wa-al Din'* (Light of the Nation and Religion),[1] its form of government was 'a military aristocracy'.[2] Its present borders were not settled until the beginning of the twentieth century and were a direct outcome of imperial considerations of two great powers—Great Britain and Czarist Russia.

A circle with Kabul as its centre and a radius of 1000 miles would have within it unparalleled diversity of geographic, linguistic, religious, cultural, political, and economic frontiers. To this day, the people of Afghanistan are paying the price for the birth of their country and for its geo-strategic location.

The Mughal Empire considered the Kabul-Ghazni-Qandahar line the strategic and logical frontier of India. It was for this reason that Qandahar was always the bone of contention between the Mughals and the Safavids.[3]

A somewhat different set of strategic considerations confronted the British after they established their control over the Indian subcontinent. Various foreign policy options were explored: 'The controversy led to the emergence of two distinct schools, commonly called the Forward and Stationary, and thus began the vital conflict over the question of political strategy along the north-west frontier.'[4] In the closing decades of the nineteenth century, however, the general thrust of policy was on the twin need 'to prevent rival encroachments and to establish the predominance of British influence'.[5] This was reflected with particular vehemence in regard to Afghanistan, and was also responsible for some painful setbacks.

In 1880, the British compelled Amir Abdur Rahman Khan to abandon his exile in Central Asia and to assume control of the Afghan state.[6] He had at that point pleaded, unsuccessfully, with the chief political officer of the Indian government to 'define my limit and duties and responsibilities in a treaty'.[7] Subsequently, he became increasingly undependable in the eyes of the British. But wider policy considerations compelled the Indian government to do nothing about his intransigence as long as he was alive. Instead, an attempt was made with his successor to restrict matters and to renegotiate the arrangements.

This did not work either. The new Amir, Habibullah, deferred an invitation to visit India, leaving the British with no choice but to send Foreign Secretary Louis Dane as special envoy to Kabul. The brief given to him spelt out in detail the British interests and concerns relating to Afghanistan and the necessity of having a friendly ruler in Kabul: 'The conversations should therefore be of friends and allies. You should proceed upon the assumption that the objects, interests, and the enemies of the two countries are identical, and their policy therefore should be one of harmonious cooperation.'[8] Furthermore, 'our object throughout is to bind the Amir by the ties of self-interest' and in return for the subsidy and the facility for the import of some arms, obtain a *quid pro quo* in the form of (a) control of his foreign relations (b) abandonment of intrigues with frontier tribes (c) maintenance of a power friendly to Great Britain as a formidable barrier to the defence of India and (d) possible commercial facilities.[9]

In the final analysis, however, Habibullah 'had his way'[10] and his draft treaty—declaring that the old engagements of his father's period would continue—was accepted by the British government in preference to their own, much to the annoyance of Lord Curzon for whom it was seen as a defeat and who described it as 'an abject and humiliating surrender'.[11] The episode highlighted the complexity of dealing with Afghanistan in the context of Central Asian politics. The treaty, noticeably, did not further British India's commercial interests in Afghanistan, and even the suggestion of a telegraph line was found unacceptable, as was the proposed railway line.[12]

The same mix of power play and negotiations went into the making of the Anglo-Russian Convention of 1907, which sought to stabilise the situation in Central Asia.[13] The British affirmed that 'they have no intention of changing the political status of Afghanistan' or 'of interfering in the internal government of Afghan territory' or encouraging Afghanistan to take any measure which might threaten Russia. The latter, on its part, conceded that Afghanistan was outside the Russian sphere of influence and that its political relations with Afghanistan should be conducted through the Britannic Majesty's government. It further engaged not to send any agents to Afghanistan. The convention highlighted the commitment of the two parties 'to the principle of equality of commercial opportunity in Afghanistan and they agreed that any facility which may have been, or shall be hereafter obtained for British and British-Indian trade and traders, shall be equally enjoyed by Russian trade and traders'.[14]

The entire exercise was initiated and concluded without a reference to the Amir of Afghanistan. After the signing of the convention, the British government instructed the Viceroy of India to break the news to the Afghan ruler 'to persuade him to look upon it with a favourable eye' since it secured the integrity of Afghanistan between Russia and India, and to give his concurrence without the least possible delay to Articles III and IV (relating to non-political Afghan-Russian relations of a local nature at frontier posts and to Afghan-Russian trade, respectively). The Amir, clearly annoyed, replied after a year and sought clarifications about the advantages that might accrue to him. In the subsequent years, the Amir's silence continued and 'ultimately the Afghan resentment against the conduct of the Indian government resulted in the Third Afghan War.'[15]

The outbreak of World War I propelled Amir Habibullah to proclaim Afghanistan's neutrality for 'as long as the honour, existence, independence, and freedom of Afghanistan were in no way jeopardized or threatened'.[16] Public opinion, however, reflected pan-Islamist sentiments on account of Ottoman Turkey's involvement on the side of Germany; and was also reflective of strong anti-European sentiments.[17] The arrival of a Turko-German Mission in Kabul signalled an effort on the part of Germany and Turkey to draw Afghanistan into the war and cause a major upheaval in the tribal belt on the Indian frontier. The mission established contact with some Indian revolutionaries (Mahendra Pratap, Obaidullah Sindhi and Barkatullah) who had set up a provisional Indian government in Kabul in 1916. The Turko-German Mission, however, was unsuccessful and the Amir successfully maneuvered to maintain benevolent neutrality towards both the British and the Germans.

The Russian Revolution in 1917, and the disintegration of the Czarist regime, had important implications for the Afghan nationalist forces. The Amir saw in it an opportunity to project Afghan influence in Central Asia. He also wrote to the Viceroy of India in February 1919 seeking British cooperation in obtaining international recognition of the 'absolute liberty, freedom of action, and perpetual independence of Afghanistan' at the Paris Peace Conference. The British, who had suspended in early 1918 the Anglo-Russian Convention of 1907, responded with gratitude to Habibullah's wartime neutrality and declared that Britain 'looked forward to Afghanistan playing a continued positive role in the defence of India, possibly even a role of political leadership in Central Asia'.[18]

Habibullah's policy of gradualism, his insistence on the observance of treaty obligations with the British, and his failure to assuage Islamist feelings, aroused on account of Turkey's defeat, bred resentment amongst the nationalist sections of the Afghan population whose expectations were heightened during the war years. This, eventually, led to his assassination in February 1919. He was succeeded by his reformist-modernist son Amanullah who, as a first act, informed the Viceroy of his accession and proclaimed full independence for Afghanistan.

The British response was 'evasive and made no direct reference to the proclamation of independence' on the ground that the Dane-Habibullah Treaty being a dynastic agreement, could not be abrogated unilaterally.[19]

The new Soviet government, on its part, immediately recognised the new status of Afghanistan.[20] The disagreement with Britain soon led to an armed conflict, which was of a short duration and was confined to a series of small engagements on the Indo-Afghan border. The matter was finally resolved through the Treaty of Rawalpindi (8 August 1919) which recognised Afghanistan as a fully sovereign state. The Amir, in turn, recognised the Durand Line, and also had to forego the British subsidy.[21]

He crafted the contours of an independent, balanced foreign policy based on the establishment of diplomatic relations with the Soviet Union, the gradual normalisation of relations with Britain and the development of solidarity with the Muslim world. This latter dimension was personally encouraged by Lenin![22]

The Soviets and Indian revolutionaries like M.N. Roy also explored the possibility 'of using Afghanistan as a base of operations to promote revolutionary activities in India'.[23] The Amir, however, would have none of this and ordered the Indian revolutionaries who had set up a provisional government in 1916 to leave Kabul. Lenin, on his part, had no illusions about the British capacity to influence the Amir. They would, he told Roy, 'bombard Amanullah's citadel with silver and gold bullets'.[24] Despite this, the Soviet-Afghan Treaty of September 1920 placed Afghanistan in a considerably stronger bargaining position with Britain. Similarly, the treaties with Turkey and Persia (both in 1921) strengthened the Amir's hands in his endeavour to usher in modernity in Afghanistan through Islamic solidarity abroad.

This quest for modernity, and the administrative and social reforms which came in its wake, produced complex results. It diluted the 'Islamic legitimacy' and the tribal support base of the Amir,[25] and led to his ouster by the Tajik Bacha-i-Saqao who reversed Amanullah's social and administrative reforms and took steps to re-establish the rule of Islamic law 'in all its purity'. The Soviet Union denounced this seizure of power but the British extended *de facto* recognition even though the British diplomatic mission was withdrawn from Kabul. Bacha's support base however was limited. The Muhasiban branch of the

Durranis was therefore able to rally Pushtun support against him, leading to his ouster in October 1929. 'I underestimated the power of greed,' he said after his capture. 'Large rewards were offered for my capture, and it was unarmed hill-men who eventually took me, and not sabre thrusters from Kabul.'[26]

The new king, Nadir Shah, enunciated his foreign policy carefully in the Afghan National Consultative Assembly in July 1931:

In my opinion the best and most useful policy that one can imagine for Afghanistan is a policy of neutrality. Afghanistan must always entertain good relations with its neighbours as well as all the friendly powers that are not opposed to the national interest of the country. Afghanistan must give its neighbours assurances of its friendly attitudes while safeguarding the right of reciprocity. Such a line of conduct is the best one for the interests of Afghanistan.[27]

There is enough evidence to suggest that Nadir Shah's accession was fully endorsed by the British who also gave him financial assistance. He was soon to show that his policies 'were highly compatible with British interests and plans in India'. More specifically, the British were interested in knowing if Afghanistan proposed to champion the Khudai Khidmatgaran (Red Shirt) movement of Khan Abdul Ghaffar Khan as well as the Afridi and Mohmand tribal struggles. The Afghan response, on both counts, was very satisfying: 'The whole frontier policy of the Afghan Government would be actuated by a desire of peace on both sides of the frontier and a spirit of true friendship towards His Majesty's Government.'[28]

British Indian officials were candid in their acknowledgement of this approach: 'The present ruler, King Nadir Shah, has honourably lived up to his engagements and shown himself most fair and loyal. Indeed he has kept his firebrands on his side of the border much better than we have on ours. It is greatly due to his influence that the Red Shirt movement has not spread into independent territory to a greater extent than it has.'[29]

A similar policy, of non-intervention in Soviet Central Asia, was adopted towards the Soviet Union and was formalised through the non-aggression pact of 1931 as well as through a 1933 agreement on the definition of aggression. Efforts were made to further cultivate existing relations with Turkey and Iran—and to seek openings for developing relations with Germany, France and Italy on the one hand, and with the United States and Japan on the other. The objective in each case was to explore opportunities of assistance in Afghanistan's modernisation within the straitjacket of the requirements of the tribal interests and of the religious establishment.

The pressures generated in the process eventually led to King Nadir Shah's assassination in 1933. He was succeeded by his 19-year-old son Zahir Shah who ruled with the help of two effective prime ministers—his uncle Hashim Khan and his cousin Sardar Mohammad Daud. The policies of King Nadir Shah were continued. A new dimension, however, was added by Afghanistan's membership of the Saadabad Pact (1937) and by the intensification of the economic relationship with Germany.

The outbreak of World War II put various pressures on Afghanistan's desire for neutrality. These pressures emanated principally from the Axis Powers. The Afghan government was anxious to complete the economic assistance projects initiated by the Germans. And, the Germans (along with Italy) sought to enhance their anti-British activities in Afghanistan and in the tribal belt on the borders of British India. The gullibility of the Afghan public in the tribal areas and its propensity to succumb to the influence of the mullahs and pirs was fully exploited.

Saeed al-Gailani from Syria presented himself as a descendent of Sheikh Abdul Qadir al-Gailani of Baghdad and was promptly hailed as the Shami Pir. He incited the tribes against the Kabul government and the Indian government eventually had to pay him 20,000 pound sterling to leave the area and go back to Syria. The Italians tried a similar game with the Fakir of Ipi.[30] Some senior officials of the Afghan government were also not averse to anti-British intrigues. Nazi documents now available reveal that the Minister of Economy and President of the Afghan National Bank, Abdul Majid Zabuli, negotiated with the Germans about 'the possible territorial changes resulting for Afghanistan from the war' to include the Indus as the new Afghan border with the port of Karachi incorporated in the Afghan territory.[31]

The War disrupted Afghanistan's modernisation programmes and caused serious economic dislocation. The end of the War and the impending British withdrawal from India propelled the Afghan government to review its security environment. In a representation made to the British government in November 1944, it argued that the Pushtuns in the tribal areas should be given the choice of becoming independent or reuniting with their 'motherland'. It also suggested that Afghanistan should be given a corridor to the sea through Baluchistan. When Pakistan sought the membership of United Nations in September 1947, Afghanistan initially cast a negative vote. It also demanded that the Pushtun-inhabited frontier areas be constituted into 'a free, sovereign province'; that Afghanistan be given a corridor to the sea through West Baluchistan or be allotted a free zone in Karachi; and that the two countries enter into a treaty which would permit one party to remain neutral if the other was attacked.

In July 1949, the Afghan National Assembly passed a resolution repudiating all treaties, conventions and agreements signed between the Afghan and the British governments before the birth of Pakistan and rejected the Durand Line as the international frontier.[32] The resulting tensions prompted Afghanistan to reduce its economic dependence on Pakistan. And, with this objective in view, to sign a trade agreement with the Soviet Union in July 1950. This gave considerable impetus to Afghan-Soviet trade and economic cooperation. (As a result, by 1978 the USSR accounted for 64 per cent of Afghanistan's total imports and 34 per cent of total exports. By that year, the total Soviet credits to Afghanistan had reached a figure of US

$1.26 billion; the comparative figure for US credits and grants was $470 million).

Notwithstanding these economic linkages, and despite sharing a long border with the USSR, Afghanistan managed to maintain its distance from the Soviet Union in its foreign policy pronouncements in the peak years of the Cold War up to 1978. It was thus easy for Afghanistan to convert its traditional policy of positive neutrality into a non-aligned position when the Non-Aligned Movement took shape in 1961. Afghanistan played a constructive role in the NAM summits from Belgrade (1961) to Colombo (1976). Kabul's position, however, was generally dented after the revolution of 1978 and particularly in the aftermath of the Soviet-Afghan Treaty of Friendship, Good Neighbourliness and Cooperation of 5 December 1978. This became evident when, after the Soviet intervention, an effort to raise the matter in the NAM Coordinating Bureau resulted in a deadlock and led to a decision that the issue would only be discussed in the meeting of NAM Foreign Ministers in New Delhi (February 1981).

Afghanistan's relations with the United States were slow to take off. The US withheld recognition till 1934 and did not open a mission in Kabul on the ground that Afghanistan 'is doubtless the most fanatic hostile country in the world today'.[33] Wartime requirements eventually led to the opening of an embassy in Kabul in 1942. After the War, Afghanistan sought a US loan for its economic development plan as a way of balancing Soviet offers of assistance. This did not make much headway in Washington. A similar fate awaited an Afghan offer to buy surplus American military equipment left over in India after the War. In November 1950, the US offered to assist Kabul and Karachi as an 'informal go-between' in resolving their problems.[34] In 1954, an appeal for military aid elicited the response that such aid 'would create problems not offset by the strength it would generate. Instead of asking for arms, Afghanistan should settle the Pushtunistan dispute with Pakistan.' To add insult to injury, a copy of this communication was given to the government of Pakistan. A month later, in January 1955, Afghanistan accepted a long-standing Soviet offer of military aid.[35] Notwithstanding this, the US perception of strategic disinterest in Afghanistan continued through the sixties.

Pakistan's Afghan policy, since the inception of the state in 1947, has to be seen in the context of this backdrop of recent history. Pakistan viewed itself as the inheritor of the British rights and duties in the north-western frontier areas of the former British India. More important, it tended to subscribe to some of the British Indian Forward Policy perceptions that were so eloquently criticised by Lord Elgin as early as 1862:

I am wholly opposed to that prurient intermeddling policy which finds so much favour with certain classes of Indian officials. It is constantly thrusting us into equivocal situation in which our acts and our professions of respect for the independence of other nations are in contradiction—and in which our proceedings become tainted with the double reproach of inconsistency and selfishness. Nothing in my opinion can be more fatal to our prestige and legitimate influence. [36]

As a result, from its inception, the relationship was one of 'almost continuous hostility'.[37] In an emergency cabinet meeting as early as September 1947, Jinnah chose to define the border problem in the context of the Cold War and asserted that 'the safety of the North West Frontier (is) of world concern and not merely an internal matter for Pakistan alone.'[38]

Ayub Khan, in his talks with Eisenhower in 1959 and with Kennedy in 1961, urged the United States to adopt a hard line with the Afghans. Kennedy offered good offices and deputed a special envoy in 1961 who found that the problem was 'difficult and complicated' and did not recommend putting 'excessive pressure' on a staunch ally like Pakistan.[39] The Pak-Afghan relationship thus remained tense and difficult throughout the sixties and up to the Indo-Pak War of 1971.

The advent of Zulfiqar Ali Bhutto as prime minister in the post-Bangladesh period also witnessed insurgencies and political problems in Baluchistan and the NWFP. 'These three events—the breakup of Pakistan, the ousting of NAP governments in Baluchistan and NWFP, and Daud's assumption of power (in Kabul)—became the basis of renewed Pakistan-Afghanistan conflict.'

The Pakistan army presented to Bhutto 'an Afghan invasion plan involving a quick occupation of certain Afghan areas including Jalalabad' in order to force Daud 'to accept the Durand Line and withdraw his support for Baluch and Pushtun nationalists'. Bhutto rejected this suggestion and 'decided to tackle Daud politically'.[40] To begin with, he appointed a secret committee of his most trusted advisors 'to find a satisfactory long term solution of Baluchistan – an honourable and lasting solution without being cornered'.[41] He countered the alleged Afghan subversive activities in Pakistan by establishing contacts with extreme left- and right-wing elements in Afghanistan and funded them generously. He also visited Moscow in an effort to persuade the Soviet leadership to use its influence with Daud on the question of Pushtun demands. 'I have cut the string which flew the (Afghan) kite,' he said on his return.[42]

The move appeared to produce results. None of Afghanistan's traditional friends were willing to adopt an activist posture on the Pushtunistan question. Bhutto visited Kabul in June 1976 and Daud reciprocated the gesture two months later. According to one account: 'Daud had abandoned his advocacy of an independent Pusthunistan and Baluchistan and was now content with the release of Pushtun and Baluch leaders in return for his acceptance of the Durand Line as the international border between the two neighbours.' Both leaders, however, were soon out of office and the understanding therefore remained unimplemented.[43]

A similar effort was made by Zia-ul Haq and Hafizullah Amin after the revolution of April 1978 in Afghanistan The Soviet intervention in December 1979, however, definitively put an end to these overtures. Zia decided to oppose the Soviet action publicly and 'provide clandestine military assistance to the insurgents while denying that (Pakistan) was doing so'.[44] For the next 10 years, Pakistan was a frontline state against the Soviet presence in Afghanistan and pursued, with considerable success, 'a dual-faceted Afghan policy'[45] of supporting the Afghan resistance on the one hand, and, of pursuing a negotiated settlement through UN channels for a Soviet withdrawal, on the other.

There can be, as has always been, more than one image of Afghanistan in the minds and hearts of the people of India. Readers of Rabindranath Tagore would forever cherish the loveable Kabuliwala. Another set of Indians would show no empathy for the Afghan moneylender and his usurious ways. Students of history relish the flavour of *Babarnama*'s ecstatic description of the Arghawan blossom and of the peerless beauty of Kabul. The same students would recount with admiration the administrative genius of a Sher Shah Suri and, with horror, the destructive fury of an Ahmad Shah Abdali.

In later times, the refuge given in Kabul to freedom fighters like Raja Mahendra Pratap, Obaidullah Sindhi and Barkatullah touched responsive chords, as did the Frontier Gandhi's participation in the national movement. It should also not be overlooked that right across northern and central India are individuals and communities claiming an Afghan ancestor in the remote or proximate past. The same holds good for people of Indian origin in Afghanistan whom the Indian government officially chooses to refer to as 'Afghan Hindus and Sikhs'.

In such a matrix where political, social and familial relationships constantly overlap and bear the imprints of wide-ranging cultural interaction and unstated Kautiliyan prescriptions, the delineation of foreign policy perceptions would often be in general rather than in specific terms and occasionally may even be taken for granted. This was the case in the early years after the independence of India. The two countries signed a treaty of friendship in 1950. King Zahir Shah visited India in February 1958 and the joint communique stressed that 'no differences disturb these good relations' which they resolved to strengthen.[46] Nehru reiterated this with greater vigour a year later when Prime Minister Sardar Daud came to India:

'Ever since India's independence, we have grown closer to each other, for a variety of reasons. The long memory of our past contacts was there, and the moment it was possible to renew them, we renewed them. And then came mutual interest, which is a powerful factor. There has also been a very great community of interests between our two countries in the many important matters which affect the world. Both our countries decided that we should not become a part of the international conflicts, of what is known as the Cold War, and of military alliances and blocs of the great countries. This basic identity of views between us brought us nearer to each other, and we have followed these policies in spite of difficulties and pressures. Whether in the United Nations or elsewhere, we have often seen eye to eye with each other.'[47]

Despite this, both countries remained cautious and avoided involvement in each other's disputes with other countries. India did not support Afghanistan on the Pushtunistan issue or on the question of the revision of the 1893 Durand Line Agreement. 'During the 1961 Pakistan-Afghan crisis, Nehru refused to comment on the relations between those two states, noting that Pakistan inherited the interest that undivided India had in the Durand Line, a remark interpreted in Karachi as an affirmation of Pakistan's legal position.'[48] Afghanistan adopted a similar approach to Indo-Pak matters. Zahir Shah 'was not supportive of India in its conflicts with Pakistan in 1947-49, 1965 and 1971. He equivocated on the Kashmir issue.'[49] During the negotiations on the 30-mile Sino-Afghan border in the Wakhan area, Afghan negotiators 'refused the Chinese request to designate a point on the boundary as adjacent to territory defended by Pakistan, thus maintaining its perfect neutrality on the Kashmir controversy'.[50]

Despite these unstated reservations, bilateral relations between New Delhi and Kabul remained good and substantive. President Radhakrishnan visited Kabul in May 1963. Prime Minister Indira Gandhi paid an official visit to Afghanistan in June 1969 and readily accepted an Afghan suggestion to set up a joint commission for economic, trade and technical cooperation charged with the responsibility of working out programmes of cooperation in the fields of agriculture, irrigation and power, health, industrial cooperation and training of personnel. India undertook to (1) assist in the setting up of agricultural research stations in Bamiyan, Qandahar and Kabul for rice, wheat and potato (2) execute the Charde Ghorband irrigation cum micro-hydel scheme and some other irrigation projects (3) build an industrial state in Kabul and (4) build and commission a 100-bed children's hospital in the Afghan capital. On political matters, she and Prime Minister Etemadi 'steered clear of controversial issues' like Kashmir and Pushtunistan but reaffirmed their faith in the principles embodied in the Tashkent Declaration for finding solutions to differences between states and expressed the hope that the implementation of that declaration would lead to peace in the region. Indira Gandhi also sidestepped Soviet Premier Kosygin's suggestion for regional cooperation between India, Pakistan and Afghanistan by saying that there should be bilateral cooperation before it could be widened into a regional one.

Bilateral relations were developed vigorously in 1972. A new trade agreement was signed in February in which the two governments agreed, besides measures to strengthen trade, on 'healthy lines' to provide facilities for the setting up of a joint venture for the production of extracts of medicinal herbs and plants grown in Afghanistan which India undertook to use in its pharmaceutical industry.

In April, Foreign Minister Swaran Singh reviewed in Kabul the totality of the relationship with particular emphasis on economic and technical cooperation. New avenues for this were identified. These included the setting up of an isotope-dispensing unit in Kabul, the despatch of 60 additional teachers and technical experts and assistance in the restoration of the Bamiyan monuments.

In July, nine days after the signing of the Simla Agreement, President V.V. Giri was in Kabul saluting Afghanistan 'as the originator in this part of the world of a policy of independent development, free from the overbearing influence or control of any foreign power'.[51] He spoke of the challenges of the future, of the avenues of cooperation between India and Afghanistan and stressed that peace and prosperity were indivisible and that 'the problems of the subcontinent affect also our Afghan brethren'.

Finally, towards the end of the year, the Afghan crown prince visited India and it was noted on that occasion that bilateral trade and economic cooperation was 'growing rapidly'. Five years later, notwithstanding changes of government in Kabul in 1973 and in New Delhi in 1977, the commonality of perception on global and regional issues was reiterated during Foreign Minister Atal Behari Vajpayee's visit to Kabul in September 1977. 'We,' he said, 'understand and have stood by each other in moments of crises.'[52]

The imperatives of a comfortable relationship with the Daud government may have led India to underestimate the developing contradictions within the Afghan political system, which led to his overthrow and assassination in April 1978. The change 'came as a surprise to the Indian government' and India had 'to cope with it as best as it could'.[53] Even more distressing for India was the Soviet intervention on 27 December 1979. Caretaker Prime Minister, Charan Singh, described the act as 'unacceptable' and urged the withdrawal of Soviet troops.[54] A government statement on 28 December attempted a balancing act and stressed that 'India has always opposed any outside interference in the internal affairs of one country by another. It was also the Indian government's earnest hope that no country or external power would take steps which might aggravate the situation.'

On 30 December, the official spokesman said: 'We are not supporting or opposing anyone. We are still assessing whether the Soviet assumption that they extended their help and assistance on the request of the duly constituted authorities in Kabul, is right or wrong.' He added: 'We have, however, taken note of the justification given by the Soviet Union.'[55] On 12 January 1980, the Indian permanent representative told the UN General Assembly that India had no reason to disbelieve the Soviet commitment to withdraw its troops when asked to do so by the government in Kabul; that India hoped that the Soviet Union would respect the independence of Afghanistan by not keeping its troops a day longer than necessary; and that India was gravely concerned over the response of the United States, China, Pakistan and others and over the arming of Afghan rebels and the expansion of naval activities in the Indian Ocean, all of which intensified with the Cold War and posed a threat to India. The Indian speech, and the abstention on the resolution—carried by 104 votes to 18, with 18 abstentions—caused surprise and dismay in non-aligned circles.

Faced with a dilemma of reconciling conflicting policy considerations Prime Minister Indira Gandhi 'temporised'[56] in her public stance. Behind the scenes, however, a more nuanced response to the crisis was soon developed. Foreign Secretary Sathe who was sent to Islamabad on 5 February, to ascertain Pakistani thinking, was told by his counterpart that 'Pakistan and India have different perceptions regarding the situation which had developed.' Soviet Foreign Minister Gromyko, who came to Delhi on 13 February, had difficulty in convincing the Indian leadership about the virtues of Soviet action—so much so that in the joint communique issued after the visit, Afghanistan was only indirectly alluded to. The communique said the two sides 'reviewed international situation including developments in the region and around it'.[57] India is said to have urged the Soviet Union to make a token withdrawal along with a public pledge that the bulk of the troops would be withdrawn within a specified period.[58]

A new and complicating dimension to the problem was added in April with the conclusion of the Soviet-Afghan Treaty formalising the presence of Soviet troops in Afghanistan. On 14 May, an Afghan government statement suggested that the only solution to the problem would lie in direct talks between Afghanistan and Pakistan on one side, and between Afghanistan and Iran on the other. This was rejected out of hand by the governments concerned as well as by the OIC that convened a special meeting to consider the crisis. Faced with this situation, India made another effort in June to persuade the Soviet leadership to see the merit of an immediate troop withdrawal and put some multilateral security arrangement in place to establish a non-aligned government in Kabul.[59] This was done during Foreign Minister Narasimha Rao's visit to Moscow. No progress however was discernible. Instead, 'there was a turgid assertiveness in the Soviet stand.'[60] Once again Afghanistan was not specifically mentioned in the joint communique and the divergence of views was made known when Narasimha Rao reported to the Lok Sabha on his Moscow visit on 17 June. He said the expectation that the presence of Soviet troops in Afghanistan would be 'limited in time' was not coming true and was of concern to India:

It is time for us to ask ourselves the question whether the Soviet troops meant for assistance in Afghanistan have not become, or are not likely to become, pretext for those who wish to create further instability in that country.

He went on to add that the Soviet Union recognised that 'it was natural for a non-aligned country to have a different perspective on some international questions.'[61] When Brezhnev visited New Delhi in December he said in his speech to members of Parliament that Afghanistan's 'southern neighbours' (i.e., Pakistan and its allies) should have 'good neighbourly agreement with the Afghan Government. As a result, prerequisites will emerge for a full normalisation of the situation including withdrawal of Soviet troops.' The joint declaration, however, again avoided a direct reference to

Afghanistan and stressed the opposition of the two countries to 'outside interference in the internal affairs of the countries of the region'. It said a negotiated political settlement alone could guarantee a durable settlement.[62]

Faced with this persistent clash of perceptions, India opted to isolate the Afghan factor from the totality of the Indo-Soviet framework of wide-ranging cooperation, developed a six-point conceptual framework for the conduct of its Afghan policy and conveyed it at the highest level to the government of Afghanistan. This stressed that India:

a) had primary interest in the continuance of people-to-people relations;
b) wished to help the process of the development of Afghanistan to bring about prosperity and stability;
c) had no desire to interfere in the internal affairs and would deal with the *de facto* government in power. While being generally supportive of the objective of the Afghan Revolution, it opposed violence and the Soviet intervention;
d) conveyed its serious reservations about the Soviet action but without saying so in public;
e) was convinced that an Afghanistan dominated by external Islamist forces and the US was not in India's interests; and
f) wished to continue bilateral cooperation particularly in health, hydel power and small scale industrial sectors.[63]

Such an approach was compatible with the perceived imperatives of India's national interest. It did however extract a price. The average Afghan and the non-PDPA elite nursed a sense of betrayal. On the diplomatic front, India 'remained marginalised on the Afghan crisis in terms of international processes dealing with it'.[64] On the bilateral-political front, visits from New Delhi to Kabul were few and invariably below the top level. Afghan visitors, however, were received at all levels and a modicum of non-military cooperation and assistance was sustained during the war years to the extent possible given the ground realities. The Afghan leaders were candid enough to tell

Indian visitors that 'the sustenance of wide-ranging relations with India is perhaps the only means by which Afghanistan can retain some credibility about its non-aligned independence status.' Such a relationship, they felt, was also necessary because of 'common interests, common security perceptions and common political, economic and strategic threats that India and Afghanistan face in the current regional and international situation'.[65]

Although Pakistan had rejected Kabul's 14 May proposals, efforts to initiate a dialogue to resolve the crisis were continued by the parties concerned as well as by the UN. These resulted in a diplomatic process of indirect negotiations between Pakistan and Afghanistan which commenced in June 1982 through the good offices of the UN and which finally led to the Geneva Accords of 14 April, 1988 incorporating:

(1) A bilateral agreement between Afghanistan and Pakistan on the 'Principles of Mutual Relations in Particular on Non-Interference and Non-Intervention';
(2) A Declaration of International Guarantees by the USSR and USA;
(3) A bilateral agreement between Afghanistan and Pakistan on the voluntary return of refugees and;
(4) An agreement on the Inter-relationships for the Settlement of the Situation Relating to Pakistan and Afghanistan and witnessed by the US and USSR. Paragraphs 5 and 6 of the latter laid down the schedule for the start and conclusion of the Soviet troop withdrawal from Afghanistan.

The completion of the Soviet troop withdrawal on 15 February 1989 was followed by a major mujahideen offensive in the Jalalabad sector. It failed and the Najibullah government 'displayed unexpected staying power'.[66] It gained some support for its policy of national reconciliation that was announced in 1987. In the process, it completely abandoned the PDPA's plans for the social transformation of the countryside and the president 'presided over the reversal of virtually every aspect of the revolutionary process'.[67] On the other hand, the seven

Sunni groups of the mujahideen in Pakistan gave the impression of being visited by a death wish.

In the period immediately after the completion of the Soviet withdrawal everything they did went against their own interests. They went to the battlefront contemptuous of, and blissfully unaware of the fighting capability of the government forces. They failed to close their own ranks or develop an integrated command and control structure so essential in a military conflict. Their inability to entice the Tehran-based resistance groups into a working arrangement was matched by their incomprehension of the post-withdrawal scenario and its new imperatives. Above all, their failure to motivate the local commanders to continue the fight against the PDPA government helped the latter not only to concentrate its energies on Jalalabad and Khost but also seemed to convey an impression to the average man that the interests of the local commanders and of the Peshawar leadership did not necessarily coincide.

The Peshawar groups were eventually cajoled into convening a *shura* through which an Interim Islamic Government of Afghanistan (IIGA) was chosen. It reflected 'ISI and Saudi manipulation' and the latter were reported to have spent $ 26 million on the exercise besides paying $1 million per month to it.[68]

Having survived the initial onslaught, the Najibullah government endeavoured to take the initiative and to suggest a dialogue with its opponents on the basis of the new realities. It put forward as many as 30 proposals in the next two years. The common ingredients in all of these was a ceasefire or a cooling down period, negotiations between the government and the opposition groups, the setting up of a joint supervisory body charged with the responsibility of drafting a new constitution and an electoral law, and the holding of elections under UN supervision.

The peace plan of 23 June 1990 asserted the government's willingness 'to relinquish our monopoly of power and share power, but we are not prepared to sacrifice power in favour of anarchy and chaos'. The same viewpoint was reflected in the US-USSR talks in July 1990 with the latter taking the position that the Afghan resistance could not obtain at the negotiating table what it failed to achieve in the battlefield.

In its external policy and apart from the dependence on the Soviet Union for political and military assistance, Najibullah looked to India for political support and assistance in the post Soviet withdrawal period. This support was given by New Delhi in ample measure. The joint communique issued after the Afghan president's visit to New Delhi in August 1990 expressed India's support to his policy of national reconciliation. It reiterated the Indian position that a negotiated political settlement, based on existing realities and legitimate interest of all, was the only viable solution for the Afghan question.[69] India sent medicines and food supplies to Afghanistan immediately after the visit. Wider economic assistance, however, was hampered by the complexity of the supply route (overland through the Soviet Union) and the accompanying delays.

In the final analysis, however, the Najibullah government failed to survive. Its collapse came about, not due to external pressure from the south, but because of the Soviet state's disappearance from the world stage and the support which it provided to Afghanistan. The internecine conflict between the Pushtun and the non-Pushtun factions of the PDPA did the rest and sealed its fate in April 1992.

The UN's plan for an orderly transfer of power to a transitional authority was thus frustrated. The control of Kabul passed into the hands of forces loyal to Ahmad Shah Masood. And, on 26 October, the mujahideen factions meeting in Pakistan concluded the Peshawar Accord on a rotational arrangement and proclaimed the establishment of the Islamic Republic of Afghanistan: 'Perhaps this entity was Islamic, but it was hardly a state and it certainly did not rule Afghanistan.'[70] It was, nevertheless, recognised by many countries, including India, with whom it expressed the intention of having 'warm and cordial relations'. This was the outcome of an exercise undertaken earlier to 'establish contact with leaders of all groups and remain in touch with them so that eventually India could deal with whosoever came to power'.[71]

Under the terms of the Peshawar Accord, Mujaddidi relinquished the presidency after two months in favour of Burhanuddin Rabbani who, in turn, declined to carry the cycle of change further. Rabbani's fragile authority in the 1992-96 period was constantly challenged, internally, by his own prime minister, Gulbuddin Hikmatyar, who had longstanding ISI connections and, externally, by Pakistan 'which from the start distrusted the Rabbani Government and was determined to replace it with one which would be under the control of one of its protégés'.[72] Consequently, relations between Islamabad and the Jamiat-i-Islami-dominated government in Kabul deteriorated noticeably to the point that, in early 1995, Prime Minister Benazir Bhutto publicly attacked Rabbani's policies and declared his government 'illegitimate'.

The regional dimension of Afghanistan acquired a new significance altogether on account of the independence of Central Asia and the emergence of a new state system in the region. 'The independence of ethnically defined Central Asian states strengthened ethnic identities in Afghanistan. Competition for control over trade and pipeline routes from Central Asia transformed relations between Iran and Pakistan.'[73]

Nasirullah Babar, Interior Minister in Benazir Bhutto's government, explored Pakistan's interest in an alternate overland route to Central Asia going from Quetta to Turkmenistan through Qandahar and Herat. This exercise was undertaken in the autumn of 1994. A group of six Western ambassadors in Islamabad (including the American ambassador) were taken to both places to demonstrate the viability of the project and to seek funding for it. Route security was guaranteed by a small band of madrasa students (Taliban) whose attitude was reflective of the resentment of Pushtun tribes, both against the corruption of the mujahideen leaders and against the domination of the government in Kabul by non-Pushtun elements.

This new force was able to overcome the resistance of the local warlords and captured Spin Boldak and Qandahar. The movement was essentially a military enterprise, proclaimed as a crusade to reunify the country by firepower as much as by exhortion. 'How that firepower was acquired and deployed is basic to the understanding of the Taliban phenomenon.'[74] Its particularly noticeable aspects were a unified command and control system, good logistics support and an overwhelming speed of a type not seen in 17 years of war in Afghanistan. 'To suggest that the semi-literate Taliban commanders whose military experience had never extended beyond the hit-and-run attacks of guerilla warfare could have risen to this level of planning and execution defies belief.'[75]

All serious observers agreed that this was made possible through the covert support of Pakistan that was aimed at re-establishing Pushtun predominance in Afghanistan and thus achieving a strategic as well as a commercial objective. The United States was also supportive of the new development since it helped isolate Iran and hampered Iranian ambitions of becoming the principal conduit for Central Asian energy supplies. The US also hoped that the Taliban would restore order in a war-torn country and would curb the plague of drug supplies reaching the world market from Afghanistan. Recognition and assistance soon came forth from Saudi Arabia and the UAE also. The ferocity, the extremism, and the intolerance displayed by the Taliban rulers gradually disillusioned its external supporters with the exception of Pakistan. It also alarmed Iran, Russia, the Central Asian states (with the exception of Turkmenistan) and India—all of whom came together to render political and material support to the Northern Alliance, a grouping of anti-Taliban forces in the northern areas of the country.

A careful student of the Afghan scene had observed in 1995 that 'if the international community does not find a way to rebuild Afghanistan, a flood tide of weapons, cash and contraband will escape the state's porous boundaries and make the world less secure for all.'[76] This prediction took shape with the success of the Taliban, as the international community—for reasons ranging from indifference to hard commercial and strategic interests—ignored the dangerous dimensions of the new force whose eventual nemesis, ironically enough, finally emanated from the source of its greatest perceived strength and notoriety in the public mind.

What commenced as a refuge soon transformed itself into a launch pad for daring terrorist acts using committed Islamist extremists of different nationalities. It started with the bombing of the US embassies in East Africa in 1998 and culminated in the dramatic destruction of the World Trade Center on 11 September 2001. The US reaction, supported by the UN, sounded the death knell for the Taliban and the destruction of whatever was left of a war-torn Afghanistan. Along with it Pakistan's dream of acquiring strategic depth through a pliant government in Kabul changed overnight into a strategic nightmare whose wider implications have yet to unfold.

India's relations with the Rabbani Government in the 1992-96 period were of a limited nature and lacked substance. A relationship with the Taliban was not attempted though a section of the Taliban leadership made some exploratory gestures that were negated early enough as a result of the treatment meted out to the Afghan Hindus and Sikhs. Much more serious in Indian eyes were the Taliban pronouncements on Kashmir, the training of Kashmiri, Pakistani, and foreign militants in camps in Afghanistan and their induction into Jammu and Kashmir. And, the hijacking to Qandahar of the Indian Airlines plane, these touched the core of India's vital interests and compelled New Delhi to strengthen its support and assistance to the predominantly non-Pushtun Rabbani-Masood forces. This produced rich dividends particularly in the post-September 11 period and was aptly summed up by Yunus Qanooni during his visit to New Delhi in December 2001: 'We want countries that were our friends during our bad times to remain friends in the time of Afghanistan's reconstruction.'

The UN brokered the Bonn Agreement (laced with the promise of $10 billion of reconstruction assistance), and the interim government of Hamid Karzai sworn in on 22 December 2001, marks an improvement on the cumbersome and infructuous arrangement of 1991-92. Its tentativeness, however, is much too evident since equations within its various components, and between the external powers concerned; leave a lot of room for misunderstandings if not for mischief.

The past two decades have shown that recipes for Afghanistan's salvation do not fructify and that a saner cause may yet lie in King Nadir Shah's policy of neutrality reinforced through an institutional neutralisation of Afghanistan involving (1) a proclamation of neutrality by an elected legislature (2) its endorsement by the UN Security Council (3) the acceptance of reciprocal obligations pursuant to it by the Afghan government on the one side, and the interested foreign powers (including its immediate neighbours) on the other. In such a context, suggestions of de-weaponisation leading to demilitarisation would be easier to explore.

The idea of an externally guaranteed institutionalised neutrality, for Afghanistan was suggested by the EEC and the US in early 1980 and by the Soviet Union in 1986. Pursuant to the latter, the Pakistan foreign office 'prepared a concrete proposal' incorporating 'a declaration closely following the Laotian declaration of 9 July 1982 and the subsequent Treaty of Guarantors' and 'envisaging a role for the Security Council to act in case of a threat or breach of neutrality status'. Copies of the proposal were given to the Soviet Union, the United States, China, Saudi Arabia and Iran. 'The idea was dismissed unanimously by the seven Alliance leaders as contrary to the Islamic ethos. It did not appeal to their image of Afghanistan as a virile nation.'[77] Fifteen years later and in a transformed world, the Afghans themselves may have a more mature view of the Islamic ethos and of their virility!

It could be said, in relation to Afghanistan, that everyone's first wish is to influence and the second to assist. A uniform denial of the first would thus enhance the capacity of the second and respond to what the Afghan poet Khalilullah Khaleeli poignantly described as the 'promise of tomorrow'. In such an endeavour, India as a traditional friend of the Afghan people can play itself back as a country of relevance to assist in the reconstruction, in the training of cadres and eventually in welcoming Afghanistan into the community of South Asia nations—and as a dependable bridge between south and central Asia.

---

1. Kakar, Hasan M. *Afghanistan: A Study of Internal Political Developments 1880-1896* (Kabul 1971) p. 4.
2. Ibid., p. 208.
3. Islam, Riazul *Indo-Persian Relations* (Lahore 1970) pp. 176-186 and pp. 210-225.
4. Ghose, D.P. *England and Afghanistan: A Phase in Their Relations* (Calcutta 1960) p. 3.
5. Gopal, S. *British Policy in India 1858-1905* (Cambridge 1965) p. 228.
6. Kakar, op. cit., p. 271.
7. Ibid., p. 269.
8. Tripathi, G.P. *Indo-Afghan Relations 1882-1907* (New Delhi 1973) p. 175.
9. Ibid., pp. 181-182. For the full text of the instructions given to the Foreign Secretary, see pp. 175-187; paragraph 13 spelt out in some detail 'certain grounds of misunderstanding' which needed to be cleared up.
10. Gopal, op. cit., p. 285.
11. Tripathi, op. cit., p. 159. The text of the British Draft, and of the Treaty, is given on pp. 188-190.
12. Ibid., p. 126.
13. Ibid., p. 161.
14. Ibid., pp. 191-192 for the text.
15. Ibid., pp. 166-167.
16. Gregorian, Vartan *The Emergence of Modern Afghanistan* (Stanford 1969), pp. 216-217.
17. This was expressed bluntly in an article written by the Amir's nephew Sheikh Ahmad Abdullah entitled 'Asia and the War' in the Harper's Weekly of 11 December 1915: 'We are unmoved by the slaughter, the

losses and the untold sufferings, the wholesale destruction. The reason for this is simple and obvious. Whatever hurts the Occident helps us. Therefore it pleases us... We hate the European because we consider him an intolerable barbarian, who bullies where his wheedling is unsuccessful... The European has taught us with the sword. Presently we shall teach him with the sword.' (Gregorian, ibid., p. 216).

18. Gregorian, ibid., pp. 225-226.
19. Ibid., p. 229.
20. Rubin, Barnett, R. *The Fragmentation of Afghanistan* (Yale 1995), p. 54.
21. Gregorian, op. cit., pp. 230-231.
22. Ibid., p. 232.
23. Roy, M.N. *Memoirs* (Bombay 1964), p. 407.
24. Ibid., p. 493.
25. Rubin, op. cit., p. 57. Gregorian, op. cit., pp. 263-274.
26. Gregorian, ibid., p. 286. Oliver Roy (*Islam and Resistance in Afghanistan* Cambridge 1986, pp. 66-68) disagrees with the general view. The Bacha-i-Saqao affair, according to him, 'was first and foremost a cultural revolt, rather than a political one' and should be seen as a manifestation of the fundamentalist network, pp. 66-68.
27. Gregorian, op. cit., p. 321.
28. Ibid., pp. 322-323.
29. Ibid., p. 329 quoting Sir Michael O'Dwyer.
30. Ibid., pp. 384-385. Also, Olaf Caroe *The Pathans* (1958) pp. 408-409 for the Shami Pir episode.
31. Gregorian, ibid., pp. 386-389.
32. Burke, S.M. *Pakistan's Foreign Policy: An Historical Analysis* (London 1973), pp. 72-74. The Afghan contention was rejected by the British. In a statement in the House of Commons on 30 June 1950 it was stressed that 'Pakistan is in international law the inheritor of the rights and duties of the old Indian government and of His Majesty's Government in the United Kingdom, in these territories, and that the Durand Line is the international frontier'. Olaf Caroe, op. cit., p.465.
33. Poullada, Leon, B: 'The Road to Crisis 1919-1980' in Raousanne Klass (ed), *Afghanistan: The Great Game Revisited* (New York 1987) p. 40.
34. Kux, Dennis The *United States and Pakistan 1947-2000* (Washington 2001), p. 42.
35. Poullada, op. cit., p. 43.
36. Gopal, op. cit., p. 41.
37. Burke, op. cit., p. 68.
38. Kux, op. cit., p. 20. In August 1948 Pakistan told the UN Commission

for India and Pakistan (UNCIP) that the reason for the entry of the regular Pakistan army in the territory of Jammu and Kashmir was to prevent the possibility of India establishing a physical link with the movement for independence in Pushtunistan as also to avoid 'pincer movement against Pakistan by India and Afghanistan'. See Josef Korbel, *Danger in Kashmir* (Princeton 1966), pp. 138-139.

39. Ibid., pp. 109, 125.
40. Raja Anwar *The Tragedy of Afghanistan: A Firsthand Account* (London 1988), pp. 78-79.
41. Wolpert, Stanley *Zulfi Bhutto of Pakistan* (Oxford 1993), pp. 216-217.
42. Raja Anwar, op. cit., pp. 80-81
43. Ibid., p.82. The change in Daud's worldview is cited with approval by Henry Kissinger in his *Years of Upheaval* (Boston, 1982), p. 677.
44. Kux, op. cit., p. 246, quoting Gen. K.M. Arif.
45. Khan, Riaz M. *Untying The Afghanistan Knot: Negotiating Soviet Withdrawal* (Lahore 1993) p.11. The book gives a detailed account of the negotiating process as observed by a member of the Pakistan delegation. He gives some interesting details about the ISI's 'autonomous interest in the success of military operations' to the exclusion of political process and objectives.
46. Text in A. Appadorai: Select Documents on India's Foreign Policy and Relations 1947-1972 (New Delhi 1985), Vol. II, pp. 3-4.
47. Ibid., p. 5. Also Heimsath, Charles H., and Mansingh, Surjit *A Diplomatic History of Modern India* (New Delhi 1971), pp. 293-294.
48. Ibid., p. 294. Khan Abdul Ghaffar Khan said in New Delhi in 1969 that 'India was never serious about Azad Pushtunistan, but used the slogan only as a stick to beat Pakistan with.' Kuldip Nayar *Report on Afghanistan* (New Delhi 1981), p.123.
49. Dixit, J.N. *An Afghan Diary: Zahir Shah to Taliban* (New Delhi 2000), p. 19.
50. Heimsath and Mansingh, op. cit., 294.
51. Text of Banquet Speech in Satish Kumar (ed) Documents on India's Foreign Policy 1972 (New Delhi 1975), pp. 286-287.
52. Vajpayee, A.B. *New Dimensions of India's Foreign Policy* (New Delhi 1979) p. 198.
53. Dixit, op. cit., p. 19. Equally surprised was the United States Government which had assessed, a month before the coup that the internal situation was stable with no significant opposition to the President. Kuldip Nayar *Report on Afghanistan* (New Delhi 1981), p.19.
54. Dixit, Ibid., p. 21.

55. Mukherjee, Sadhan *Afghanistan from Tragedy to Triumph* (New Delhi 1984), pp. 203-204.
56. Dixit, op. cit., p. 22.
57. Asian Recorder, vol. XXVI, No. 11, p. 15355.
58. Sen Gupta, Bhabani, *The Afghan Syndrome: How to Live with Soviet Power* (London 1982), p.123.
59. Dixit, op. cit., p.28.
60. Dixit, J.N. *Across Borders: Fifty Years of India's Foreign Policy* (New Delhi 1998) pp. 139-40.
61. Asian Recorder, vol. XXVI, No. 31, pp. 15572-73.
62. Ibid., vol. XXVII, No. 2, pp. 15827-29.
63. Dixit, op. cit., pp. 142-143.
64. Ibid., p. 144. See also Riaz M. Khan, op. cit., p. 20: 'the New Delhi meeting of NAM Foreign Ministers in February 1981 also represented the high watermark of India's involvement with Afghan issue in an international forum. Despite its status a major regional power, India remained on the sidelines of the diplomatic process on Afghanistan which was dominated by the OIC and UN-oriented initiatives.
65. Dixit, ibid., pp. 388 and 430.
66. Khan, Riaz M., op. cit., p. 302.
67. Rubin, op.cit, p. 147. This process of the retreat of the State, as also of its appropriation of the Islamic and traditional Afghan discourse, is traced in some detail on pp. 146-175.
68. Ibid., pp. 249-250.
69. Asian Recorder, vol. XXXVI, No. 44, pp. 21408-9.
70. Rubin, op. cit., p. 272.
71. Dixit, J.N. *My South Block Years: Memoirs of a Foreign Secretary* (New Delhi 1996), p. 108.
72. Saikal, Amin: 'The Rabbani Government 1992-1996' in William Maley (ed) Fundamentalism Reborn? Afghanistan and the Taliban (New Delhi 1999), pp. 29 and 38-39.
73. Rubin, Barnett, R.: 'Women and Pipelines: Afghanistan's Proxy Wars,' International Affairs 73.2 (1997), p. 284.
74. Davis, Anthony: 'How the Taliban Became a Military Force' in William Maley (ed), op. cit., p. 43.
75. Ibid., p. 68.
76. Rubin (1995), op. cit., p.280.
77. Khan, Riaz M., op. cit., pp. 239-241. Also Sen Gupta, op. cit., p. 127 and Selig S. Harrison: 'Dateline Afghanistan: Exit Through Finland?' in Foreign Affairs, 41, (Winter 1980-81) pp. 163-187.

Bangladesh

Deb Mukharji

The emergence of Bangladesh has, arguably, drawn the final boundaries of South Asia, ending the anomaly of the increasingly estranged cohabitation between the two wings of erstwhile Pakistan. The logic of the emergence of Bangladesh has a bearing both on the future of the country as also on its relations with the outside world, most notably India. India's understanding of the historical forces operating in Bangladesh, which admittedly pull in different directions, remains coloured by its own role in 1971 and the tendency to see the creation of the new state not so much in objective terms as in the construct of Indo-Pakistani relations. As a consequence, many in India oversimplify the emergence/liberation of Bangladesh in terms of the military victory over Pakistan. This, even if unstated, has been resented both by the genuinely nationalist Bangladeshi and also by those who never reconciled themselves to the break-up of Pakistan (despite the benefits which they may have reaped) and consider the creation of Bangladesh as the most visible proof of Hindu India's aspirations. If these perceptions (or misperceptions) have to be corrected, then India will have to become more cognisant of and sensitive to the diverse forces in operation. Much will also depend on how Bangladesh eventually projects the roots of its origin. It would be useful to take a brief look at history.

From the early thirteenth century, the area now comprising Bangladesh had been under Turkic/Afghan/ Mughal rule, sometimes independent and sometimes under Delhi. This went on until the advent of the British in the mid-eighteenth century when the last independent ruler of Bengal was defeated at Plassey. There was thus uninterrupted rule by sultans and emperors of the Islamic faith for over 500 years. It was a period of relative peace, prosperity and harmony, particularly under the independent sultanate from the mid-fourteenth to the mid-sixteenth century. It was the period when the wealth of Bengal, including its famous muslin, became renowned and attracted worldwide attention. Sufism and the Bhakti movement took root and flourished. But Plassey changed all that. In the century-and-a-half that followed, sections of the Hindu Bengali found warmth under the British sun not only as landed gentry but also in services and professions and the Bengali renaissance brought about remarkable achievements in every field. Meanwhile, the Muslims of Bengal continued to nurse their grievances—real and perceived—and their aspirations remained, in a sense, outside the mainstream in almost all spheres of activity. The excitement as well as the challenges and opportunities of adapting to western education passed them by. The resentment and resulting distance grew and in 1905 came the partition of Bengal. Perhaps Viceroy Curzon intended it to be a lesson to the now increasingly recalcitrant Hindu Bengali, and win Muslim gratitude. Or perhaps it made administrative sense. Either way, it provoked bitter protests and had to be annulled six years later. For the Muslim Bengali, the partition of Bengal had brought forth the possibility of Dhaka being revived and a future away from the embrace of Calcutta. However, this was not to be, as yet.

The years leading to Partition saw the Muslim Bengali's increasing political assertion though it had a largely economic rationale vis-à-vis the landed gentry. What is too often ignored—and this has a direct bearing on Bangladesh polity today—is that without the sheer mass of support from Bengali Muslims, Pakistan may have remained a dream. The only others to believe in the new state (besides the activists of Bihar and UP, both of which were to remain in India) were neither from Punjab, nor from Sind, and certainly not from the North West Frontier Province (which required a referendum). It is the great Calcutta killings that made Partition inevitable. And, if there would have been no Pakistan without Muslim Bengal, there were some, even in the Bengal Muslim League who would have preferred a united and independent Bengal, distinct from India or Pakistan, an outcome acceptable to neither the Congress nor the Muslim League.

But the Bengali Muslim, whose elite even disdained to acknowledge that they knew the native language and proudly traced their ancestry at least beyond the Hindukush, discovered soon after Partition that he was not to be a grade-one citizen of Pakistan. Thus was born the language movement, symbolised by *ekushey* on 21 February 1952, when the police in Dhaka University shot students agitating for a rightful place for Bengalis. The movement was to lead to, as one analyst said in the sixties, 'the homecoming of the Bengali Muslim' where his cultural and linguistic roots became, if not the primary, then at least equal to his religious identity. This assertion of identity together with West Pakistan's exploitation led, through many twists and turns, to the savage military crackdown in March 1971. Even if those fighting for their rights had not envisaged a new nation, this was now inevitable.

For India, the choice initially may not have been as clear as it may appear. The opportunity presented by the enemy, the temptation to 'disprove' the two-nation theory and the heavy burden of the increasing influx of millions of refugees were compelling reasons for action. Against this would have been the advice that a Pakistan internally riven would be a permanently disabled Pakistan. But all this was overtaken by events. No government of India could stand by and cynically watch the horrors perpetrated across the border whose victims came in an unending stream to the refugee camps.

Yet another aspect needs to be borne in mind. In West Pakistan itself, there was a feeling among some, particularly in Punjab, that since further exploitation of East Pakistan was not feasible, it may be better to let it go. There was shock when the draft Third Five Year plan of Pakistan actually suggested transfer of resources from the West to the East. The need for disassociation became a political imperative with the 1970 elections actually positing a Bengali Prime Minister. This was anathema to Zulfikar Bhutto's ambitions and I recall the editor of his newspaper suggesting to me in Islamabad in March 1971, days before the military crackdown, that would India please take over East Pakistan and rid Pakistan of these pestilential Bengalis. The chain of events flowing from Islamabad's bad faith under Bhutto's blackmail and Bengali anger, together with the arrogance of the Pakistani military, may have prevented a mutually acceptable arrangement and led to the inevitable denouement. It was an amicable parting that, it is said, Bhutto tried to sell to Sheikh Mujib-ur-Rahman as he was released from a Pakistani prison. Mujib was to see the reality of the previous nine months when he returned to now free Bangladesh.

The sequence of events in 1971 needs no recounting. Some perceptions do. There was, for long, resentment at what was seen as India's preferential treatment of Bengali freedom fighters associated with the Awami League, in terms of training and provision of arms. If this has any basis, it would be entirely understandable as the Awami League had just won an overwhelming mandate from the people and Mujib was the undisputed leader. It would nevertheless indicate inadequate insurance for the future in Indian planning. Such a feeling may also have been coloured by the ideological attachment to

China felt by some left elements among the freedom fighters (despite China's role in 1971). This perception, based on reality or otherwise, gave rise to the impression of a very special relationship between the Awami League and India. The fact is that Mujib never compromised with what he perceived to be the national interest of Bangladesh. If there was cordiality between the post-liberation government of Bangladesh and India (as also the Soviet Union), it also has to be seen in the context of the active hostility of China, the United States and sections of the Islamic fraternity to the emergence of Bangladesh, a hostility that continued to simmer until Mujib could be removed. This was achieved in August 1975 and a new direction was sought to be given to Bangladeshi society and polity. Two instances of the ambivalence of Bangladeshi thinking are illustrative. Some believe that by engaging the Pakistan army, India cut short the revolution that would have changed traditional Bangladeshi society. One interlocutor, himself a refugee in India in 1971, felt that while India's intervention was welcome, it was a pity that for the first time the sword of Islam had been blunted by Hindus. (Led by a Parsee, a Jew and a Sikh, I had responded to alleviate his anguish). It is also sobering to reflect that in less than two decades, by the end of the eighties, there were instances of schoolchildren believing that the marauders of 1971 were Indians—a conclusion derived from constant anti-Indian propaganda and the fact that history books only referred to the 'allied' forces assisting the freedom fighters without naming any country. Such instances may not reflect the public feeling but are indicative of the forces at work. One must also recall that perhaps the first public acknowledgement of the Indian role in 1971 was made by then Prime Minister, Sheikh Hasina, in her banquet speech at Hyderabad House on 12 December 1996. This was subsequently followed by a public speech in Dhaka.

Mujib's assassination was the precursor to fundamental shifts in the direction the fledgling state could have been expected to take. Had the emergence of Bangladesh resulted from a negotiated settlement with Islamabad, it may have been plausible to expect that its foundation would continue to have been seen in the two-nation theory. This was not so. Bangladesh was born in blood and tears and seen as the culmination of over two decades of struggle based largely on language and culture. The Bangladeshi who had sought to establish that adherence to its traditions did not, in any way, come in the way of being a good Muslim. Such a philosophy was systematically subverted in the next two decades by succeeding governments. The changes in the constitution in April 1977 by the decree of the Chief Martial Law Administrator, Major General Zia ur Rahman, removed secularism and re-designated the citizens from a Bengali to a Bangladeshi. Zia made the significance of this abundantly clear in the coming months with the enunciation of 'Bangladeshi nationalism'. This nationalism was based on the identity of a Muslim Bengal and, in effect, went back to the Lahore Resolution of March 1940, calling for the creation of one or more Muslim majority states. The process was carried further by Ershad who declared Islam as the state religion. Born in the cantonment, the Bangladesh Nationalist Party was to become the latter day torchbearer of the ideology of the Muslim League.

It is important to understand that Bangladesh polity has been vertically split on the question of identity since 1971 (despite the relative homogeneity and inter-connectivity of the elite). The situation may have been different if there had been a process of catharsis after 1971; an acceptance and internalisation of all that had gone wrong; and a reconciled society thereafter owing allegiance to mutually acceptable norms and a common vision of the future. If this did not happen, the primary responsibility must lie with Mujib whose magnanimity and image as the father of the nation did not permit necessary action to be taken against the collaborators and killers of fellow Bengalis in 1971. The release of even the

195 Pakistani war criminals, whatever the international compulsions, was the gravest of errors. Consequently, there was, on the one hand, the large numbers who had suffered but whose sacrifice received at best token acknowledgement. A recent documentary on freedom fighters has the poignant story of a man who lost a leg fighting the Pakistanis in 1971 and has since earned his living driving a rickshaw. On the other hand, were the forces, defeated in 1971, which bided their time, with Pakistan happily providing the required support for dissension at no cost to itself. Thus, with the processes set in motion by Zia under the rubric of Bangladeshi nationalism, be it through conviction or political expediency, many with the blood of their countrymen on their hands came to hold positions of authority, something that continues to this day. For the votaries of Islam as the primary identity, the linguistic/cultural definition that had germinated and flourished remains anathema. It is not surprising that a senior minister in Bangladesh should say recently that the emergence of Bangladesh was primarily the result of Indian moves to disintegrate Pakistan, thus implicitly disowning the movement for self-assertion for over two decades and rubbishing the sacrifices of his own people.

In a sense, of course, this is jousting with mirages. It is an indisputable fact that there was unlikely to have been a Bangladesh if there had been no Pakistan. It is also self-evident that Bangladesh is a vastly Muslim majority country with a deeply religious people. But to define Bangladesh, even if implicitly, simply as independent East Pakistan runs in the face of Bengali linguistic/cultural identity. Pakistan has been on a self-destructive mode by not being able to assert its existence on its own merits—to be able to say, we are because we are, (to which Bangladesh can add, because we always have been) and instead trying to justify why it is not India. Though a far more homogenous Bangladesh does not quite face the same consequences, a negative self-definition, instead of pride in and assertion of its linguistic/cultural heritage (not by any means excluding Islam) would not lead to the self-assurance that is so readily available. The use or even creation of emotive issues, including religion, is not unknown in politics, as indeed we see in India today. But in Bangladesh the consequences are more severe. The polity could remain permanently and irreconcilably riven, its potentials unrealised.

Seen against this backdrop, it is not difficult to see how internal developments in Bangladesh so directly affect relations between India and Bangladesh and why these go beyond the normal cool calculations of tangible national interests that determine foreign policy. Even at the best of times, relations between neighbours acquire non-rational dimensions, particularly if there is substantial disparity in size. It can become intractable if the very basis of the state is implicitly predicated on non-reconcilability.

India's attitude to Bangladesh was unduly influenced by the circumstances of its birth. East Pakistan had been seen as a victim of Islamabad's exploitation and persecution and there was insufficient appreciation of the complex impulses that motivated even liberal Bangladeshis—who did not all look towards India without suspicion. India's ability to reach out to a wider cross-section of people appears to have been limited.

Indo-Bangladesh relations can be classified into several phases. The first was from 1971 to 1975, when each basked in the warm glow of having defeated the enemy. Indian troops left Bangladesh within a remarkably short space of time. A 25-year treaty of Friendship, Cooperation and Peace was signed, as also the Indira-Mujib agreement on the land boundary. The Joint Rivers Commission was set up to promote cooperation in water resources, while the Joint Economic Commission was to encourage and ensure economic cooperation. The Planning Commissions of the two countries made serious efforts to concretise proposals and projects for mutual benefit and it appeared that a new chapter had truly begun. Political (introduction of a one party state and deteriorating law and order) and economic (severe drought) constraints in Bangladesh and India, which was on the threshold of the Emergency, prevented rapid movement.

The second brief phase lasted from Mujib's assassination to the assumption of office by the Janata government in Delhi in March 1977. Indira Gandhi may not have been surprised (it is said that Mujib had been dismissive of the cautions conveyed by Delhi) but was certainly shocked and probably surmised correctly that there was more to the assassination than the action of a few disgruntled junior officers. Zia was virtually in charge shortly after the jail killing of the Awami League leaders in November 1975 and suspected India of actively supporting elements trying to overthrow the regime. It was a period of mutual suspicion and hostility.

The third phase was coterminous with the Janata government in Delhi until the return of Indira Gandhi in January 1980. Morarji Desai, both by conviction as much as to show that his government was more neighbour-friendly than his predecessor, tried to generate confidence and Zia would have felt reassured about India's non-involvement in the internal affairs of Bangladesh. This period saw the consolidation of Zia and the propagation of Bangladeshi nationalism. The five-year agreement on the sharing of the Ganges waters at Farakka was also signed in November 1977.

The period from 1980 to 1995 could best be described as one of non-engagement with no progress of substance in any area of cooperation. In Bangladesh, it spanned the last years of Zia, who was assassinated in May 1981, eight years of Ershad and five years of Khaleda Zia. In India, this coincided with the governments of Indira and Rajiv Gandhi, V.P. Singh, Chandrashekhar and Narasimha Rao. It saw the fracas over New Moore island/South Talpatty connected with the determination of the still unresolved maritime boundary. This period also saw the influx of Chakma refugees into India resulting from state-sponsored migration of Bengalis to the Chittagong Hill Tracts, and brutal army action (with Bangladeshi charges of Indian training to Chakma guerillas, the

Shanti Bahini), the establishment and consolidation of ISI activities in Bangladesh, acting both to influence local politics as also using Bangladesh territory against India. Then there were the Indian charges of Bangladesh complicity in the insurgencies in North East India, the short-term revalidations of the 1977 agreement on Ganges waters with revised clauses and its final lapse. Bangladesh was livid at the withdrawal of Ganges waters at Farakka even after the lapse of the agreement, and raised the issue at all available international fora.

The assumption of office by the Awami League in Bangladesh in June 1996 coincided with the arrival of the coalition under Deve Gowda in Delhi. The activist I.K. Gujral, then Minister for External Affairs, visited Dhaka in September, followed by several high-level visits in both directions. The landmark 30-year agreement on the sharing of the Ganges waters was signed by Prime ministers Deve Gowda and Sheikh Hasina on 12 December 1996.

Doubts and recriminations seemed to belong to the past and a new era seemed to be dawning. A year later followed the courageous peace agreement between the government of Bangladesh and the dispossessed of the Chittagong Hill Tracts, heralding peace and confidence after 20 years of conflict, and facilitating the return of the more than 50,000 refugees from camps in Tripura. Thereafter, as far as Indo-Bangladesh relations were concerned, Dhaka seemed to lose its way in a maze of political apprehensions that did not seem warranted. The confidence shown in achieving the agreement on water sharing appeared to evaporate in the heat of internal political calculations while Delhi, with its own rapid changes of government, appeared only perfunctorily concerned with moving ahead. Mutual respect and understanding was only marginally translated into concrete steps.

It remains to be seen what equation is reached between the new BNP-led government in Dhaka and the BJP-led coalition in Delhi in its last years. Both have in common the use of religion for political purposes.

A look at some of the major issues dealt with or awaiting resolution between India and Bangladesh can be instructive.

As is often said in Bangladesh, there are 54 rivers that flow into Bangladesh from India and are the lifeline of the country. This is factually quite correct though the number of people dependent on each would vary widely. Besides agriculture, the ecology of Bangladesh, particularly the problem of salinity, and navigation must remain issues of concern to any government. Bangladesh quite rightly feels that its present and future must be protected against any action that India might take which may diminish flows of water with adverse consequences.

India, on the other hand, has to calculate the increasing requirements of its growing population. It also feels that overall, Bangladesh has far greater availability of water than, for example, the densely populated areas of the Gangetic plains. The maximalist Bangladesh demand is for the maintenance of existing flows of the rivers. The Indian position is that Bangladesh has far more water than it could possibly use, to which the Bangladesh response is that water requirements cannot be simplistically judged by adding up the annual total including floods and droughts.

Issues relating to water sharing have always remained vexed, one reason being the absence of any binding and unambiguous international guidelines or laws. The Helsinki rules, as well as the recent unratified UN initiative, do not provide any clear framework within which parties concerned are obliged to negotiate. Within India itself we have seen continuing conflicts over the sharing of waters. In the case of Bangladesh, the situation becomes more tenuous because of political sensitivities and the more than willing attitude of the lower riparian to attribute negative motivations. (Demonstrations were held in Sylhet and Dhaka in the mid-nineties over the disastrous effects of the Indian construction of the Tipaimukh project in upper Barak, when, in fact, the dam is still not beyond the drawing board. Moreover, if it materialises, the dam would provide substantial relief in the dry season to both the countries as well as some protection against floods). It needs to be added that the Indian propensity to be non-communicative on water-related issues does not contribute to promoting confidence.

The single most fraught question confronting Bangladesh and India was the sharing of Ganges waters at Farakka. Being people who best understood commerce, the British had concluded long before their departure from the sub-continent that the future of the port of Calcutta would require a degree of flushing during the dry season. This could be best achieved by diverting water from the main channel of the Ganges, which becomes the Padma in Bangladesh, and that the most appropriate location for effecting this diversion would be at Farakka in the district of Murshidabad in Bengal. With this in view, the Muslim majority district of Murshidabad was allocated to India, and Pakistan received instead the Hindu majority district of Khulna. Farakka was not by any means simply a ploy by the Indians to cause desertification in Pakistan/Bangladesh as was sometimes made out to be subsequently. While India took up the construction of the barrage at Farakka, negotiations with Pakistan on the quantum of withdrawal made little headway with each rejecting the technical arguments of the other. Farakka was operationalised in 1975 following an interim agreement with Bangladesh, but the quantum of water withdrawn by India was well below both the capacity of the feeder canal and the stated requirements of Calcutta port. India continued to withdraw water after the expiry of this interim agreement (after the political changes following Mujib's assassination), to the great dismay of Bangladesh who took the issue to the United Nations. The Desai government at Delhi took great pains to resolve the issue and prove its bonafides. The resultant agreement of November 1977 was also interim in nature, being valid for five years. But it skirted the main issue of permanent sharing with the pious hope that mutually agreed means of augmenting the scarce flows at Farakka would be found. The preferred Indian suggestion was for upstream storages on the Brahmaputra in Arunachal with a link canal, through the territory of Bangladesh, to bring the augmented flows to the Padma. Bangladesh, at best sceptical of Indian requirements, saw no reason why its scarce land should be used for a link canal to replace water that India had taken away and suggested that the augmentation be through storages in Nepal. India wanted the availability of the Ganges and the Brahmaputra to be considered together, while Bangladesh wanted them to be kept discrete. Subsequent discussions predictably led nowhere and the agreement was revalidated for short periods, after removal of the minimum guarantee clause, in 1982 and 1985. India was not able to meet the essence of the Bangladeshi intent of perpetuating the interim agreement of 1977—which was predicated on the prospect of augmentation, however differently understood -- and withdrew water into the feeder canal without an agreement from 1989. This led to a further decline in the already cool Indo-Bangladesh relations with the growing conviction in Dhaka that India intended to desertify Bangladesh. Every normal water shortage almost anywhere in Bangladesh during the dry season was attributed to Farakka. Saline intrusion and even the increase in the number of mosquitoes were blamed on Farakka. Intractable Farakka was fast becoming the Kashmir of Bangladesh vis-à-vis India. The likely fact that Indian withdrawals at Farakka, even if unilateral, had not been irresponsible or quite unmindful of Bangladeshi interests, was of no consequence as the process was without joint monitoring.

It is believed, at least by some in Bangladesh, that India was waiting for an Awami League government to come to power in Bangladesh before concluding an agreement on Farakka. This is factually incorrect. The respective foreign offices had started exploring possible solutions. Within days of my assuming charge in Dhaka in March 1995, I was discussing, under my government's instructions, the possible parameters of an agreement. A month later, then BNP foreign minister, late Col. ASM Mustafizur Rahman told me that while he appreciated my efforts, elections were due in a year and this was not the time for his government to negotiate an agreement on such a sensitive and politically charged issue. He was confident that a conclusion would be reached soon after the BNP returned to power. Whether this would have materialised must remain a matter of conjecture.

Due to the extreme emotions aroused on the issue, many considered a lasting agreement on Ganges water sharing at Farakka to be more than merely difficult. Any government in Bangladesh was likely to run the gauntlet of being charged with selling out on the country's interest. There were interests which were not unhappy with the perpetuation of the continuing sore in Indo-Bangladesh relations. Calcutta was no less firm that the port would not be allowed to die. A fortuitous combination of circumstances eased the way to the Farakka agreement. The Awami League, which came to power in June 1996, was keen to prove that it could deliver on this issue of vital national interest and prepared to face the political fall-out provided it could get a reasonable agreement. The Deve Gowda government, which simultaneously came to power in Delhi, was also anxious to remove the irritant. And Foreign Minister Gujral, long a member of track two diplomacy, was not only conversant with the nuances but also keen to give a practical demonstration of the Gujral doctrine. Not the least important, the Jyoti Basu government in West Bengal was on cordial terms with Delhi. There was a flurry of visits between Dhaka, Calcutta and Delhi. Jyoti Basu's visit to Dhaka in the last week of November set the stage for the negotiations in Delhi in early December and the signing of the agreement on 12 December 1996.

The agreement was possible because each, while protecting its own interests, was assured of the bonafides of the other. Bangladesh was assured of a reasonable deal without unduly straining Indian interests. Besides the sharing of water on an agreed basis, the 30-year span of the duration of the agreement made it virtually permanent, ensuring that Bangladesh would never again have to face the uncertainties of a no-treaty regime and could embark on its own development programmes with a degree of certitude. The agreement also ensured that even if there were to be future disagreements during reviews, 90 per cent of the release to Bangladesh would be assured during its lifetime. There was, of course, opposition and criticism on both sides. The BNP predictably focussed on the absence of a guarantee clause, ignoring the fact that the guarantee clause had ceased to operate on the renewal of the 1977 agreement. Moreover, its own five years in power from 1991 to 1996 had seen a no-treaty regime with, according to its own allegations, massive withdrawals by India leading to the desertification of Bangladesh. In India, the treaty was opposed by the BJP. It is interesting to recall that when criticism of the treaty was voiced in a track two meeting in Dhaka in 1997, some of those now occupying senior positions in the Indian government responded by saying that if Bangladesh felt unhappy with the treaty, so did they. And, that they would be quite willing to consider termination if Bangladesh so wished.

The issue of illegal migration from Bangladesh is likely to be one of the major points of contention in the years to come. The enforcement agencies on both sides have either permitted, or have been unable to prevent, large-scale movement of Bangladeshi nationals to India over two decades and more. Today, the numbers would be in the millions. Though there is now greater appreciation of the magnitude of the problem, the fact is that for many years political parties in the neighbouring states of India for their electoral calculations may well have encouraged such migration. The migrants are largely Muslim, who move due to economic reasons, though Hindus are proportionately more in terms of their share of the population of Bangladesh and move also due to reasons of security. The demographic changes in some of the Indian districts bordering Bangladesh bear out the dimensions of the movement of people. Some of the migration is also seasonal. It is an issue that is routinely raised by the Government of India and equally routinely denied by Bangladesh, though at times the nuances are visible. There are no easy answers and the best way out could be legalising the movement by the issue of work permits. This is an idea voiced sometimes in India but somehow not pursued. This would at least ensure that foreign nationals do not acquire Indian citizenship.

The Indira-Mujib Land Boundary Agreement of 1974 sought to clean up boundary related questions. These were not difficult to identify, being leftovers from 1947. It is a reflection of the apathy of the respective administrations that nearly 30 years down the line, India is yet to ratify the agreement on the grounds that this will have to be preceded by demarcation of all areas, while the early ratification by Bangladesh is without value as it also requires demarcation before taking effect. The areas of difference are few and could be resolved by mutual accommodation and political will. But local pressures and non-engagement by the central governments have so far precluded forward movement. One may argue that the attention of the two governments had been so overwhelmed by the Farakka issue—particularly given the Bangladeshi position that no movement was possible anywhere without its resolution—that the boundary question had to wait. But this is no longer tenable after the water-sharing agreement of 1996.

Related to this is the question of Teen Bigha. Under the land boundary agreement, all enclaves mutually held in the territory of the other were to be exchanged. However, India was to retain south Berubari, a Bangladeshi enclave in India. In return, Bangladesh would retain Dahagram and would be granted lease in perpetuity of a strip of land measuring 178 m x 85 m (*teen bjgha)* to provide connectivity from the mainland of Bangladesh. While south Berubari remained with India, it found it difficult to part with Teen Bigha as it was found that on the ground its transfer to Bangladesh would render the populated Indian area of Kuchlibari virtually an enclave within Bangladesh with no connectivity to India. While the Indian dilemma could be understandable, the temperatures raised on the subject by some political parties in West Bengal were entirely avoidable. After years of discussion, which included suggestions of over-pass and under-pass, a methodology of providing Bangladesh access to its enclaves was evolved. Here again, India should have found its way to providing far more liberal access than it was inclined to for a long time for reasons that do not bear scrutiny. Teen Bigha could be a case study of how a larger country needs to be alive to the sensitivities of its smaller neighbours and maintain credibility.

The discussions on transit facilities to India for goods and people to the North East could be considered to border on the absurd, if they did not have such substantial economic implications for both countries. A look at the map indicates that transit facilities would considerably save time and money for Indians and would be of direct benefit to Tripura, Meghalaya, Mizoram and parts of Assam as well as relieve pressures on the Siliguri corridor. It would bring very substantial revenues to Bangladesh and be an incentive to India to invest in the transport infrastructure of Bangladesh with all its concomitant benefits. At one point transit was sought to be linked to the resolution of Farakka and tacitly accepted by Bangladesh. Any such linkage was rightly removed. In some way, Bangladesh considers the grant of transit facilities to be its main trump card vis-à-vis India with some yet undefined *quid pro quo* to be extracted. Political parties have made it appear that transit would be some kind of abnegation of sovereignty. There is little or no informed discussion on the practical aspects of the proposition and the economic benefits to Bangladesh. What is also ignored is the fact that should India make substantial investments in upgrading the existing connectivity to the North East, transit through Bangladesh may lose some of its importance.

Indo-Bangladesh trade showed a sharp upward swing in the mid-nineties following liberalisation in the Bangladesh import policy, with the major share going to Indian exports. After the surge of the initial years there has been a plateau, though the product mix has tended to vary. Under the South Asian Preferential Trading Arrangement (SAPTA), India has offered duty concessions on a large number of items, many of which are of interest to Bangladesh exports. Citing the substantial trade gap (imports $1170 million, exports $62 million in 2001), Bangladesh has consistently sought special dispensation in reduced tariffs for items of specific interest. However, Dhaka has not shown any active interest in pursuing the model of the Indo-Sri Lanka trade agreement, which provides for zero-duty access to each other's products and also ensures a preferential time frame for the smaller economy. Lately, there has been emphasis on preferential access to some items of export interest to Bangladesh, citing an assurance by the visiting Indian prime minister in June 1998 that this would be considered out of context. The background to this is glossed over. During the April 1998 visit of the Bangladesh Commerce Minister, the two countries had agreed that committees would look into the question of preferential access as also, *inter alia*, multi-modal transport and border trade. Bangladesh has declined to move in the areas of interest to India.

While noting that the whole issue of balancing trade is quite outmoded in the present global context and the downward trend in India's own tariffs, there could be different ways of looking at and proceeding further with the issue. It could be argued that India should demonstrate generosity in dealing with a smaller neighbour and that the welfare of the neighbour is also of benefit to India. In fact, one of the arguments by Bangladeshi interlocutors, albeit not publicly discussed, for investments in Bangladesh and freer access to its goods into India, used to be that this would diminish illegal migration. But Dhaka's disinclination to move in the areas of interest to India does not provide the requisite stimulus for making gestures. It can also be noted that there is scarcely a word said in Bangladesh about its rapidly increasing trade deficit with China (imports $700 million, exports $14.2 million in 1999).

Discussion of trade would be incomplete without a reference to the 'informal trade' between the two countries. Such exchanges are by definition impossible to quantify precisely, but estimates place this as perhaps twice the volume of legal trade. Such trade deprives the governments of revenue and leads to the obvious gray transactions with all its negative connotations. It is, however, of some benefit to the Bangladeshi consumer. I am aware of one instance when, at a time of food shortages, the Bangladeshi enforcement agencies had stopped a convoy of several dozen trucks carrying smuggled rice from across the border and had been instructed to release them in the larger national interest. There is also the curious case of the movement of cattle. Cattle export is not permitted by India but that does not prevent substantial 'exports' from as far as Punjab and Haryana and there are officially designated corridors in Bangladesh for their 'import' as also a schedule of levies. Given the nature of the border, it may not be possible to entirely eliminate such movement of goods, but upgradation of transport facilities and greater openness and understanding between the governments could reduce this substantially.

The long pending possibility of export of natural gas from Bangladesh to India is another instance of the absence of clear economic thinking. Bangladesh continues to claim proven recoverable reserves of about 13 trillion cubic feet, whereas it is understood to be well in excess of 50 trillion, with large areas still unexplored. There cannot be, obviously, any question of Bangladesh exporting gas without ensuring at least a minimum degree of self-reliance for the future. The discussion is not always on rational economic terms. At one extreme are those who say that selling gas would simply make India more powerful and must, therefore, be avoided. Even a senior minister said recently that Bangladesh would be forced to export gas because of the faulty agreements signed by the previous administration with the multinationals. The fact that Bangladesh would be able to virtually wipe out the trade deficit with India (assuming it has sufficient reserves) with even moderate gas export and create a state of some dependency of its larger neighbour is rarely touched upon. What should be a clear and relatively simple economic decision gets bogged down in politics.

Mutual security concerns play an important role in both perceptions and decision-making. India's training and support to the Bangladesh freedom fighters and its eventual military action, however beneficial to Bangladesh, also remains a reminder of the vulnerability of the state to Indian intervention, a concern fuelled by interested parties. This concern was reflected in the shrillness of the analysis of the terms of the Indo-Bangladesh friendship treaty before it was laid to rest in the fullness of time. Bangladesh also nurtures memories of the assistance it claims was provided by India to the opponents of the regime after Mujib's assassination as also to the Shanti Bahini. On her part, India feels that at various points of time, the government of Bangladesh has turned more than a blind eye to the sanctuaries enjoyed by insurgents of the North East and the flow of arms from the coast. There is credible evidence of the ISI of Pakistan operating from Bangladesh in creating trouble for India with, at times, the likely support of elements of the government. The matter is further complicated by some uncertainty with regard to the role of the Bangladesh armed forces, which though removed from the position enjoyed by its counterpart in Pakistan, may not be completely amenable to civilian control. Pakistan has been able to use its past connections with a fair degree of success and at little cost in furthering its interests even if these have been prejudicial to the interests of Bangladesh both with regard to her relations with India as also her internal polity. Indo-Bangladesh dialogues at the political level have been far too sporadic to allay mutual concerns and suspicions and promote confidence on a lasting basis. (At the time of going this book to press, and as 2002 draws to a close, one notes the recent statements made by India about Pakistan's renewed vigour in promoting subversive activities through Bangladesh. While one may question the wisdom of such diplomacy through the media, the facts themselves do not augur well for the future.)

CONCLUSION

Seen from Bangladesh's point of view, India is a gigantic neighbour with great potential for influencing events. Such potential is usually seen in negative terms and not as providing challenges and opportunities. That Bangladesh is itself among the 10 most populous countries of the world is often forgotten. Those less certain of their heritage, consider the common linguistic/cultural affinities with India to be a potential threat. Those still imbued with the pathological compulsions of Pakistan see India in inimical terms. The self-assured nationalist sees possibilities of cooperation for mutual benefit.

The geographical importance of Bangladesh is insufficiently appreciated in India. Its territory is embedded in the most populous and, considering the North East, the most volatile part of India. Events in Bangladesh would always have repercussions at least in the neighbouring states, if not beyond. But New Delhi's preoccupation with its western neighbour has not permitted the degree of attention which Bangladesh (or indeed its other neighbours) merit in India's own interest.

Elements in Bangladesh voice suspicions about India seeking an *akhand bharat,* which is ironical as elements in India are even now trying to prove their own version of the two-nation theory. The dream of *lebensraum* in the North East does exist among some Bangladeshis. It is this that may have prompted some BNP leaders to assert in 1997 that, as a nation born of a war of independence, it was the bounden duty of Bangladesh to assist the freedom-loving people of the North East. Bangladesh has always evinced special interest in extending its economic influence in the North East—on this count even minimising the importance of transit. Clearly, however, the future will not be determined by any such aspirations but by how the state of India conducts its affairs.

With the resolution of water sharing at Farakka, there are no issues with a capital 'I' between Bangladesh and India. Those that do exist are normal among neighbours and capable of resolution with a modicum of political direction and will. Where perceptions cause problems, these can be resolved by painstaking confidence-building by both sides. Fortunately, the large extent of travel, particularly by Bangladeshis to India and increasingly to areas beyond the immediate neighbourhood, is helping to foster greater understanding.

There is one area of influencing Indian policy-making that Bangladesh has not addressed. Looking at the forbidding mass of India, Bangladesh (and other neighbours of India) often fails to recognise that the particular interests of the constituent units of this mass can be effectively utilised to gain leverage and influence. The only effort made in this direction has been to look benignly at the centrifugal forces in the North East. This is counter-productive as it can only result in an adverse reaction from Delhi and can bear fruit only in the event of Indian disintegration. It would be far more useful to look at the genuine economic problems of the neighbouring states of India and thus create an effective lobby in India for cooperation with Bangladesh. As a sovereign state, Dhaka obviously has to deal with Delhi. But that should not preclude positive economic diplomacy with the neighbouring states.

Water sharing will remain a difficult issue and the discussions have tended so far to be a platform for the sterile assertion of expertise by experts on both sides rather than a meaningful dialogue for understanding. Both the countries constructing barrages on the Teesta within miles of each other where the total available water can barely meet the potentials of one structure exemplify the absence of mutual understanding. Bangladesh, quite understandably from its perspective, wants assurances that traditional flows will not drastically diminish and is not willing to talk of management. It is impossible for India to give such an assurance over a long period because of the needs of the nearly 300 million people who inhabit the Ganga-Brahmaputra basins. The answer has to lie in management, augmentation and, not the least, in cooperation and understanding of the genuine needs and concerns of all the parties involved. Much of this has been conspicuous by its absence. It is a curious phenomenon that Bangladesh has always wanted Nepal to be associated with discussions on the development of water resources, usually opposed by India, while Nepal—again understandably from its point of view—wants nothing to do with augmentation but only gathering revenues from the sale of electricity. Nor are schemes of augmentation, involving high dams, too popular in the North Eastern states of India. China, from whose territory of Tibet flows the mighty Brahmaputra, remains outside any discussions so far. Political will and sagacity might be able to resolve an individual problem like Farakka, but finding any just and sustainable long term solution to the vital issue of water management will require infinite patience, understanding and cooperation of all parties concerned.

Speaking at a meeting of the chamber of commerce in Dhaka in late 1995, a senior member of the BNP had said that too often we forget that before 1947, the economy of the region was one whole and lines on the map do not alter the essential needs of people. This is something which opinion makers—and governments—on both sides of the border need to internalise. Bangladesh has to realise that suspicion alone or the use of anti-Indian rhetoric for political purposes does not confer long term benefits and must demonstrate greater confidence in its nationhood. Delhi has to take greater cognisance of the cost of non-engagement or indifference, which is borne by the states bordering Bangladesh. What is needed is both realism as well as a vision of prosperity that is not exclusive. One must be able to visualise an upgraded port at or near Chittagong serving the needs at least of the seven sisters of India and of the free movement of people going about their legitimate business without being perceived as a threat. One would hope that the passion fruits would no longer decay in the forests of Mizoram but be processed for export by Bangladeshi entrepreneurs. One would even hope for a degree of constructive engagement between businessmen and governments where investments are placed for optimum benefit. Enhanced economic interaction for mutual benefit will lay to rest many past ghosts. But the conviction and the will to prove that this is not a zero-sum exercise has to be demonstrated in a more convincing manner than we have seen over the past 30 years.

April 2002 Delhi

Bhutan

Salman Haidar

Bhutan is the last surviving jewel of the Himalayas. Its mountains retain their forests, its streams and rivers run clear, it air is fresh. Remoteness has long been Bhutan's greatest ally in it preserving itself. Moreover, a deliberate policy of isolation has kept the world at bay and permitted the evolution of Bhutan's distinctive culture and way of life.

This isolation could not last forever and, in the last century, Bhutan warily opened to the world. After a slow and measured evolution, when it finally felt it was ready, the country assumed its proper place in the international community. However, this does not mean that Bhutan has shed its traditional caution about the world outside. Nor does this lessen its deep commitment to values and traditions.

Enfolded within the Eastern Himalayas, Bhutan is an entirely mountainous kingdom, with India to its south and the Tibet region of China to its north. Its area of some 47,000 sq km is divided laterally into three broad regions—the alpine, largely barren north leading to the high mountains beyond which lies Tibet; the temperate central zone with fertile upland valleys where the bulk of the population lives; and the thickly forested sub-tropical lower reaches bordering India which is also well-populated.

Geographical variety makes for great diversity of flora and fauna. Bhutan is rich in medicinal plants and is the last refuge of some rare animal species. A number of major rivers flow down from the high mountains through the valleys and debouch into the Duar region of the Indian states of Assam and West Bengal, and then on to Bangladesh. It is a rugged country, the valleys being separated by steep mountains that make lateral movement and communication difficult.

The population has been variously estimated at between 600,000 and 1 million. The bulk of the inhabitants are of Tibetan stock. Dzongkha, related to the languages of Tibet and predominant in the western part of the country, is the national language of Bhutan. People in the central and eastern parts have their specific languages, also derived from Tibetan sources. In the southern region are the people of Nepali origin, who are relatively recent settlers and speak their own language. Thus, within a comparatively small area, there is considerable diversity of setting and inhabitants.

For Bhutanese annalists, the first important event in their history is the advent of Buddhism, brought to this land by Guru Padmasambhava. He came to Tibet in the eighth century from the Swat Valley in what is now Pakistan, to spread the message of the Buddha in the esoteric Mahayana form that took root there. His journeys took him to Bhutan where he founded what are today the most ancient temples in the country. The Guru's coming and the message he brought are deeply embedded in the consciousness of the Bhutanese, and his image is everywhere to be seen in the country's numerous temples and shrines. Buddhist doctrine is the source and fountainhead of Bhutan's culture.

The religion spread and became firmly established, but Bhutan lacked identity and any sort of political unity. Several religious sects struggled for primacy. It was not till the seventeenth century, when Shabdrung Ngawang Namgyel came there from Tibet that Bhutan acquired the distinctive features it has retained ever since. The Shabdrung is revered as the founder of the Bhutanese state. Under his powerful guidance, the numerous contending religious schools gave way to the Drukpa Kargyupa school, which, till today is the established doctrine of the country. From his base in the western part of the country, he expanded his reach to cover virtually the entire territory that constitutes the Bhutan of today.

He gave Bhutan a system of administration that endured well into the twentieth century and only now has been substantially modified to meet modern requirements. He built the first of the dzongs that have come to be regarded as characteristic of Bhutan—vast structures that serve a defensive purpose and also house the civil administration and the monk bodies. He devised a system of rule whereby authority was divided between a religious and a temporal leader, each with a subsidiary hierarchy. This complex system was further complicated by the Tibetan-style reincarnation of high lamas who had their own sphere of influence. All this led to a confused and fractured authority. Yet the system endured for over two centuries until the emergence of the hereditary monarchy that is now in place.

The Shabdrung came to Bhutan as a fugitive from the important monastery of Ralung in Tibet where he had been recognised as the reincarnate ruler, only to be forced to flee in the face of threats from a rival. He made himself supreme in Bhutan but his rivals followed him. There were repeated invasions of his territory from Tibet, for both political and doctrinal reasons. The Shabdrung successfully defended his realm.

The dzongs he built are located along potential invasion paths from Tibet, which reveals where the threat to Bhutan came from. Several further attempts were made after the Shabdrung's time, to restore Tibet's rule over Bhutan but these were firmly resisted, and none had any lasting effect.

The powerful personality of the Shabdrung had an impact in regions far removed from his seat of government. His renown as a healer led the king of Ladakh to invite him to treat a disease from which the latter was suffering. The Shabdrung could not go himself but sent medicines and a skilled doctor to cure him. In gratitude, the king, whose domains extended far into western Tibet at that time, gifted five villages in the area of the holy Lake Mansarovar to the Shabdrung. Revenues from these villages were to sustain a Bhutanese monastery at the lake. These villages remained in Bhutanese possession until as late as 1959 when Chinese control was forcibly extended right across Tibet.

The contact between Ladakh and Bhutan in that early era reflected their common adherence to the Kargyupa school of Buddhist teaching. This link has not ceased to exist. The high, largely barren plateau of Ladakh and the distant lush mountains of Bhutan show remarkable religious and cultural affinities till date. The deification of the Shabdrung in Bhutan, as shown in his numerous formalised images in places of worship, finds an echo in Ladakh. Thangkas (religious painted scrolls) carrying his portrait can be seen in shrines in the remote Zanskar valley of Ladakh. They continue to bear testimony in this distant place to the name and aura of the founder of the Bhutanese state.

For more than a century, Bhutan's independence was challenged only from Tibet. However, the next great trial was to come from the opposite direction—the British as they advanced into the Duars. Bhutan had long been accustomed to exacting tribute from this tract, and was not inclined to give up what it regarded as its established rights. This led to a confrontation with the British, eventually culminating in military action in 1773, when a small British force attacked and expelled a Bhutanese contingent from the Duar state of Cooch Behar.

Bhutan sought assistance from the Panchen Lama, who wrote on its behalf to Warren Hastings. This paved the way for the first direct contact between the British and Bhutan. Warren

Hastings, who was in Calcutta, sent an emissary to Bhutan to regulate affairs and to find out more about the place. Bogle, the man sent, was a meticulous and sympathetic observer, and his account of his visit is of great historical value. There were others who followed him, for the Duars continued to remain a bone of contention. Besides, Britain was looking for new access routes to Tibet, the traditional one through Nepal having developed some problems. In this early phase, despite their initial clash, the British showed a friendly and sympathetic interest in Bhutan.

But by mid-nineteenth century, in the aftermath of the Great Uprising of 1857, Britain adopted a much more censorious attitude. Natives everywhere were to be denigrated and kept in check. Continued friction between the hill people of Bhutan and the plainsmen seemed to warrant stern action to put the Bhutanese in their place.

It was under these inauspicious circumstances that the Honorable Ashley Eden was nominated to lead a British mission to Bhutan in 1864. He was repeatedly discouraged by the Bhutanese, but could not be deterred—in the post-1857 setting, natives were to be cowed down, not conciliated.

The outcome was a rare disaster for Eden. When he eventually struggled his way through to meet Bhutan's notoriously fractious leaders, he was totally unable to parley with them, let alone get anyone to accept the treaty he had taken with him. Instead, he had to suffer an incredible number of personal humiliations—there is no other recorded instance of a British envoy having wet dough rubbed on his face and hair.

Today we may find his travails amusing but at the time they provoked the sternest response. A punitive expedition was sent. It fared poorly to begin with, but overwhelming British firepower eventually prevailed. Ultimately, the Treaty of Sinchula (1864) put the relations between the two parties on a different basis. Bhutan was deprived of any rights in the Duars, for which compensation was given in the form of an annual subsidy. A small tract of land at Dewangiri in eastern Bhutan was ceded to the British where they established a cantonment, the aim being to keep an eye on the turbulent Bhutanese and to ensure that they remained bottled up in their hills. (Dewangiri was restored to Bhutan by independent India in 1949.)

While the British sought to exert control, they did not wish to assimilate Bhutan into their Indian domain. It suited them better to maintain Bhutan as a buffer with Tibet. As for Bhutan, its emphatic assertion of independence was plainly seen during the Eden visit. Yet mutual interest drew it closer to the British. The subsidy provided under the treaty was a valuable asset to Bhutan's rulers, who in turn were able to offer a useful channel of contact with Tibet. By the time of the Younghusband Expedition to Lhasa in 1903-04, Bhutan had become a trusted and valued mediator between British India and Tibet.

This change in the relationship with British India reflected important internal developments in Bhutan. The system of succession established by the Shabdrung had made for complexity and uncertainty. There were always rival claimants, none of whom was ordinarily able to either assert control or to be wholly counted out of the reckoning. Provincial governors in their separate valleys were usually uncaring of any central authority. Revolts and insurrections were common, and unchallenged rule by a single person was rare.

Eventually, Bhutan found a powerful individual who was to put an end to this endemic confusion and lead the country towards a more centralised system of rule. This was Jigme Namgyel, the Penlop (ruler) of the strategically located province of Tongsa in the centre of the country. He assumed office in the middle of the nineteenth century. And, through his formidable strength and courage, to which were allied a canny ability to conciliate or to eliminate opponents, progressively outstripped all rivals. His methods were not always pretty but it was a rough era. By the time he ended his days, Jigme Namgyel had made himself virtual master of all Bhutan. He had prepared the groundwork for a new form of rule and was fortunate in his son and successor, Ugyen Wangchuk, who was able to build on his legacy to emerge as the first hereditary monarch.

After the turbulent era of his father, Ugyen Wangchuk adopted a rather different method to strengthen his hold. He worked to pacify his enemies, not crush them, and succeeded in bringing to an end the ceaseless civil strife that had plagued Bhutan for so long. Some rebels who had earlier fled to Tibet were encouraged to return. Such actions set a trend that his successors on the throne have emulated. Ugyen Wangchuk was shrewd and adaptable enough to adjust to the changed circumstances in which Bhutan found itself.

The major test was the Younghusband Expedition to Lhasa of 1903-04 when, spurred by imagined fears of Russian activity, a British army was pushed into Tibet, rudely introducing a decisive new force into the regional balance. Ugyen Wangchuk accompanied the expedition and accomplished the difficult task of serving as an interlocutor between the invaders and the hapless Tibetans—and to win a position of trust and esteem from both.

The resultant enhancement in his status helped him to assume the role and title of hereditary monarch in 1907. In this he received incalculable assistance from Ugyen Dorji of Paro, who had settled and prospered in Kalimpong where he was designated Bhutan Agent by the British. His knowledge of the world and his shrewd advice proved very helpful in the elevation of Ugyen Wangchuk, who rewarded Ugyen Dorji and his heirs with high office in Bhutan. The actual enthronement, a decisive new step for Bhutan, was endorsed in writing by all the leading Bhutanese and took place in the presence of a British representative. Thus British blessings, though no guarantee, were obtained.

Improving ties between the two countries were strengthened by a treaty in 1910 whereby Bhutan's annual subsidy was substantially increased. The country also undertook to be guided by Britain in its foreign relations, in effect becoming part of the British imperial system. (This 'guidance' clause was repeated in the 1949 Indo-Bhutan treaty, and is thus technically still in effect in the post-Independence era, but no longer with any great practical significance). While accepting restraints on its foreign relations, Bhutan remained an independent entity, in this respect crucially different from the princely states of India.

With the setting up of the monarchy, the modern phase of Bhutan began. The initial emphasis was on consolidation. The traditional leadership that had been eclipsed by the newly crowned king was restive but unable to mount a challenge. Ugyen Wangchuk maintained his ascendancy and succeeded in handing over smoothly to his son and heir at the end of a reign of some 20 years. He is rightly respected as founder of the dynasty, which he established on a firm and enduring basis.

The second king, Jigme Wangchuk, who reigned from 1926 to 1952, continued on the path laid down by the founder. Fairly early in his reign, he was confronted with a difficult problem when a reincarnation of the Shabdrung was identified in eastern Bhutan and attracted popular support as a rival source of authority. Eventually, the matter was resolved by the departure of the individual, into exile in India.

Another problem arose shortly after Indian Independence when a few people in southern Bhutan tried to start a political agitation, using ideas and methods associated with similar groups in India. This fizzled out for lack of interest, and the ringleaders decamped to India to continue a fitful movement until some years later when they were permitted to return. These incidents showed how insulated Bhutan had remained from the great tide of events that had convulsed the entire world in the 1930s and 1940s. It also demonstrated how a good understanding with India helped maintain orderly and stable relations in Bhutan.

Jigme Dorji Wangchuk, third in the line, was crowned King at the young age of 24. He rapidly initiated a series of reforms that responded to the spirit of the age and, in fact, anticipated popular demands that his people themselves were yet to express.

The instruments of government, often dating back to the first Shabdrung, were thoroughly revised and new ones instituted. The need for modern education and development was recognised, and measures to improve the economic and social status of the people were put into effect. The age-old isolation of the country was cautiously reduced. All this was done in a distinctively Bhutanese way, drawing on, but not blindly, the example of others. The third king was a remarkable leader and Bhutan, as we see it today, derives in large measure from the vision and the direction that he provided.

Internally, there were concealed threats to the king's programme, for sweeping reforms were bound to affect established interests. In the first part of his reign, the king had the highly respected and well-known figure of Jigme Dorji, Prime Minister and scion of the family of Ugyen Dorji by his side. The prime minister became the target of those opposed to reform and was assassinated in 1964, when the king was in Switzerland recuperating from a heart attack.

This dreadful crime had severe repercussions. For a while, it looked as if internal strife could not be avoided. However, the king was eventually able to bring the situation under control. Fortunately, there was no outside power seeking to take advantage of the situation; indeed, the major external influence—that of India—was unwaveringly supportive of the king's plans for order and stability. The emergency was a reminder that development and reform in a highly traditional society like Bhutan could be destabilising. Whatever the risks, the country continued on the path of change.

The departure of the British from India left Bhutan in some uncertainty. It had never been fully equated with India's princely states. Hence there was no question of following the others into the Indian Union. Yet, it had a crucial treaty relationship with British India, which had provided important support to the monarchy, politically and financially.

How independent India would view its ties with Bhutan was not clear. In the event, the two countries rapidly made 'standstill' arrangements to continue the previous agreement, pending the negotiation of a new treaty. This was finalised in 1949 after a smooth negotiation, to the satisfaction of both parties. The 'guidance' clause of the 1910 Bhutan-Britain treaty was maintained; it looks anachronistic today but it was perfectly acceptable at the time. The annual subsidy from India was increased substantially and, as already mentioned above, the Dewangiri strip was restored to Bhutan. Thus, the 1949 treaty essentially provided for continuity of relations, with some incremental advantages to Bhutan.

The geo-political dimension of the arrangement came into sharp focus a couple of years after the treaty was signed when China sent its armies into Tibet. Bhutan was greatly perturbed, not only because many Tibetans were forced to take refuge on its soil but also because of the threat to the sacred centres of the religion it shared with Tibet. From that time, barriers came up to secure its age-old religious contacts across the Himalayan range. India had its own concerns about these events, and Bhutan's role as a buffer between India and China took on a new significance. Nehru's affirmation in Parliament in 1950 that India's security frontier lay along the Himalayas and that it could not permit that barrier to be penetrated, was received with satisfaction in Bhutan as an Indian commitment to the maintenance of its security.

Sino-Indian relations went through the euphoria of the *Bhai-Bhai* days in the early 1950s, only to degenerate into the tension and armed clashes at the end of the decade. Bhutan remained aloof from these swings in their ties. It was affected by the unsettled conditions in Tibet, including armed resistance to Chinese rule in locations close to its border. To add to the uncertainty, as Sino-Indian ties deteriorated, historical claims of hegemony over Bhutan were sometimes revived in China.

It was in these circumstances that Jawaharlal Nehru visited Bhutan in 1958. His was an arduous journey, much of it on horseback, for he was obliged to come through Sikkim and then across the Chumbi Valley of Tibet into western Bhutan. For all that, it was a memorable occasion. Nehru clearly enjoyed himself in Bhutan. His romantic love for the mountains was fully indulged and his appreciation of Bhutanese culture was much in evidence. His talks with King Jigme Dorji Wangchuk were to have far-reaching consequences.

Nehru encouraged the king to embark on a programme of development activity. To overcome the problem of Bhutan's shortage of resources, virtually the entire cost of the early projects was to be undertaken by India. A process of five-year development planning was initiated soon after: a development wing was established in the Bhutan government, and Indian experts came in good numbers to provide technical support.

Thus development activity had the effect of bringing the two countries closer together. Road communications southward were developed, built and maintained by India's Border Roads Organisation, and the route through India became the exclusive outlet for Bhutan. Agriculture, horticulture, power, health, education were among the areas that received attention. Simultaneously, a cadre of Bhutanese officials was created, most of them trained in India, expected to progressively take over from foreign experts. The formation of a small army, wholly equipped and trained by India, was another significant development. Through such measures, the long-standing southward orientation of Bhutan received a decisive boost.

In this phase, the biggest challenges for Bhutan came from events outside the country. The flight of the Dalai Lama from his capital Lhasa in 1959 was one such challenge. The Dalai Lama did not himself come out through Bhutan but several of his followers did. Many sought to stay there as refugees. And, despite the obvious sensitivity of the issue, several thousand were given permission. They remained there, a distinct and unassimilated group, till Mrs. Indira Gandhi agreed in the early 1980s to their moving to India.

Less long-lasting in its impact, but much sharper and more dangerous when it happened, was the 1962 Sino-Indian border war. Stragglers from the Indian Army routed by Chinese forces in neighbouring Arunachal Pradesh had to pass through Bhutan to find a safe way home. The Bhutanese Army, primitively armed though it was, moved to the frontier to defend the land. Fortunately, it was not put to the test of a battle for which it was totally unequipped (for the unilateral Chinese ceasefire brought hostilities to an end). In this great crisis, Bhutan had stood by India. Thereafter, when India vowed never again to be exposed as it was in 1962, the defence plans of the two came into closer alignment and so, by and large, they have remained, as underlined by the presence of an Indian military training team in Bhutan.

However close to India it was driven by circumstances and by its own interest, Bhutan was consistent in ensuring that it was not wholly within the Indian embrace. It did not make the mistake of trying to play off its giant neighbours India and China against each other. It chose instead to work with India and obtain Indian support for its policy of gradually increasing its international exposure.

One of the first moves in this direction was Bhutan entering the Colombo Plan in 1961 with Indian sponsorship. By a similar process, Bhutan joined the Universal Postal Union in 1969. The big step thereafter was membership of the United Nations, which was achieved in 1971, once more with Indian backing. The deliberate heightening of its international profile, in particular through membership of the UN, was important chiefly for the sense of national affirmation and security that it provided. India was seen as a benevolent friend but Bhutan's people were anxious to see international acknowledgment of their sovereign status, which the UN membership conveyed.

With it came a measured expansion of diplomatic ties. Before joining the UN and setting up its Permanent Mission in New York, Bhutan had exchanged plenipotentiaries with India but had no other diplomatic missions. The emergence of Bangladesh gave an opportunity Bhutan was quick to seize: diplomatic relations were established and the two countries exchanged ambassadors. This was done without formal consultation with India but it could hardly object. Thereafter, a few more missions were established. Today, Bhutan has half-a-dozen or so missions. From the start, Bhutan refused to have formal ties with any permanent UN Security Council members or with any other major power, which could suck it into issues and problems of no direct relevance to the country.

Notwithstanding these limitations, diversification of external relationships has been fairly extensive. Several UN agencies are active in Bhutan and many countries that do not have formal ties run aid programmes in that country. This has given Bhutan many more options for the training of its personnel and has also broadened the sources of aid. India remains the largest contributor but it is no longer the exclusive provider of economic and technical support as it was in the early days.

An organisation of which Bhutan has become a member, perforce, is SAARC. From the start, Bhutan has had its reservations. Its previous ventures into membership of international organisations had a clear goal and purpose. SAARC offers less clear and measurable advantages. Moreover, it has tended to line up the smaller countries of South Asia against India, which has never been part of Bhutan's purpose in the shaping of its external relationships. So, it has been a punctilious but somewhat sceptical member of the organisation.

King Jigme Singye Dorji, the fourth in the line, succeeded his father in 1972 when he was just 16 years old. He was in full command from the start, a confident and forward-looking ruler despite his lack of years. Modern Bhutan's foundations had been well laid by his father, and the present king continued along the established reformist path. In the 30 years that he has been on the throne, the pace of change has picked up significantly and Bhutan has moved some way from being the simple, remote society that it was only a generation earlier. The challenges of external policy and of internal development have been met with increasing self-assurance. Steady progress has been recorded in this period, though some new and difficult problems have challenged the state at different times.

Among these was the impact of the integration of neighbouring Sikkim into India in 1975. This caused alarm in Bhutan. By that time, a new generation of Bhutanese had come into prominence, with genuine friendship for India and an equally genuine desire to reduce the Indian hold. For them, and for other Bhutanese, the events in Sikkim seemed to be a warning. The implications of the 1949 treaty came under scrutiny, for the notion of Indian 'guidance' in foreign policy that it embodied seemed incompatible with the sovereign equality conferred by UN membership. Some unthinking Indian officials complicated the issue by seeking to put a literal interpretation to this provision. Wisely, the leaders of the two countries never permitted the issue to go beyond control and it was tacitly agreed that there was no advantage in tampering with the 1949 treaty. In practice, Bhutan's right to run its own affairs was not in question, and India had no reason to fear that its defences in a sensitive part of its perimeter were at risk of being exposed.

Indo-Bhutan economic projects proved highly successful but also presented some initial difficulties, especially the huge Chukha Hydel Project that dwarfed all other projects. In the eyes of some Bhutanese, this scheme seemed too large for Bhutan's needs and thus seemed designed essentially for India. There was understandable concern that Bhutan's natural resources should be reserved for its own use. Such anxieties were soon laid to rest, however, for the project went well from the start and now yields good revenue. The result is that subsequent projects of similar or even greater size have been welcomed by the Bhutanese for the economic benefit these are expected to provide.

There are no border problems between Bhutan and India. However, Bhutan's border with China, like that of India, has never been formally defined and there are areas of overlapping claims. The revival of Sino-Indian border talks in the 1980s posed a particular test for Bhutan. During earlier such talks, Bhutan's claims had been linked to those of India and taken up by Indian negotiators. China, however, never accepted India's right to speak on behalf of Bhutan, insisting instead on direct talks. In both New Delhi and Thimpu, this demand could not be accepted as it threatened to complicate the hitherto seamless joint approach of the two countries.

Nevertheless, India came to acknowledge that direct talks were unavoidable in the circumstances and did not demur when Bhutan decided to send a team to Beijing for initial border talks in 1983. For Bhutan, this was an initiative that demonstrated its growing confidence but was full of complexity. Bhutan had boldly taken on itself the task of talking to a neighbour that had been seen as a threat to its political and religious institutions. Moreover, relations between India and China had improved but many problems remained between them, and Bhutan had to be careful not to be pulled into controversies that offered no gain. In the event, Bhutan conducted the talks in a manner that enabled it to maintain good relations on all sides while retaining the pattern of diplomatic and official relations with which it was comfortable. The negotiation is not yet concluded—mirroring in that, the protracted Sino-Indian border talks—but considerable progress has been made in providing Bhutan with a clearly defined border to its north.

After a long period of reform, a distinctive institutional structure has emerged in Bhutan that seems likely to endure. The most significant institution that emerged in Bhutan in the twentieth century is that of the monarchy. It has been at the helm of the modernising process and at the centre of the state apparatus.

Nominally equal in status to the king—the only other person entitled to wear the yellow scarf, insignia of supreme rank—is the Je Khempo, or Chief Abbot, head of the official monk body. The post today is a far cry from that of the spiritual leader who at one time shared—and disputed—authority with the temporal leader. The Je Khempo is selected by the monk body and reigns for a three-year period, though the term can be extended. The official monk body itself took its present shape during the reign of the first king. Its impact on affairs of state is slight but it represents something that runs deep in the beliefs and values of Bhutan.

Major political reforms and innovations came to Bhutan in the reign of the third king. He created institutions that represented a radical new departure from the old ways. Prominent among these is a National Assembly (or Tshogdu), which has a three-part membership of people's representatives, senior figures from the administration and delegates of the monk body. The people's representatives are chosen not by suffrage but by a process of consultation, which differs between northern and southern Bhutan to reflect the varying cultural patterns of the two regions. While the Assembly is essentially a consultative body, the monarch tried from the start to give it authority and responsibility. It has thus grown in stature, and assumed the significant role of a watchdog.

Government ministers are not appointed by the Tshogdu nor are they answerable to it. However, ministers in charge of the various departments have to make policy presentations to the Assembly, and deal with this increasingly assertive body. In shoring up the authority of the Assembly and in modernising the structure of the government, the present king has continued—and accelerated—the work begun by his father.

He still appoints ministers and can remove them, but gradually a structure of official departments has been created that looks very much like similar structures elsewhere—ministries of Foreign Affairs, Home, Finance and so on. Earlier, ministries and their equivalent bodies tended to be headed by a traditional type of servant of the Crown who had often risen from household service in the palace. These have been replaced by a new generation of younger, well-educated ministers who can comfortably hold their own in the world at large. Until recently, the king was, in effect, head of government for there was no prime minister. A rotating prime ministership has now been introduced, with each of the five or six ministers getting one year. These changes have not come about as a result of pressure from below; they represent a forward-looking policy on the part of the monarch to establish and strengthen the representative institutions that Bhutan will require for its future. He has also kept in existence a Royal Advisory Council of nominated elders of a more traditional orientation to provide advice and assistance.

As part of the process of distancing himself from the day-to-day affairs of the state, the king has taken steps to institutionalise processes that were earlier a matter of grace and favour. Thus, appointment to the civil services has been entrusted to a Royal Civil Service Commission, which has introduced objective testing procedures.

The administration has also been decentralised to permit greater local participation in the planning and implementation of development projects. The financial devolution to the local level that accompanied these measures initially permitted a great deal of corruption. Stern remedial measures appear to have had effect and Bhutan seems less plagued by this scourge of developing societies than many others.

Like the civil administrative arrangements, till not so long ago, the legal processes in Bhutan were neither objective nor predictable. This has been remedied in recent times by establishing a system of courts with a Supreme Court at the apex. No legal profession has come into being, no lawyers and no elaborate court procedures. A written legal code is only now being drawn up. The system is bound to evolve further as society's demands become more complex. However, the measures already taken have served to establish the rule of law, as they were intended to, and, to that extent, to modify earlier reliance on essentially personal rule.

The social sectors command priority attention in development and education in particular. Bhutan has been concerned about setting up its own institutions of learning and not being obliged to send its young people to India or elsewhere for higher education. India has cooperated in the endeavour and has helped set up a college which is set to evolve into

Bhutan's first university. Some institutions of technical education have also been established. Health services are as yet not well developed but as more medical personnel become available, the situation will change.

Bhutan started its economic planning process in 1961. It has made steady progress ever since. It is obvious to any informed visitor that life for the average citizen has improved a good deal in the past few decades. The effort has been progressively to involve the people closely in development activity. The intended beneficiaries are involved in both the framing and the implementation of plans and projects. At the same time, Bhutan has tried to free itself of the rigmarole and jargon of economic planners, preferring its own yardstick for measuring progress.

Thus, it has come up with the concept of 'Gross National Happiness' as the goal of its development activity. This is an attractive idea and it should not obscure the fact that Bhutan shows up well even by more conventional measures of progress.

The country's renewable resources are being used to the optimum, and Bhutan remains the only part of the region that seems immune from the spreading ecological malaise. Stringent controls have preserved its forest wealth and there has never been any readiness in Bhutan to earn easy, but temporary riches by the reckless felling of trees for timber. The country has huge hydroelectric resources and its location above the power-starved Indian plains means that it has a ready market for all the electricity it can produce. Already electric power has proved to be its largest and most enduring source of revenue. One major hydroelectric project is successfully in operation, and soon several more will be completed. The contiguous parts of India look to Bhutan for their power needs. None of these hydroelectric schemes requires large storages that can drown forests and displace humans. The proceeds from sales of power to India, even without taking into reckoning the stimulus to economic activity within the country that is provided by abundant cheap power, seems set to transform Bhutan's future.

While Bhutan's management of its affairs has shown up well

and has earned international respect, there are some difficult, unresolved items on its agenda that have proved controversial. Prominent among these is the complicated issue of persons of Nepali origin, euphemistically known as 'Southern Bhutanese', who have perforce left Bhutan and now live in refugee camps in Nepal.

This group of people descended from Nepalese settlers who were encouraged to move into insalubrious tracts of southern Bhutan in the latter part of the nineteenth century. They were able to deal with the difficult conditions they faced, settling in, clearing the area and establishing themselves as successful agriculturists. The revenue they provided made them a significant asset to the state. With Bhutan's open borders of that time permitting continuous immigration from outside, these 'first comers' were followed by many others.

Something similar was taking place elsewhere in the region, especially in nearby Sikkim. The Nepali settlers were restricted to the southern part of the country where the Bhutanese from the higher reaches were unable to live and work. They thus lacked the right of mobility within Bhutan. But efforts were made to integrate them within the country by means like providing employment in the civil and military services, and by establishing a place for them in institutions like the National Assembly.

This worked well enough until recently and the two communities seemed satisfied with the situation. However, there were some divisive tendencies at work that became more marked with time. For one thing, the number of immigrants seemed to have increased beyond the authorised limit, raising the fear that Bhutan could be swamped by these Nepali settlers. There were also questions of loyalty with the new arrivals being regarded as having divided allegiance between their adopted land and their place of origin.

The example of Sikkim where the indigenous population had been forced to yield to the numerically superior immigrants was there in the background. When some clashes that threatened long term consequences took place in the early 1990s in the southern part of the country, Bhutan decided on pre-emptive action and moved to get rid of those who, in its view, had no right to be there. This created a panic and many Nepali settlers left Bhutan because of a sense of insecurity and moved to UN-aided refugee camps in Nepal where they continue to live.

The cause of these refugees has been taken up by Nepal and has become a divisive and controversial issue between the two Himalayan kingdoms. Extensive negotiations have not as yet yielded any final result though the last round of talks offered some better prospects. The international expectation is that genuine refugees will be allowed to go back. As matters seem to be progressing in that direction, this whole issue could become a lesser source of concern and criticism as time goes on. For the present, however, it remains an unresolved problem in the region. Easy access to Bhutan from nearby Assam has brought an entirely new and unexpected set of problems in the last few years. Assam's insurgent ULFA and Bodo groups have infiltrated into remote areas of Bhutan where they have set up camps and training areas. Bhutan is a reluctant host to these groups and would be glad to get rid of them. There is considerable public resentment against their illicit occupation of Bhutanese territory. However, they are formidably well armed, and removing them by force could be difficult. It could also lead to lasting complications for Bhutan in its dealings with the adjacent region of Assam through which its people have to frequently come and go. Bhutan has therefore moved cautiously and is reluctant to rush into immediate military action against the intruders. Handling the consequences of the overspill of Assam's insurgency can become an increasingly awkward matter and no early solution is in sight as yet.

Probably more than any of its South Asian neighbours, Bhutan seems to have a fair prospect ahead. There are no looming dangers that could threaten to distort its expectations. Internally, under the enlightened rule of King Jigme Singye Wangchuk, steady and orderly progress is being made. The instruments of governance, including the National Assembly, the law courts and the administration, are becoming continuously more effective, so that power and authority can be permitted to devolve away from the throne towards popular and accountable institutions. The king remains an immensely popular symbol of the nation and continues to exercise final authority but he has deliberately encouraged the democratic and consultative processes that are expected to assure the country's future. At the same time, Bhutan's deep commitment to its religion and its traditions find expression in its state institutions.

The country has developed a successful strategy of economic development that has already paid dividends and could transform the country's future. Substantial investment has been made in developing the infrastructure, and in sectors such as education and health. This has boosted the 'Gross National Happiness' that is Bhutan's developmental goal.

An even tempo of growth and development is dependent on the maintenance of good relations with its next-door neighbours. In this, Bhutan has succeeded very well indeed. Its all-important ties with India have never been strained. Stability in this relationship has permitted Bhutan the leeway it needed for its internal modernisation and for accelerated economic growth. The relationship with China, also a key to Bhutan's future, has been handled with proper care.

Bhutan has emerged fully on the international stage. It plays its part in the UN and its agencies. It is also part of the regional structure, SAARC. Bhutan's approach to these organisations has been practical and down-to-earth. It has succeeded in pursuing matters of interest without becoming unnecessarily embroiled in affairs from which it has little to gain.

Today, Bhutan is set to emerge as a parliamentary democracy with a constitutional monarchy at the top.

On the whole, Bhutan's future prospects appear bright and it seems set to emerge as an enviable enclave of prosperity and good governance in South Asia.